Edward II's Nieces: The Clare Sisters

Edward II's Nieces: The Clare Sisters
Powerful Pawns of the Crown

Kathryn Warner

First published in Great Britain in 2020 by
Pen and Sword Transport
An imprint of
Pen & Sword Books Ltd
Yorkshire - Philadelphia

Copyright © Kathryn Warner, 2020

ISBN 9781526715579

The right of Kathryn Warner to be identified as Author of this work has been asserted by her in accordance with the Copyright, Designs and Patents Act 1988.

A CIP catalogue record for this book is available from the British Library.

All rights reserved. No part of this book may be reproduced or transmitted in any form or by any means, electronic or mechanical including photocopying, recording or by any information storage and retrieval system, without permission from the Publisher in writing.

Typeset in 11.5/14 Ehrhardt by Vman Infotech Pvt. Ltd.

Printed and bound in the UK by TJ International Ltd.

Pen & Sword Books Ltd incorporates the Imprints of Pen & Sword Books Archaeology, Atlas, Aviation, Battleground, Discovery, Family History, History, Maritime, Military, Naval, Politics, Railways, Select, Transport, True Crime, Fiction, Frontline Books, Leo Cooper, Praetorian Press, Seaforth Publishing, Wharncliffe and White Owl.

For a complete list of Pen & Sword titles please contact

PEN & SWORD BOOKS LIMITED
47 Church Street, Barnsley, South Yorkshire, S70 2AS, England
E-mail: enquiries@pen-and-sword.co.uk
Website: www.pen-and-sword.co.uk

or

PEN AND SWORD BOOKS
1950 Lawrence Rd, Havertown, PA 19083, USA
E-mail: Uspen-and-sword@casematepublishers.com
Website: www.penandswordbooks.com

Contents

Introduction vii

Chapter 1: The Clare Sisters 1
Chapter 2: The New King 13
Chapter 3: Journeys to Ireland 21
Chapter 4: Two Young Widows 30
Chapter 5: The Earl of Gloucester's Heirs 38
Chapter 6: The First Abduction 43
Chapter 7: Widowed Again 49
Chapter 8: Two Favourites, Two Weddings 54
Chapter 9: A Rich Inheritance 61
Chapter 10: The New Favourite 67
Chapter 11: The Despenser War 76
Chapter 12: Contrariants 83
Chapter 13: In the King's Favour 91
Chapter 14: Unequal Treatment 99
Chapter 15: A Secret Lover 108
Chapter 16: Intruder and Pharisee 119
Chapter 17: A Protest Against the Regime 126
Chapter 18: The End of Hugh Despenser 131
Chapter 19: Deposition 141
Chapter 20: Rebellion and Abduction 149
Chapter 21: The King Lives 156
Chapter 22: A Belated Funeral 161
Chapter 23: Death of an Earl 167

Chapter 24:	A Third Abduction and a Death	171
Chapter 25:	The Young Generation	176
Chapter 26:	The Last Sister	184
Chapter 27:	The Final Years	192
Appendix 1:	*Brief Biographical Details of the Clare Sisters*	202
Appendix 2:	*The Sisters' Children*	203
Appendix 3:	*The Descent of the Sisters' Inheritances*	205
Abbreviations		208
Endnotes		209
Bibliography		242
Index		249

Introduction

Between 1292 and 1295, three women were born who were granddaughters of the reigning king of England, Edward I, and daughters of the greatest English nobleman of the late thirteenth century, Gilbert 'the Red' Clare, Earl of Gloucester and Hertford. Eleanor, Margaret and Elizabeth Clare's lives were full of drama, intrigue, conflict and tragedy. The death of their brother the Earl of Gloucester at the Battle of Bannockburn in 1314 made the women hugely rich and therefore highly desirable as marriage partners—two of the three sisters, and the daughter and heir of the third, were abducted and forcibly married for their wealth. All three women spent time in captivity during the turbulent reign of their uncle Edward II and its aftermath: the regime of their aunt-in-law Queen Isabella. The sisters were married to a total of seven men, four of whom were involved in intense and perhaps sexual relationships with Edward II, and Eleanor was even said by one chronicler to have had an incestuous affair with her own uncle, a statement which finds some support in his accounts. Events of the early 1320s destroyed the sisters' relationship forever when they and their husbands found themselves on opposite sides of a bloody conflict between Edward II and some of his barons.

The youngest Clare sister, Elizabeth, is by far the best known of the three, as she lived much longer than Eleanor and Margaret and founded Clare College at Cambridge, and because many of her household accounts fortuitously survive, revealing much more about her life than is the case for her two older sisters. She has been the subject of an excellent monograph, *For Her Good Estate* by Frances Underhill, while Jennifer Ward has done much work on Elizabeth's household accounts and has published a useful translation of some of them under the title *Elizabeth de Burgh, Lady of Clare (1295–1360)*, in addition to her many articles about Elizabeth. It is much harder to delve into the personal lives of Eleanor and especially Margaret as the records simply do not exist, though much of Eleanor's life in the 1320s, when her husband was the powerful and despotic favourite of her uncle Edward II and she herself was high in the king's favour and perhaps even his mistress, can be reconstructed. Married women of the fourteenth century do tend to disappear from the written record, sadly, and it can be frustrating for author and reader alike to have to delve frequently into a welter of 'probablys' and 'she might haves', and to run the risk of writing what amounts to a biography of the women's husbands rather than the women themselves. With these limitations in mind, this is an account of the lives of three wealthy and fascinating women, and the tumultuous times they lived in.

Chapter 1

The Clare Sisters

**Westminster Abbey, Sunday, 30 April 1290
(Eighteenth year of the reign of King Edward I)**

T he bride wore a second-hand dress, the groom was a divorcé almost thirty years her senior, and she spent the days before the wedding squabbling with her sisters. Not, perhaps, the most auspicious-sounding of occasions, yet this was a wedding of great significance: that of the king of England's daughter and the most powerful nobleman in the country.

Joan of Acre, the bride, was the second eldest of the five surviving daughters of King Edward I (1239–1307) and his Spanish queen Leonor of Castile (*c*. 1241–90), and the first of them to marry. At the time of her wedding, Joan had either recently turned 18 or was shortly to turn 18: she was born in the spring of 1272 when her father, accompanied by her mother, was leading the last major Christian crusade to the Holy Land. Joan's birthplace of Acre or Akko was then the sole remaining important port and stronghold of the Crusader kingdom of Jerusalem, and is now a town in northern Israel and one of the oldest continuously inhabited sites in the world, first mentioned around 2000BC. Just over a year after Joan's wedding, in May 1291, her birthplace fell to the Mamluks, a Muslim dynasty of former slaves who ruled Egypt and Syria from the middle of the thirteenth century until overthrown by the Ottomans in 1517. A few weeks after her birth, in fact on his thirty-third birthday on 17 June 1272, Joan's father Edward had survived an assassination attempt in Acre by an emissary sent to him by the Egyptian general Sultan al-Zahir Baibars. Edward was stabbed with a poisoned dagger and sustained serious injury, but survived and managed to kill his attacker. The knife used to stab him was kept and was still held in the English treasury at Westminster in the early 1340s.[1] On 16 November 1272 when Joan of Acre was about

2 Edward II's Nieces: The Clare Sisters

6 months old, her grandfather Henry III (b. 1207) died after a reign of fifty-six years and her father succeeded to the English throne, though he did not return to his realm until 2 August 1274. He and Leonor were crowned king and queen of England at Westminster Abbey seventeen days later.

Joan did not travel to England with her parents in 1274 but stayed for some years in northern France with her maternal grandmother Jeanne (or 'Joan' in English) of Ponthieu, dowager-queen of the Spanish kingdoms of Castile and Leon, and Countess of Ponthieu in her own right. Joan of Acre was presumably named after her grandmother. Queen Jeanne (*c*. 1217/20–79) had left Castile in 1254 two years after the death of her husband Fernando III (r. 1217–52), following a dispute with her stepson Alfonso X (r. 1252–84). She returned to her own county of Ponthieu, bordering Normandy, which she had inherited from her mother Marie and would bequeath on her death in 1279 to her daughter Leonor of Castile and ultimately to her grandson Edward II of England (r. 1307–27), Joan of Acre's younger brother and their father's successor. Joan arrived in England for the first time when she was 6 years old in 1278, when her father had already begun arranging a future marriage for her with one of the sons of the German king Rudolf I (r. 1273–91). Sadly, her 18-year-old husband-to-be, Hartmann von Habsburg, drowned in the Rhine in 1281 before their wedding could go ahead.

The man Joan married instead was Gilbert 'the Red' Clare, Earl of Gloucester and Hertford, born on 2 September 1243 in Christchurch, Dorset and hence 46 when they married in April 1290.[2] He was known as 'the Red' as much for his choleric disposition and touchiness as for his flaming hair, and he and his new father-in-law Edward I, only four years his senior, had long had an uneasy relationship. During the baronial wars of the 1260s, Gilbert had at first supported Henry III's brother-in-law Simon Montfort, Earl of Leicester (*c*. 1208–65), against the king and his son Edward, though switched sides and played an important role in the royalist victory of 1265. He commanded one of the divisions which defeated the Earl of Leicester at the Battle of Evesham in August that year; Leicester, who fell during the battle, supposedly exclaimed 'This red dog will eat us today.'[3] When he was only 9 years old in the early 1250s, Gilbert had been married to Edward I's French cousin Alice Lusignan (*c*. late 1230s/early 1240s–1290), whose father Hugues, Count of

La Marche, was a younger half-brother of Henry III. This was a famously unhappy match which resulted in the couple living apart for many years from about 1267 onwards and ultimately in the annulment of their marriage in 1285. Gilbert and Alice's daughters Isabella and Joan, born in 1262 and *c*. 1264, were a few years older than their new stepmother. At the time of Gilbert's wedding to Joan of Acre, his second daughter Joan MacDuff née Clare, Countess of Fife in Scotland, had already borne at least one child, Duncan MacDuff; Gilbert was already a grandfather.

Gilbert surrendered his many lands to Edward I before his wedding to the king's daughter, and on 27 May 1290 they were granted back to him and Joan jointly with the condition that any children Gilbert had with Joan would inherit them. This grant gave precedence to any children Gilbert might have with his second wife over his two daughters with his first, who had probably been disinherited anyway by the 1285 annulment of their parents' marriage, and the question of who exactly the correct Clare heirs were became a pressing matter in and after 1314. Well into the 1400s, 150 years after Gilbert Clare and Joan of Acre's wedding, royal officials often examined and confirmed Edward I's May 1290 grant of Gilbert's lands back to him, the birth order of Gilbert's three daughters with Joan, and the subsequent ownership of his lands by his daughters, their husbands and their descendants.[4]

The Clares were one of the greatest families of medieval England. They had held the earldom of Hertford since the twelfth century and the earldom of Gloucester since the early thirteenth, and owned lands in England—in every county of the south of England—Wales and Ireland. Gilbert 'the Red' was the second child and eldest son of Richard Clare, Earl of Gloucester and Hertford (1222–62), and Maud Lacy (b. 1223), daughter of Margaret Quincy (*c*. 1206–66), Countess of Lincoln in her own right. Maud Clare née Lacy appears to have had a personality as prickly, difficult and hostile as that of her eldest son, and Gilbert had an ongoing feud with her over her dower lands (Henry III unfairly assigned Usk in Wales and Clare in Suffolk, two of Gilbert's chief lordships, to Maud as part of her dower in 1262 which was a major factor in Gilbert's decision to join Simon Montfort against Henry and his son Edward in 1263/64). Mother and son went so far as to sue each other on occasion, and although Gilbert had five daughters he named none of them after his mother. This is so unusual and unconventional for the era that it reveals much about their unamicable relationship. Maud played favourites among her children, going out of her way to promote the career of her third son Bogo, a rich cleric who held numerous offices, to the exclusion of Gilbert, her daughters Isabella, Margaret and Rohese, and the remaining son Thomas, lord of Thomond in Ireland. Gilbert was perhaps not too distraught when Maud died in early 1289, and he could finally, in his mid-40s, take possession of his entire inheritance including the third of it she had held as dower.[5]

The April 1290 wedding of Joan of Acre and Gilbert Clare was a private affair, only attended by Joan's parents the king and queen, her elder sister Eleanor and younger sisters Margaret and Elizabeth, and her much younger brother Edward of Caernarfon, the future King Edward II and the only survivor of Edward I and Leonor of Castile's four sons, who turned 6 years old five days before the wedding. (The remaining royal sister, Mary, who was 11, had been veiled at Amesbury Priory in Wiltshire in 1285 and was not present.) The gowns of Joan and her sisters were not new, but a tailor had spent a full nine days making them ready for the wedding, and a magnificent headdress with rubies and emeralds and a belt of gold also with rubies and emeralds had been especially made for Joan in Paris. Joan gave 3 shillings as an offering at a Mass she attended on her wedding day, and the three of her sisters who were present each gave a shilling to 'poor widows' in alms.[6] A wedding party was held afterwards in a temporary hall built at Westminster for the occasion, at which one guest enjoyed himself so much he somehow managed to break several tables.[7]

Soon after the wedding, Joan and Gilbert left court without royal permission and took themselves off to Gilbert's castle of Tonbridge in Kent, to the annoyance of her parents: an example of Joan's determination to do what she wanted to do rather than what she was told to do, which she would demonstrate again and again. The king and queen retaliated by confiscating seven gowns laid aside for her and giving them instead to her 15-year-old sister Margaret, whose wedding to the future Duke John II of Brabant took place also at Westminster a few weeks later.[8] The couple eventually returned: Gilbert the Red held a banquet at his mansion in Clerkenwell to celebrate his marriage on 3 July 1290, and a few days later rode with 103 knights in the wedding procession of his sister-in-law Margaret and John of Brabant.[9] Edward I, who loved his daughters dearly and was often very indulgent towards them, had obviously forgiven Joan by then for leaving court without permission. He gave her a large amount of plate and other equipment for her household at Clerkenwell, including four beds, forty-six golden cups, sixty silver spoons, many bowls of silver and one of pure gold.[10] The daughters of Edward I and Queen Leonor were headstrong and independent women. As well as the numerous examples of this demonstrated by Joan of Acre, the third daughter Margaret decided to stay in England for more than three years between 1294 and 1297 without her husband the Duke of Brabant, and the fifth and youngest daughter Elizabeth also flatly refused to join her own husband in the county of Holland in 1297, to her father's annoyance. The fourth daughter Mary, although veiled as a nun at a young age, did what she wanted and went where she pleased, incurred numerous gambling debts, and lived a luxurious life at Amesbury Priory with servants and hunting-dogs. She also spent much time as an adult at the court of her brother Edward II.

Joan of Acre became pregnant around late July or early August 1290, about three months after her wedding. Unfortunately, the queen of England did not live long enough to see the birth of her first grandchild. Leonor of Castile died at Harby in Nottinghamshire on 28 November 1290, at the age of 49. Joan, despite her pregnancy, rushed to see her mother before she died.[11] Leonor was buried at Westminster Abbey on 17 December. Her grieving widower, the 51-year-old king to whom she had been married for thirty-six years, poignantly referred to her in a letter to the abbot of Cluny in France as 'whom in life we dearly cherished, and whom in death we cannot cease to love'.[12] He remained a widower for nine years, only remarrying Philip IV of France's half-sister Marguerite (1278/9–1318) when it became necessary to do so as a means of ending a war against Philip. Philip's only daughter Isabella was betrothed to Joan of Acre's brother Edward of Caernarfon at the same time and for the same purpose.

Joan gave birth to her first child sometime between 23 April and 13 May 1291, a year after her wedding and just before her birthplace of Acre fell to the Mamluk besiegers and the Holy Land was lost to the Christians, on 18 May 1291.[13] It was a boy, called Gilbert after his father (though it would have been more conventional by the standards of the era to have named him Richard after his paternal grandfather Richard Clare, Earl of Gloucester and Hertford) and who, from the moment of his birth, was heir to Gilbert the Red's earldoms and vast landholdings in three countries. Edward I, delighted at the news of his first grandchild, gave a hugely generous gift of £100 on 21 May to Joan's messenger 'William son of Glay' who informed him.[14] Young Gilbert was only seven years younger than his uncle the future king, Edward of Caernarfon, and when he was 10 years old in 1301, his grandfather sent Gilbert to live in the household of the boy's step-grandmother Queen Marguerite, whom the king married in September 1299. Edward I also granted the queen the right to arrange Gilbert's future marriage.[15] The king's order had to be repeated to make a reluctant Joan of Acre give up custody of her son to the queen, and Marguerite informed Edward that she had sent two men to find Gilbert and bring him to her.[16] It seems that Joan's relationship with the stepmother who was about seven years her junior may not have been particularly harmonious. Gilbert, however, as grandson of the king and heir of the great Earl of Gloucester, lived in some style: he was attended by five squires, five valets and sixteen other servants, and was given six greyhounds, ten running dogs and thirteen horses.[17]

Between 1290 and early 1292, Gilbert 'the Red' Clare (b. 1243) clashed violently with Humphrey Bohun, Earl of Hereford, concerning their rights in the Marches (Wales and the English-Welsh borderlands), and both men were summoned to parliament in January 1292 and condemned to temporary imprisonment.[18] The king also made Gilbert acknowledge a huge debt to him of £10,000 which he pardoned Gilbert's executors after the earl's death at Joan of Acre's request.[19] Edward I could not long imprison his own son-in-law, however, and the matter did not impede Gilbert and Joan's marital relations: their second child and first daughter was born on or a little after 14 October 1292 at the earl's mighty South Wales stronghold of Caerphilly. Gilbert himself had built the castle twenty years previously to aid his conquest of Glamorgan and his struggle against Llywelyn ap Gruffudd (d. 1282), the last native Prince of Wales.[20] Caerphilly Castle still exists and broods magnificently, the second largest castle in Britain after Windsor and the first of concentric design. Gilbert designed it to be surrounded by two artificial lakes and to be virtually impregnable.

Gilbert and Joan named their second child Eleanor after her maternal grandmother Leonor of Castile and great-grandmother Eleanor of Provence (Edward I's mother and Henry III's widow, who had died the year before), and she was the king's first granddaughter. In contemporary spelling, her name was Alianor, Alianore or occasionally Alienore. Shortly after Eleanor Clare's birth, Gilbert 'the Red' sent a letter to Robert Burnell, chancellor of England and a close ally of Edward I, apologising for being unable to attend the king as he should. He explained that he had been forced to remain in Glamorgan for longer than anticipated as when he had travelled there from London, he had found one of his children ill.[21] Wishing to keep this reason private, however, he asked Burnell to make excuses for him in public. Whether the earl meant his son Gilbert, now 18 months, or the newborn Eleanor, is unclear, but the letter lends a pleasantly affectionate touch to a famously irascible man.

Not long after Eleanor Clare was born at Caerphilly, Gilbert 'the Red' was driven out of Wales by a rebellion there; Edward I finally suppressed it the following June. In the early summer of 1293, Gilbert and Joan of Acre began making plans to visit Ireland, where they stayed until April 1294.[22] Before they left, Joan probably attended the wedding of her elder sister Eleanor in Bristol on 20 September 1293. Eleanor was now 24, and married Henri III, Count of Bar, a part of the Holy Roman Empire in eastern France, with its capital at Bar-le-Duc, in the region of Lorraine. She had long been betrothed to King Alfonso III of Aragon, second largest of the four Spanish kingdoms, who died suddenly in June 1291; perhaps it was something of a disappointment for Eleanor to marry a mere count when she should have married a king. Eleanor and Henri's marriage produced two children: Edouard, born probably in 1294 and his father's successor to the county of Bar, and Jeanne or Joan, later Countess of Surrey, born in 1295 or 1296. Edouard and Jeanne de Bar were the cousins closest in age to Joan of Acre's daughters, the Clare sisters. The three girls never knew their aunt Eleanor, who died in 1298, and probably had little if any contact with their cousin Count Edouard in eastern France, but knew their cousin Jeanne de Bar well. She came to England in the early 1300s after the death of her father, and spent most of the rest of her life there.

Joan of Acre and Gilbert's third child, Margaret Clare, was born sometime between the autumn of 1293 and the autumn of 1294; she is the only one of the four Clare siblings for whom we have no recorded date of birth. Perhaps a date in the spring or summer of 1294 is most likely which would assume a regular spacing between the Clare children, and

8 Edward II's Nieces: The Clare Sisters

Margaret may have been born in Ireland. In her own lifetime, her name was usually spelt 'Margarete', and she was presumably named after her mother's sister the Duchess of Brabant, or after her father's grandmother Margaret Quincy, Countess of Lincoln, and his sister Margaret, Countess of Cornwall. Around Christmas 1294, Gilbert 'the Red' and Joan conceived their last child, who was born at Tewkesbury in Gloucestershire on 16 September 1295, two weeks after Gilbert's fifty-second birthday.[23] It was another daughter, Gilbert's fifth and Joan's third, and they named her Elizabeth after Joan of Acre's youngest sister. In the fourteenth century, the name was spelt Elizabet, Elizabeth, Elizabethe or Elyzabeth.

Gilbert 'the Red' Clare, Earl of Gloucester and Hertford, the wealthiest and most influential English nobleman of the era, died on 7 December 1295 just two-and-a-half months after the birth of his youngest child. His son and sole heir Gilbert the younger was only 4-and-a-half years old, and when a tenant-in-chief died with his heir underage, the revenues of his lands went to the king until the boy turned 21. None of the four Clare children except perhaps Gilbert can have had any memories of their father, though they would have been raised to know exactly who he was and to recognise their own exalted birth and importance. The sisters would also have been very aware of the strong, capable and independent women in their family: their mother and aunts, both their grandmothers, and their great-grandmother Margaret Quincy, one of the greatest English noblewomen of the thirteenth century.

Edward I granted Bristol Castle to his daughter for her and her children's sustenance, so possibly the Clare sisters grew up there, at least part of the time. They may also have spent time at Amesbury Priory in Wiltshire, where their aunt Mary, the king's fourth daughter, was a nun. It was not planned to give any of them to the Church, but Amesbury was a place where they could be educated and where they—and, crudely but importantly by the standards of the era, their virginity—would be safe. Nothing at all is known of the sisters' upbringing and education, but in likelihood they learned to read, and perhaps to write, in French, and would have learnt some Latin, though not to the extent of being able to read it fluently. Later in life, there is evidence that Elizabeth, the third sister, enjoyed books, and perhaps Eleanor and Margaret did as well. They must also have spoken English, but the written language of the nobility in their era was French. Sometime in about early 1297, their mother Joan of Acre caused a huge scandal when she wed a squire named Ralph Monthermer without her father's permission and while the king was negotiating a second marriage for her with Amadeus, Count of Savoy. On 16 March 1297 the future marriage to Amadeus was still under discussion, even though Edward had already heard about his daughter's illicit wedding.[24] Ralph was of obscure parentage, and apparently illegitimate; the London annalist called him 'the bastard of Monthermer'.[25] It was unheard of for a great royal lady to marry a man of such low birth and standing, and Edward I raged when he heard about it. Ralph Monthermer was briefly imprisoned, but as the king could not unmarry the couple and as Joan was probably already pregnant, he eventually had to accept the situation, and Monthermer was released and acknowledged as Earl of Gloucester by right of his wife. Supposedly, Joan sent her three little Clare daughters to the king to soften him up before she approached him in person.[26]

Joan and Ralph's first child Mary Monthermer was born around October 1297, only two years after her half-sister Elizabeth Clare, and later married the Scottish nobleman Duncan MacDuff, Earl of Fife, who grew up in England. Most confusingly, Duncan was the grandson of Gilbert 'the Red' Clare via his mother Joan MacDuff née Clare, Gilbert's second daughter from his first marriage to Alice Lusignan. For the three Clare sisters Eleanor, Margaret and Elizabeth, this meant that their half-sister married their half-nephew, who was born in 1289 and was older than they were. Joan of Acre and Ralph Monthermer had three younger children: Joan, who became a nun at Amesbury Priory, probably born in 1299; Thomas, born in 1301; and Edward, born in 1304.

Eleanor Clare was the first of the four Clare siblings to marry, and her wedding took place on Thursday, 26 May 1306 when she was 13 years 7 months old. Her grandfather Edward I had arranged the marriage and attended the wedding in his own chapel at Westminster Palace, and paid for the minstrels who entertained the guests, including two harpists called Richard Whiteacre and Richard Leyland. The king gave Eleanor a generous £29 for clothes and jewels and another £10 to dress her attendants, and also gave her three pieces of red silk to line a quilt and sixteen more pieces to make a dorsal curtain round her bed.[27] Eleanor's mother Joan of Acre and almost certainly Joan's much younger brother Edward of Caernarfon, Prince of Wales, Duke of Aquitaine, Earl of Chester and Count of Ponthieu, heir to the throne of their aged father, also attended the wedding. The Prince of Wales was then 22, and all four Clare siblings were closer in age to their uncle than their mother, his sister, was.

Eleanor's groom was Hugh Despenser, known to history as Hugh Despenser the Younger to distinguish him from his father of the same name. He was about four years Eleanor's senior, born in the late 1280s and probably 17 or 18 years old in May 1306, and was the maternal grandson of the late Earl and Countess of Warwick, William Beauchamp (d. 1298) and Maud FitzJohn (d. 1301). Hugh's paternal grandmother Aline Basset (d. 1281) was Countess of Norfolk by her second marriage, and his older half-sister Maud Chaworth (b. 1282) married Edward I's nephew Henry of Lancaster (b. *c.* 1280/81) in early 1297, so Hugh had some impressive family connections, yet would not himself inherit an earldom. Warwick passed to his uncle Guy Beauchamp in 1298, and Norfolk escheated to the Crown on the death of his childless stepgrandfather Roger Bigod later in 1306.

As the eldest granddaughter of the king and daughter of the great Earl of Gloucester and Hertford, Eleanor Clare might have expected to make a rather better match and to marry an earl, but Edward I paid Hugh Despenser the Elder £2,000 for his son's marriage and evidently believed the young man to be a satisfactory husband for his granddaughter.[28] Eleanor's first cousin Jeanne de Bar, who was no more than 11 years old and perhaps younger, married John Warenne, Earl of Surrey, also at Westminster the day before Eleanor wed Hugh Despenser. The Surrey marriage would prove to be an unhappy and childless disaster, and the couple lived apart from 1313, perhaps earlier. By contrast, Eleanor and Hugh Despenser formed a good and solid partnership over the years, and certainly a fruitful one. Their marriage of two decades produced at least ten children, the first of whom was a boy born sometime before July 1309 and probably in 1308, and named Hugh after his father, grandfather and great-grandfather. Their second child was Edward Despenser, named after Eleanor's maternal grandfather and uncle, and altogether they had four sons and five daughters who survived childhood. Eleanor was as fertile as her mother and her aunt Elizabeth, Countess of Holland and Hereford (b. 1282, the youngest daughter of Edward I and Leonor of Castile), who between them had eighteen children. Her grandmother Queen Leonor also gave birth to at least fourteen children, perhaps more.

Depending how physically and emotionally mature Eleanor was in 1306, her marriage may not have been consummated, and she may have remained with her mother for some time yet or retreated to Amesbury Priory. Eleanor turned 15 in October 1307, and either became pregnant not long afterwards or perhaps already was.

Hugh Despenser the Younger, Eleanor's uncle Edward of Caernarfon and 265 other men had been knighted in Westminster Abbey four days before her wedding. One of the new young knights was Edward of Caernarfon's beloved friend (and probably lover) Piers Gaveston, a nobleman of Béarn in the far south-west of France and a subject of the English Crown who arrived in England with his father in late 1297.[29] Gaveston would be exiled from England in April 1307 by Eleanor's grandfather the king, who was concerned about the young man's relationship with his son. Edward of Caernarfon, however, recalled him as soon as he possibly could, and Gaveston would become Eleanor's brother-in-law later in 1307. Gaveston probably also attended the Clare-Despenser wedding on 26 May 1306, as he had become the inseparable companion of the heir to the throne. Eleanor's father-in-law Hugh Despenser the Elder was present at her wedding and she may have briefly met her mother-in-law Isabella Despenser née Beauchamp, elder sister of Guy Beauchamp, Earl of Warwick, but Isabella died a little before 30 May 1306 just after the wedding.

Eleanor Despenser née Clare's wealthy, indomitable and immensely capable mother also did not have long to live. Joan of Acre, Countess of Gloucester and Hertford, died on 23 April 1307 at the age of 35 or almost. Given her age and the pattern of her childbearing, it is possible that she died during pregnancy or during or after childbirth, though this is only speculation, and if she did have a child in 1307 it is not mentioned in any known extant record. Edward I had prayers said for his daughter's soul on 6 May, when he heard the news.[30] Joan was buried at the Augustinian priory in Clare, Suffolk, in a chapel dedicated to St Vincent of Zaragoza (died *c*. 304) which she herself had founded.[31] This perhaps reveals Joan's interest in her Spanish heritage. Clare Priory itself was founded in 1248 by Richard Clare, Earl of Gloucester, father of Joan's first husband Gilbert 'the Red' and grandfather of her Clare daughters. It was a pity for Joan's younger brother, the future king, that she died before his reign began; Edward of Caernarfon loved and trusted her, and perhaps her advice might have gone some way to preventing his reign slipping into disaster quite as soon as it did.

Joan left her eight children; Gilbert Clare the eldest was not quite 16, and Edward Monthermer the youngest was barely 3. Joan's Clare daughters Eleanor, Margaret and Elizabeth were 14-and-a-half, 12 or 13, and 11 when they lost their mother. Not long afterwards, they also lost their maternal grandfather, the only grandparent they had known. King Edward I died at Burgh-by-Sands near Carlisle on 7 July 1307, aged 68. Only six of his many children outlived him: Margaret, Duchess of Brabant, Mary the nun, Elizabeth, Countess of Hereford, and Edward of Caernarfon from his first marriage, and the young children Thomas of Brotherton (b. June 1300) and Edmund of Woodstock (b. August 1301) from his second to Marguerite of France. The Clare sisters' uncle succeeded his father as King Edward II, and a new era was about to begin.

Chapter 2

The New King

Probably Edward II's very first act as king, when he heard of his father's death four days after it happened, was to recall his beloved Piers Gaveston to England from the exile imposed on him by Edward I some months before. At Dumfries on 6 August 1307, Edward made Piers Earl of Cornwall. It has often been stated by later writers that Edward I had intended the earldom of Cornwall to go to his youngest son Edmund of Woodstock, but the arrangements he made in 1306 for his children with his second queen Marguerite of France do not mention this, though the king did specify the earldom of Norfolk for his son Thomas of Brotherton.[1] The earldom of Cornwall belonged to Edward I and subsequently to Edward II personally: the last earl, Edmund, had died in 1300, and as he had no children, siblings, nieces or nephews, Cornwall passed by right to his first cousin Edward I as his nearest male relative and then to Edward II on his father's death.[2] The charter granting Cornwall to Piers Gaveston in August 1307 was sealed by all the English earls except Hugh Despenser the Younger's uncle the Earl of Warwick, and it reveals that the new king was already intending to marry his friend, or lover, to his niece Margaret Clare: it is decorated with the Clare arms as well as Gaveston's.[3] Edward was determined to bring Gaveston into the royal family, and Margaret was its oldest available female member in 1307. How much choice Margaret herself had in marrying Piers Gaveston is not clear; almost certainly little or none, but she would not have been raised to expect to have any say in the matter of her marriage. Even her formidable mother Joan of Acre, who chose her own second husband, had obeyed her father and married the decades-older Gilbert 'the Red' in 1290 as Edward I wished. Margaret's parents and grandfather were dead and her brother was only 16 and still underage, and therefore Edward II controlled her destiny both as her king and as her nearest adult male relative.

14 Edward II's Nieces: The Clare Sisters

The wedding of Margaret Clare and Piers Gaveston, Earl of Cornwall, went ahead on 1 November 1307, five days after her grandfather Edward I's funeral at Westminster Abbey, and six months after the death of her mother. The location was Berkhamsted, a manor which belonged to the dowager queen Marguerite, who was the Clare sisters' step-grandmother though was only a few years older than they were. Edward II was to grant custody of Berkhamsted to Piers Gaveston himself in March 1308.[4] The bride was about 13-and-a-half, and the groom much older: Gaveston was born by July 1283 at the latest and perhaps even in the 1270s, and was thus in his mid- to late-20s when he married Margaret.[5] The 23-year-old king gave his niece a fine 'roan-coloured palfrey' horse as a wedding gift, and paid £30 for rich silk cloth for her attendants and for a chaplet for Margaret. Edward also paid the large sum of £20 for minstrels to entertain Piers and Margaret and their wedding guests, and it must have been quite a wild celebration as he had to pay compensation to a local resident for damage done to his property by the guests.[6] Piers Gaveston, no doubt delighted with the marriage which made him the king's nephew-in-law, held a jousting tournament at his castle of Wallingford near Oxford on 2 December 1307 to celebrate it. He and his team of young knights—perhaps including Eleanor Clare's teenage husband Hugh Despenser the Younger, a keen jouster—defeated some of the great earls of the realm. The king was not present, being then at Langley in Hertfordshire dealing with the awkward situation of the mass arrest of the Knights Templar in England, though Piers and Margaret had joined him by 13 December.[7]

A historian claimed in 1979 that Margaret Clare was 'tragically married' to Piers Gaveston, but there is no real evidence for such a value judgement.[8] Gaveston was a nobleman by birth, wealthy, witty and clever, a renowned and brilliant jouster and soldier, and a capable administrator and leader. His modern reputation as little more than a flamboyant court fop is unfair and inaccurate, though it is surely true that he had the kind of personality which alienated a lot of people. Contemporary chroniclers were, with few exceptions, hostile to him, and there was considerable rejoicing throughout England at his death. It is difficult to understand the widespread and unrelenting hatred for Gaveston except by assuming that on a personal level he managed to repel and irritate people, as his behaviour, excepting the haughty arrogance he often displayed, does not otherwise seem to merit it. Edward II, by contrast, adored him and everything about him, and was infatuated with him from his teens onwards and for many years after Gaveston's death. One of the few chroniclers who had a good word for Gaveston was Sir Thomas Gray: in his *Scalacronica* he called Gaveston 'very magnificent, liberal and well-bred', though also 'haughty and supercilious', a common description of the royal favourite.[9] The *Vita Edwardi Secundi* described Gaveston thus: 'scornfully rolling his upraised eyes in pride and in abuse, he looked down upon all with pompous and supercilious countenance'.[10]

Geoffrey le Baker, a later chronicler who in fact never saw him, called Gaveston 'graceful and agile in body, sharp-witted, refined in manners'.[11] Edward I supposedly initially promoted Gaveston because he came from Gascony, the region *de bele manere*, 'of beautiful manners'.[12] It is worth bearing in mind that Edward I himself placed Gaveston in Edward of Caernarfon's household in 1300 or earlier when his son was a teenager, and for many years found him a suitable companion and role model for the heir to the throne. He removed Gaveston from England in April 1307 because he was concerned about the extremely close relationship that had developed between the two men, not because Gaveston had done anything wrong. Piers Gaveston enjoyed poking fun at the powerful and pompous and 'his arrogance was intolerable to the barons and a prime cause of hatred and rancour', but he was not malicious, and there is no reason to suppose that he treated Margaret poorly or unkindly.[13] Perhaps Margaret found him as irritating as many other people did; perhaps she found him amusing, and admired his athletic prowess on the jousting field; we do not know.

Piers Gaveston was, beyond doubt, the great love of Edward II's life, and now he was married to the king's barely pubescent niece. Whether Margaret knew about her husband's relationship with her uncle—whatever there was to know about it—cannot be established. From a modern perspective, the marriage of a girl barely into her teens to a much older man who was involved in an intense and probably sexual relationship with her uncle perhaps seems revolting and callous, but we do not know Margaret's own feelings on the matter. Gaveston was well-versed in courtly manners, and it seems highly unlikely that he would have humiliated her by flaunting his relationship with the king in her face. Margaret became a countess at marriage and thus outranked her older sister Eleanor, and this might have overcome any doubts she had about marrying a man who by birth was several ranks beneath her (albeit still a nobleman). Gaveston enjoyed an income of about £4,000 a year, whereas Margaret's brother-in-law Hugh Despenser the Younger only received about £200, and even that was as a gift of his father Hugh the Elder; Eleanor and Hugh owned no lands at all for the first few years of Edward's reign. As well as becoming a countess, 13-year-old Margaret thus became much richer than her elder sister. She was probably too young for her marriage to be consummated yet or to live with Gaveston as his full wife, and in sharp contrast to Eleanor—who had at least eleven pregnancies between 1308 and *c.* 1330 and gave birth to ten children who survived childhood—Margaret seems to have been not particularly fertile. She was to have one child each from her two marriages.

In January 1308, Edward II left England to marry Philip IV of France's daughter Isabella, his long-term fiancée, in Boulogne. Scandalously, on 26 December 1307 he appointed Piers Gaveston as his regent while he was outside England. The king had spent the festive season of 1307/08 at Westminster with Gaveston and perhaps also with his niece, Gaveston's new wife Margaret, unless Margaret had retreated to Amesbury Priory in Wiltshire or elsewhere until she was old enough to live with her husband. It would have been far more conventional to appoint one of his little half-brothers Thomas or Edmund as nominal regent, or his royal first cousin Thomas, Earl of Lancaster (d. 1322), but Edward cared little for convention. He brought his new bride back to England on 7 February 1308. Piers Gaveston and probably his wife Margaret, and the king's sisters Mary the nun and Elizabeth, Countess of Hereford, were among the welcoming party who greeted them at Dover. Isabella of France was much her husband's junior and only 12 years old, born probably in the second half of 1295 and thus about the same age as the third Clare sister Elizabeth, but was now the Clare sisters' aunt by marriage. One French chronicler who saw Isabella when she and her husband visited Paris in 1313 called her 'the fairest of the fair' (*des belles la plus belle*) and the most beautiful woman who could be found in the kingdom of France or the Holy Roman Empire.[14] Edward II himself was tall—probably at least 6ft—fair-haired, bearded and immensely strong. Numerous contemporary chroniclers comment on his enormous physical strength, and the *Scalacronica* says that he was 'one of the strongest men of his realm'. Unfortunately we have no idea what the Clare sisters looked like; perhaps they inherited their father's red hair, or were tall and fair like their uncle. Eleanor Despenser's seal of early 1329 depicts her wearing a floor-length gown, and her long hair falls either side of her face, topped with some kind of simple headdress.[15]

Edward allowed his 16-year-old nephew Gilbert Clare to have his earldoms of Gloucester and Hertford in March 1308, more than four years early, probably because an earl in control of his large inheritance was much more useful to him politically than an underage ward. He also gave Gilbert permission to marry whomever he wanted, which represents the king punishing his stepmother Queen Marguerite, as her husband Edward I had given her the rights to Gilbert's marriage in 1301.[16] In 1308, the dowager queen joined the baronial opposition to Piers Gaveston and even helped them financially, and Edward II never forgave her and had virtually no contact with her for the remaining ten years of her life. He deliberately gave custody of her manor of Berkhamsted to Gaveston four days after he gave Gilbert Clare permission to take a bride of his own choice.[17] The king's excessive favouritism towards Piers Gaveston was already creating much jealousy and hostility. Mere months into his reign, Edward II had lost the goodwill he had enjoyed at its start, and although he had shown considerable promise as Prince of Wales and heir to the throne, it was starting to become apparent that his leadership was definitely not all it could be. Gilbert Clare's relations with his uncle, and with his brother-in-law Gaveston, waxed and waned over the next few years: sometimes they were on good terms and sometimes not.

Piers Gaveston's baronial enemies forced him into exile for a second time in June 1308, though Edward II ensured he left the country in triumph by making him lord lieutenant of Ireland, just a day after he had appointed Richard Burgh, Earl of Ulster, to the position. Gaveston was forced to give up his earldom of Cornwall, but in compensation, Edward granted him £2,000 worth of lands in his homeland of Gascony, including the city of Bayonne and the island of Oléron, and lands worth another £2,000 in England jointly to Gaveston and his wife Margaret, so they suffered no loss of income.[18] Fourteen-year-old Margaret was not included in her husband's exile, and was to be granted £2,000 a year from the revenues of Cornwall for her sustenance if she remained in England.[19] She was the granddaughter of the old king and the sister of the Earl of

Gloucester, and nobody intended her harm or insult. However, Margaret accompanied Gaveston to Ireland, and they sailed from Bristol at the end of June 1308, waved off by the king.[20] Edward gave his beloved Gaveston a generous gift of £1,180 in cash on departure, and his itinerary reveals that he travelled with Piers and Margaret to Bristol to see them off.[21]

The marital norms of the early fourteenth century mean that it is far more likely to have been Gaveston's decision that Margaret should accompany him, rather than Margaret's own; as his wife she owed him obedience, and could not remain behind in England if he ordered her to travel to Ireland with him. Still, Piers' wish for her to go with him seems to indicate that he was fond of her and desired her company, and perhaps Margaret was pleased to have her husband to herself for once. In travelling to Ireland she may have been returning to her birthplace for the first time since she was an infant, and as she was now 14 she and Gaveston might have consummated their marriage. She and Piers spent a year in Ireland, and Gaveston excelled in his role there. There was far more to him than the useless, greedy court fop of popular imagination, and he was, or could be given the opportunity, an able and intelligent man.[22] Edward II, in England, immediately began a campaign to bring about Gaveston's return by coaxing Pope Clement V (r. 1305–14) onto his side and by manipulating his barons until one by one they consented to Gaveston coming back. It took a year, but his strategy paid off: Edward, like Gaveston, could be clever and competent when he put his mind to it, and it was a pity for his kingdom and his subjects that he only used his undoubted talents when his own personal feelings were involved.

The double wedding of the two unmarried Clare siblings to two children of the Anglo-Irish nobleman Richard Burgh, Earl of Ulster, took place at Waltham Abbey in Essex on 29 and 30 September 1308, in the presence of Edward II. Elizabeth, who had turned 13 two weeks before, married the earl's eldest son and heir John Burgh. The 17-year-old Earl of Gloucester married Maud, one of John Burgh's many sisters, who also included Robert Bruce's wife Elizabeth (d. 1327), queen of Scotland (held under house arrest in England from 1306 to 1314) and the Countesses of Kildare and Desmond. Elizabeth Burgh née Clare was, at barely 13, considered too young to travel to Ireland with her new husband, and appears to have retired to Amesbury Priory in the company of her aunt

Mary the nun for just over a year.[23] She moved to Ireland to live with her husband when she was 14, and became pregnant with her first child when she was 16. Her marriage was intended to make her Countess of Ulster, but did not as her father-in-law outlived his eldest son, and John Burgh is, like almost all medieval noblemen who died before their fathers, obscure. He was born around 1290, so was some years Elizabeth's senior and 18 or so at marriage. Probably Gilbert and Elizabeth's sister Eleanor Despenser attended the wedding, as her father-in-law's manor of North Weald Bassett lay only ten miles from Waltham Abbey, and Hugh Despenser the Elder had given the issues of it to Eleanor and Hugh the Younger. Eleanor can hardly have been pleased that her two younger sisters were both now countesses or set to become such, whereas her own husband would not inherit an earldom, and thus both Margaret and Elizabeth outranked her.

Eleanor Despenser née Clare gave birth to her eldest child sometime in 1308 or the first half of 1309, when she was 15 or 16 (she turned 16 in mid-October 1308 two weeks after the joint wedding of her two siblings) and her husband about 19 or 20. It was a boy, inevitably named Hugh, though in Edward II's household accounts his name always appears as Huchon or Huchoun, obviously his family nickname. The *Anonimalle* chronicler gave the young man the name Hughelyn or 'little Hugh' when talking about him in 1326.[24] Evidently, modern writers are not the only ones who struggle with generation after generation of medieval noblemen with the same name. It became especially confusing in the 1320s when Huchon's father and grandfather were still alive and there were three generations of Hugh Despensers active in England, and the boy was called 'Hugh Despenser, son of Hugh Despenser the son' or 'Huchon Despenser, son of the son'. Huchon was Joan of Acre's eldest grandchild and Edward I's eldest great-grandchild. Very little is known about his parents' life in the first few years of Edward II's reign, where Eleanor and Hugh the Younger lived or what they did or if they were happy together. Hugh's father Hugh the Elder gave the couple the issues of six of his manors in Essex, Cambridgeshire and Suffolk, and they had an income of around £200 a year, in line with a promise made by Hugh the Elder to Edward I in June 1306 to provide them with such.[25] This was a large income by the standards of most of the English population in the early 1300s and in modern terms is several hundred thousand pounds, but it was a small income by the standards of their class and family: Eleanor's brother Gilbert earned about £7,000 a year and her brother-in-law Piers Gaveston about £4,000. Hugh Despenser the Younger's relative poverty for more than half of his uncle-in-law's reign may be a factor in the almost pathological greed he was to demonstrate in later years when he became the king's favourite and perhaps lover.

Chapter 3

Journeys to Ireland

Eleanor Despenser, though not her younger sisters, frequently attended their aunt by marriage, Queen Isabella, as one of her ladies-in-waiting. The first evidence for this comes on 28 November 1310 when Eleanor set off to meet Isabella at Berwick-on-Tweed in the far north-east of the kingdom, where the young queen spent a year with her husband from October 1310 until September 1311. Eleanor's expenses of 100 marks (£66) were paid by her uncle, who also gave her a gift of 20 marks.[1] Most probably, she had begun attending Isabella when the young queen arrived in England in early 1308. Isabella's household accounts survive for her husband's fifth regnal year from 8 July 1311 to 7 July 1312, and reveal that Eleanor headed the list of the queen's ladies-in-waiting that year ahead of Alice, Countess of Buchan, Isabella, Lady Vescy, and Ida, Lady Clinton. Eleanor was called *Domina* [Lady] *Alianore la Despensere*, the contemporary spelling of her name, in the accounts. It is unclear how much time Eleanor spent with the queen, though it was probably at most a few weeks a year, as she had her own familial and feudal responsibilities. It was not a paid position, though she was entitled to receive robes twice a year as a member of the queen's household, and Eleanor continued attending Isabella into the mid-1320s.

There is ample evidence throughout Edward II's reign of his great affection for his eldest niece Eleanor Despenser, who was only eight years his junior. When Edward was at Windsor Castle on 1 April 1308, fortifying it against his own barons and obstinately refusing to send Eleanor's brother-in-law Piers Gaveston into exile, he found time to send her 20 marks to cover her expenses for her stay at the royal castle of Rockingham near Corby, Northamptonshire. On 8 May 1308, Edward gave her a further 10 marks to travel from Rockingham to visit him at Westminster.[2] Eleanor is likely to have been pregnant with her first child, Huchon, at this time. In the year 1313/14 when his accounts happen to survive, Edward gave his niece generous sums of money, between £3 and £10, every few days or weeks, and there is no reason to suppose that this was unique or unusual.³ The king had to give the money to Hugh Despenser the Younger as he was Eleanor's husband, but the money was specifically said to be for Eleanor alone, not the two of them. Although Edward was hugely fond of Eleanor and of her father-in-law Hugh Despenser the Elder, one of his closest and staunchest allies, for many years he seems to have distrusted and even actively disliked Eleanor's husband. Hugh the Younger followed the political lead of his maternal uncle the Earl of Warwick in the first few years of Edward II's reign and hence was quite hostile to both the king and Piers Gaveston. Given the way in later years the king came to love Despenser the Younger greatly and to allow him to rule his kingdom, it can be difficult to grasp how powerless and out of favour Hugh was for well over half the reign.

Although Piers Gaveston was still in Ireland in the spring of 1309, baronial dissatisfaction with the king persisted in many quarters, and a jousting tournament was held in Dunstable, Bedfordshire in March or April 1309 as a cover for several noblemen to air their grievances and discuss possible solutions. It was probably at Dunstable that a programme of reforms presented to the king at parliament later in 1309 was first worked out: these included grievances about escheators, purveyances, writs, petitions and the like. Edward II's nephew Gilbert Clare, Earl of Gloucester, was one of the men present at Dunstable, as was his brother-in-law Hugh Despenser the Younger. Hugh attended with a retinue of ten knights, who were all or almost all his father's retainers, rather than his own. Hugh the Elder himself, immensely loyal to the king, did not attend the tournament. Another young knight at Dunstable, competing as part of the Earl of Gloucester's retinue, was the man who one day would marry Gloucester's widowed sister Elizabeth Burgh: Sir Roger Damory.⁴

Piers Gaveston and his wife Margaret née Clare returned to England in late June 1309, a year almost to the day after he had been sent into his second exile by his baronial enemies. The besotted king restored Piers to the earldom of Cornwall at the Stamford Parliament of August 1309, and gave him and Margaret all their lands back. Neither man showed much common sense, however, and continued to behave in the same manner as they had before Gaveston's exile. Piers probably gave some of the English barons insulting nicknames, though the only one recorded in his own lifetime is the one he gave to Eleanor Despenser's uncle-in-law Guy Beauchamp, Earl of Warwick: the 'Black Dog (or Hound) of Arden'. The others were not recorded until much later in the fourteenth century and is it not impossible that they were the invention of chroniclers. Supposedly Piers called the portly Earl of Lincoln 'Mr Burst-Belly', the Earl of Pembroke 'Joseph the Jew', and Edward II's first cousin the Earl of Lancaster 'the Fiddler' or 'the Churl'. The most derogatory nickname recorded is *filz a puteyne*, 'whoreson', which many historians assume Piers gave to his brother-in-law Gilbert Clare, Earl of Gloucester. However, it seems highly unlikely that Piers would insult Edward II's beloved sister and his own late mother-in-law Joan of Acre in such a public fashion, and the Earl of Gloucester was his close ally after his return from Ireland, which would argue against the notion that Gaveston called Gloucester's mother a whore. It seems far more likely, assuming Piers Gaveston ever did call anyone 'whoreson', that he was referring to the Clare siblings' stepfather Ralph Monthermer, who was illegitimate. As well as Gloucester, another earl who grew close to Gaveston in and after 1309 was John Warenne, Earl of Surrey, husband of the Clare siblings' first cousin Jeanne de Bar. Surrey had previously been hostile to the royal favourite, and was one of the knights defeated at Gaveston's Wallingford tournament of December 1307. The author of the *Vita Edwardi Secundi* wrote in exasperation 'See how often and abruptly great men change their sides ... the love of magnates is as a game of dice.'[5]

Neither the hatred for Gaveston among many of the earls and the general populace, nor the knowledge that his friend's 'name was reviled far and wide' and that he was thought to be 'wicked, impious and criminal' bothered Edward II; the more he heard that almost everyone in the country hated Gaveston, the more he loved him.[6] Margaret Gaveston perhaps cared more about her husband's appalling reputation than her uncle did. Gaveston was at his own castle of Knaresborough in Yorkshire on 6 November 1309 when he sent a polite letter to John Langton, bishop of Chichester and chancellor of England. He called himself 'Pieres de Gavastoun, Earl of Cornwall', and the letter demonstrates that he was perfectly capable of courtesy when he chose: part of it runs 'Sire, we beseech you urgently that, if it please you, you may please let us have two letters'.⁷ The letter was written in French. This was Gaveston's native language and the language he would have spoken with the king and with his wife Margaret, though Gaveston's French would have had a strongly southern flavour. Edward II was just six miles away from Knaresborough at Great Ribston on that date – where Gaveston's itinerary in England can be established it generally coincides with the king's, or they were mere miles apart – and probably Margaret was with her husband. Her uncle adored Gaveston; whether she herself loved him or even liked him, and whether she thought that her uncle was the third person in her marriage and resented it, cannot be known.

Elizabeth Burgh née Clare set off for Ireland some months after her sister Margaret's return from there, on 15 October 1309.⁸ She was now 14 and considered old enough to join her husband John, the Earl of Ulster's eldest son and heir. Not much is known of Elizabeth's life in Ireland. John Burgh had many sisters: Maud was Countess of Gloucester and the wife of Elizabeth's brother Gilbert Clare; Elizabeth Bruce was the wife of Robert, king of Scotland and under house arrest in England; and Eleanor lived in Cumberland in northern England with her husband Thomas, Lord Multon and had a son John Multon in 1308, later the fiancé of Margaret Gaveston's daughter. John Burgh's other sisters included the Countesses of Kildare and Desmond and the future Countess of Louth, who all lived in Ireland and whom Elizabeth must have known.

Presumably Elizabeth's sister, 15-year-old Margaret Gaveston, and their 14-year-old aunt-in-law Queen Isabella, were with Edward II and Piers Gaveston at Edward's favourite residence of Langley in Hertfordshire at Christmas 1309. The king and the Earl of Cornwall passed the time 'making up for former absence by their long wished-for sessions of daily and intimate conversation'.⁹ Eleanor Despenser's father-in-law Hugh Despenser the Elder was also with the king that Christmas, as he usually was; now 48 years old, Despenser had been a loyal royal servant all his life, and was the only English nobleman of high rank to remain loyal to Edward II for his entire reign.¹⁰

Eleanor's husband Hugh Despenser the Younger left England for much of 1310, taking part in jousting tournaments abroad despite an order issued by the king on 31 December 1309 prohibiting English noblemen and knights from doing so. The disgruntled Edward II ordered Hugh's lands and goods to be seized on 9 January 1310 after he learned that

Hugh had disobeyed him, though restored the lands a few weeks later on finding out that they belonged by right to Hugh the Elder, not his son.[11] Hugh the Younger, now about 21 years old, held no lands of his own, and he and Eleanor only had the income assigned to them from a half-dozen manors belonging to his father. Hugh might have left his wife Eleanor pregnant when he departed from England at the end of 1309 or beginning of 1310, and perhaps returned to England in or after July 1310 – one tournament he certainly took part in, in the town of Mons, was held that July – to find that she had borne him a child or was heavily pregnant. A payment of 20 marks to Eleanor's messenger John Chaucomb for taking news of her to the king is recorded in the royal accounts on 21 October 1310, just after Eleanor's eighteenth birthday.[12] It is likely, though not certain, that this news related to the birth of a child: Edward II often paid messengers for bringing him news of children born to his sisters and nieces. Eleanor may have become pregnant while overseas accompanying Hugh the Younger when he went jousting. If so, she must have returned to her homeland to give birth, as English people born outside the lands ruled by their king ran into legal difficulties when it came to estates and inheritances.[13] The king's territories comprised Wales, Ireland, Gascony and Ponthieu, as well as England. As such, Eleanor herself, who was born in Wales, her sister Margaret, who was perhaps born in Ireland, her sister Elizabeth's son the Earl of Ulster, who was certainly born in Ireland, and Margaret's Gascon husband Piers Gaveston, encountered no such problems. If Eleanor did give birth in 1310, it is likely to have been to her second son Edward Despenser. Perhaps naming him 'Edward' in honour of the king was Eleanor's way of appeasing her annoyed uncle after her husband, and she herself, defied his command not to leave the kingdom to joust. Then again, Eleanor as a wife was bound to obey her husband and to go where he told her, and Edward II would not have blamed her or held her responsible if she did go abroad with Hugh. His paying her expenses and sending her frequent gifts of money in the following years reveals that the incident had not damaged Eleanor's close relationship with her uncle at all.

In the autumn of 1310, Edward II made his way north to attempt to deal with Robert Bruce, who had crowned himself king of Scotland in 1306. The kings of England claimed overlordship of the northern kingdom, though Edward had postponed campaigning there since the start of his reign, being infatuated with both Gaveston himself and protecting him (bringing him back from Ireland in 1309). Bruce, well aware that the king of England would always be able to field a larger army than he could, wisely refused to meet the English king in battle, and Edward's year spent in Berwick-on-Tweed accomplished nothing. Queen Isabella, who turned 15 in or around late 1310, accompanied her husband; she was attended by her niece-in-law Eleanor Despenser in November 1310 and possibly in other months. Eleanor's brother Gilbert Clare, Earl of Gloucester, also went north with his uncle, as did John Warenne, Earl of Surrey, and Piers Gaveston.

Gaveston was based in and around Perth, and his wife Margaret née Clare was with him. On 19 April 1311, both Margaret and her cousin Jeanne de Bar, Countess of Surrey, are recorded as visiting their uncle at Berwick.[14] It must have been almost exactly at this time that Piers and Margaret Gaveston conceived a child who was born on or a little after 12 January 1312; a 38-week pregnancy from the date of conception would be about 21 April 1311. This may have been their first child together, or Margaret—who turned 17 sometime in 1311—may have been pregnant before and had miscarriages or stillbirths. Presumably she was aware that her husband had an illegitimate daughter, whom he had named Amie after his only sister. The identity of the girl's mother is unknown, nor do we know when Amie was born, or anything about her at all until she first appears on record in 1332. Edward II presumably knew about her existence. He himself had an illegitimate son called Adam, born sometime in or before 1310, either before he married Isabella or when she was too young to be his wife in more than name only.

Eleanor Despenser attended Queen Isabella again in the far north of England for part of the period from early July 1311 to early July 1312, according to surviving queen's accounts. On 31 July 1311, Isabella paid 12 pence for ale for Eleanor's breakfast, a curiously large sum to spend on ale when a gallon of it could be purchased for a penny, so presumably it was intended for all of Eleanor's retinue as well. At Christmas 1311, a couple of months after she turned 19, Eleanor headed the list of Isabella's four ladies-in-waiting and eight damsels entitled to receive robes from the queen.[15] Eleanor had her own chamberlain called John of Berkhamsted, who appears in an entry on the Close Roll of 30 April 1311 when he was supposedly sent into retirement at Barnwell Priory in Northamptonshire after he had served Eleanor for an unspecified long time. (The manor of Barnwell belonged to Eleanor's father-in-law Hugh Despenser the Elder.) However, he still attended Eleanor from July 1311 to July 1312 as he is named as her chamberlain in the queen's accounts.[16]

Eleanor had two damsels serving her, Emma Prior and Emma's daughter Joan. Emma was known as Emote or Emmote and Joan as Jonette, affectionate diminutives of their names. Joan first appears on record serving Eleanor as a damsel in 1309, and she and her mother appear several times in Edward II's chamber account of 1324/25. One of Margaret Gaveston's damsels was called Maud Woodmancote, and later in life their sister Elizabeth Burgh's attendants included Suzanne Neketon and Anne Lexden. It seems to have been the norm for noble ladies of the fourteenth century to be attended by two damsels, sometimes more: in the 1340s, Elizabeth Burgh's daughter-in-law Maud of Lancaster employed Pernel (or Petronilla) Pagham and Agnes Waleys.[17]

The queen, meanwhile, had nine damsels who are named in 1311/12, and three who are named in Edward II's accounts in 1324/25 (this was not necessarily all of them), as well as her four ladies-in-waiting.[18] 'Damsel' was a social rank and meant a woman who was either not married or married to a man who was not a knight, and does not imply anything about the women's ages. One of Queen Isabella's damsels in 1311/12 was Alice Leygrave, who in 1284/85 had worked as Edward II's wet-nurse and who was therefore decades older than the young queen (born *c*. late 1295). Alice's daughter Cecily was another royal damsel.[19]

Although she had a chamberlain, two damsels and no doubt other attendants, before they inherited a third of her late brother's lands, Eleanor and Hugh Despenser the Younger were probably not rich enough to be able to afford a large household of servants. Eleanor was at court sometimes, in attendance to the queen and probably spent time with her uncle, but Hugh was rarely there. The London annalist stated in late 1311 that various courtiers, including Sir Edmund Bacon and Piers Gaveston's retainer Sir Robert Darcy, left court with the specific intention of assaulting Hugh Despenser the Younger.[20] Presumably this was done to punish Hugh for not supporting the king. Although his father was one of Edward II's closest allies, Hugh himself followed the political lead of his maternal uncle Guy Beauchamp, Earl of Warwick, Piers Gaveston's most implacable enemy.

28   Edward II's Nieces: The Clare Sisters

While the king was in the far north of his kingdom, a group of earls, barons and bishops calling themselves the Lords Ordainer had been working on a programme to reform the royal household and government. Edward II reluctantly travelled south to London in September 1311 to hear what they had to say. The Lords Ordainer presented their forty-one reforms or Ordinances to the king, and to his horror, they limited his royal power severely. The twentieth Ordinance banished Piers Gaveston from England for the third time, and this was the one that caused the king the most grief. On this occasion, Piers was specifically exiled from all Edward II's territories (even Gaveston's native Gascony) to prevent the king again turning disaster into triumph by appointing him as a high-ranking royal official. Gaveston may have expected his exile to be permanent, or at least drag on for some years, as on 22 October 1311 he was given letters of protection for five years and appointed four attorneys for the same length of time.[21] His wife Margaret did not accompany him abroad this time, for the simple reason that she was a few months pregnant. Gaveston's earldom of Cornwall was revoked, but financial arrangements were made for Margaret. As the Earl of Gloucester's sister and Edward I's granddaughter, she was not the target of the Ordainers' bile. Some of the barons affixed their seals to letters testifying to Gaveston's 'good character and loyalty'. At Edward II's request, his nephew and Gaveston's brother-in-law Gloucester also affixed his seal, but later changed his mind and tore it from the letters, 'excusing himself on the grounds of his minority' (the Clare sisters' older and only brother was now 20 years old).[22]

Gaveston was meant to leave England by 1 November 1311, though (as in 1308) left some days late, and there were suspicions amongst the Ordainers that he did not leave the country at all but went to the West Country. Men were sent there to search for him.[23] If this were true, presumably Margaret Gaveston was aware that her husband had not left the country, even if he could not openly join her. In November 1311, the month of Gaveston's third exile, a young knight of good noble birth joined her uncle's household and became a retainer of Edward II: Sir Hugh Audley, second son of an Oxfordshire lord.[24] He was about 18 or 20 years old. Audley would one day become one of the king's male favourites and among those called 'worse than Gaveston' by one chronicler, and would marry the widowed Margaret Gaveston.

The pregnant Margaret retired to Wallingford Castle, and Queen Isabella wrote to her there at New Year 1312, courteously calling her 'Countess of Cornwall' although her husband had, once again, been stripped of the title. Edward II resumed Wallingford, and all Gaveston's other lands, into his own hands on 10 December 1311 and appointed custodians, but as Margaret was at Wallingford weeks later he must have allowed her to maintain residence there. The queen sent Margaret 'various precious goods' as her New Year gift, and wrote to her receiver in the county of Ponthieu calling Gaveston 'the Earl of Cornwall'. She may have been aiding him financially, and Edward II rewarded his wife by giving her his palace of Eltham in Kent. Isabella set off there with Eleanor Despenser.[25] Sometime in early January 1312, Edward II collected his niece Margaret from Wallingford, and headed to Yorkshire with her. The 200-mile journey must have been dreadfully uncomfortable for Margaret, whose pregnancy was nearing full term. Presumably, Edward's motive in dragging Margaret on such an awful journey was to protect her. He must have known that Piers Gaveston was returning, probably because he had ordered him back, and wanted to keep Margaret out of the way of the Ordainers, who might use her as a hostage. Yorkshire was a safe distance from them in the south.

Margaret arrived safely in York, where she gave birth to a child on or around 12 January 1312.[26] This was, presumably, her and Gaveston's only surviving child Joan Gaveston, named after Margaret's mother Joan of Acre, and Piers' heir. Piers' former nurse Agnes received a payment on 5 February, probably for aiding Margaret during her pregnancy or labour.[27] The king seems to have met Gaveston at Knaresborough on 13 January, and the two men rushed the seventeen miles to York that same day so that Gaveston could see his wife and newborn infant.[28] On 18 January 1312, the king revoked Piers Gaveston's exile, declaring that he 'has returned to the kingdom by the king's order and is ready to justify himself before the king, wherefore the king holds him good and loyal'. Edward had his sheriffs proclaim the news, and two days later, ordered them to restore the lands of Gaveston's earldom to him.[29] The king, so determined to keep his beloved nephew-in-law with him, was about to bring his kingdom to the brink of civil war.

Chapter 4

Two Young Widows

Edward II held a huge celebration to celebrate Margaret Gaveston's purification on 20 February approximately forty days after Joan Gaveston's birth, which cost him 40 marks for the minstrels including one called 'King Robert'.[1] Margaret's sister Elizabeth Burgh also bore her first child in 1312, on 17 September, the day after her seventeenth birthday. It was a boy called William, and he became the heir to his grandfather's earldom of Ulster after his father John. William Burgh is often called William Donn, 'the Brown', presumably a reference to his hair colour.

The year 1312, in fact, proved a fertile one for all four Clare siblings. Eleanor Despenser gave birth sometime in 1312 to her eldest daughter Isabella Despenser, who was probably her third child after Huchon and Edward. She was named after Eleanor's late mother-in-law Isabella Despenser née Beauchamp (it was conventional in the early fourteenth century to name one's eldest daughter after her paternal grandmother). According to the Westminster chronicle *Flores Historiarum*, Eleanor, Margaret and Elizabeth's brother Gilbert, Earl of Gloucester, and his wife Maud Clare née Burgh had a son born in April 1312 who died before the end of the year.[2] Supposedly, the boy was called John, and the chronicle from Tewkesbury Abbey says that the boy was buried in the abbey.[3] It seems a little odd that the boy would have been called John and not Gilbert, Richard or Thomas, the usual male Clare names; the chronicler may be mistaken on this point. The queen of England, Isabella of France, was now 16 or 17, and she and Edward II also had their first child in 1312. The Clare siblings' first cousin, the future King Edward III, was born at Windsor Castle on 13 November 1312, and thus was conceived in York in late February or thereabouts, only a few days after the festivities which marked Joan Gaveston's birth.

The Ordainers pursued Piers Gaveston, and the earls of Pembroke and Surrey – normally allies of the king but infuriated now by his behaviour – besieged him at Scarborough Castle in May 1312 after Edward II rather foolishly left him there. Gaveston had to surrender after only nine days, as Scarborough was not provisioned for a longer siege. He was placed in the custody of the royal cousin Aymer Valence, Earl of Pembroke, who was tasked with taking him south to Gaveston's own castle of Wallingford, and a parliament would be held in the south of England to discuss and determine the favourite's fate. Edward and Gaveston kept in touch via messengers until 9 June, the day Gaveston and Pembroke reached the village of Deddington in Oxfordshire.[4] The whereabouts of Piers' wife Margaret and baby daughter Joan in all of this is unfortunately unknown; Margaret may have travelled south to Wallingford Castle, or remained in her uncle's retinue in the north of England. The men who had besieged her husband at Scarborough Castle met Edward II in York between about 26 and 28 May 1312. Perhaps Gaveston was also there and she was able to see him one last time, and maybe she sent him letters as he journeyed south. On the night of 9 June, the Earl of Pembroke went to visit his wife Beatrice a few miles away and left Gaveston behind at the priory of Deddington under guard; the men were now only thirty miles from Wallingford, but Gaveston would never reach his own castle or see it again, or his wife and child. Guy Beauchamp, Earl of Warwick, who loathed Piers Gaveston for his presumption and his insulting nicknames, seized an opportunity for revenge. On the morning of Saturday, 10 June, Piers Gaveston woke to the sound of chaos outside: the Earl of Warwick and a large armed force had surrounded the priory, and Gaveston heard the earl call out 'Arise, traitor, you are taken!'[5] He looked out of the window and shouted down that the 'black dog of Arden' had arrived. Warwick hurled back the not terribly witty retort that he was no dog, but the Earl of Warwick.[6]

Warwick's men overpowered the guards left by the Earl of Pembroke, dragged Gaveston out of the priory barefoot and bare-headed, and tore his belt of knighthood from him.[7] Surrounded by armed men, Gaveston was forced to walk through the streets of Deddington with a large crowd taunting him. He was then given a mangy horse to speed his thirty-mile journey to the dungeons of Warwick Castle. All the way, 'blaring trumpets followed Piers and the horrid cry of the populace', many people rejoicing at the downfall of the detested favourite.[8] The *Annales Paulini* say that Gaveston temporarily escaped from Warwick's custody, and the *Anonimalle* that he was taken to Warwick's castle of Elmley in Worcestershire first, but these statements seem rather improbable.[9] At his castle of Warwick, Guy Beauchamp cast Gaveston into the dungeon, in chains, and waited for the earls of Lancaster, Hereford and Arundel to arrive. The Earl of Lancaster was a first cousin of Margaret Gaveston's late mother Joan of Acre, and the Earl of Hereford was married to Edward II's sister Elizabeth and hence was Margaret's uncle-in-law, but her close familial relationships to them would not save her husband. Meanwhile, the Earl of Pembroke desperately tried to free Gaveston, not so much out of concern for his well-being but because he had sworn an oath to protect him and pledged his lands in support of the oath. He even asked Oxford University for help, to no avail, and in desperation turned to the Earl of Gloucester, who by now was clearly sick of his brother-in-law and refused to help even for his sister Margaret's sake. He told Pembroke that Warwick 'did this with our aid and counsel' and 'it only remains to advise you to learn another time to negotiate more cautiously', a rather condescending comment from a man who had just turned 21 to one twenty years his senior.[10]

Warwick, Lancaster and the others had every intention of killing Gaveston. Lancaster declared 'while he lives there will be no safe place in the realm of England, as many proofs have hitherto shown us'. Probably, they could see no alternative to killing him; if they exiled him for the fourth time, an obstinate Edward, who refused even to try to live without his niece's husband as a constant presence in his life, would only recall him yet again, civil war would break out, and thus they decided that 'this man alone should die, who oppressed our people with wars and battles.'[11] (What 'battles' they were referring to is unclear.) On 19 June, the Earl of Warwick sent a messenger to his prisoner. The man insolently told Gaveston 'Look to yourself, my lord, for today you shall die the death.'[12] The royal favourite was removed from his dungeon, and taken two miles along the road to Kenilworth where they reached Blacklow Hill on the Earl of Lancaster's lands. Lancaster took responsibility for the bloody act: 'Thomas, Earl of Lancaster, being of higher birth and more powerful than the rest, took upon himself the peril of the business, and ordered Piers, after three terms of exile, as one disobedient to three lawful warnings, to be put to death'. As Gaveston was the brother-in-law of the Earl of

Gloucester, Lancaster and the others agreed to grant him the nobleman's death by decapitation, rather than hanging. And so 'they put to death a great earl whom the king had adopted as brother, whom the king cherished as a son, whom the king regarded as friend and ally.'[13]

The *Vita* puts a most implausible speech in Gaveston's mouth:

> Oh! Where are the presents that bought me so many intimate friends, and with which I thought to have sufficient power? Where are my friends, in whom was my trust, the protection of my body, and my whole hope of safety; whose lusty youth, unbeaten valour, and courage was always aflame for hard tasks? They had promised to stand by me in war, to suffer imprisonment, and not to shun death. Indeed my pride, the arrogance that one single promise of theirs has nourished, the king's favour and the king's court, have brought me to this sorry plight. I have no help, every remedy is in vain, let the will of the earls be done.[14]

While the earls of Lancaster, Hereford and Arundel stood some distance away, one of Lancaster's Welsh men-at-arms ran Gaveston through with a sword, and as he lay dying on the ground, another cut off his head.[15] The earls demonstrated their contempt for Gaveston by leaving his mutilated body lying on the dusty road, and returned post-haste to the safety of Warwick Castle. A group of Dominican friars from Oxford came across Gaveston's body, either by accident or design – the Dominicans or Blackfriars were Edward II's favourite order – and took it to their house, where they embalmed it and sewed his head back on. An enormous ruby set in gold, worth £1,000 and a gift from Edward, was found on Gaveston's body, as were an emerald, a diamond 'of great value' and three more large rubies set in gold. Other items which had belonged to Gaveston and were seized by the Earl of Lancaster at Tynemouth in early May 1312 were eventually returned to the king – not to Gaveston's wife Margaret – in February 1313.[16] The Dominicans could not bury Gaveston as he had died under sentence of excommunication and hence could not be interred in consecrated ground, and ultimately he was not buried for two-and-a-half years after death even though the sentence had long been lifted by then. This was Edward II's decision, not Margaret's.

And so passed Piers Gaveston, the charismatic and notorious favourite and nephew-in-law of a king. He was in his early to mid-30s when he died, the father of a 5-month-old daughter and an illegitimate daughter, age unknown. The king heard the news on or just before 26 June, after he and the four months pregnant Queen Isabella had returned to York.[17] Edward II's primary reaction to Gaveston's death at the hands of his cousin Lancaster and his brother-in-law Hereford was utter rage.[18] Most of his subjects did not feel the same way: according to the *Vita*, 'When Piers had met his end, and the voice of the people had dinned his death into the ears of all, the country rejoiced, and all its inhabitants were glad ... The land rejoices, its inhabitants rejoice that they have found peace in Piers' death.'[19] To say that 'everyone' rejoiced is an exaggeration, but there is no doubt that Gaveston had been intensely unpopular. Edward would later demonstrate enormous concern and care for Gaveston's earthly remains.[20] He remembered Gaveston for the rest of his life, and honoured his memory; as late as June 1326, the last year of his reign, he was still having prayers said for Gaveston's soul.[21]

Unfortunately, it is far more difficult to ascertain what Gaveston's widow Margaret thought and felt, whether or how much she grieved, whether she had ever been embarrassed to be married to someone so unpopular and controversial or did not care, or even when and how she heard the news of her husband's execution. She and Edward paid for two clerks to watch over Gaveston's embalmed body, which the Dominicans dressed in a cloth of gold.[22] Margaret Gaveston née Clare was only 18 years old (or almost) when her husband was killed, and had been left alone with a young child, but no-one bothered to record her reaction to Gaveston's sudden and shocking demise.

The king granted lands worth 2,000 marks or £1,333 a year to Margaret, 'to hold, for her sustenance, and until the king shall make other provision for her'. It was difficult for Edward to give Margaret her full dower as Countess of Cornwall, as the legal status of Piers Gaveston was unclear; the king certainly believed that he was Earl of Cornwall at the time of his death, but the Lords Ordainer did not agree. The death of Margaret's aunt in September 1312 neatly solved the financial problem. The aunt's name was also Margaret and she was one of the three sisters of the late Gilbert 'the Red' Clare, and had been married to the previous Earl of Cornwall, Edward I's cousin Edmund (1249–1300). This older

Margaret had no children, and her dower lands reverted by right to the king as her late husband's heir (after Edward I's death in 1307, Edward II was Edmund of Cornwall's closest male relative). Edward gave them to his niece, and also allowed Margaret to hold the royal manor of Burstwick, Yorkshire. Burstwick had been granted to Margaret and Gaveston during their time in Ireland, and was one of the manors they gave back to Edward when Gaveston was restored to the earldom of Cornwall on 5 August 1309. So keen was Edward to look after Margaret financially that the grant of lands to her which had been her aunt's dower was made on the same day, 16 September 1312, as he and his clerks heard of the aunt's death. Margaret Gaveston also became the high sheriff of the county of Rutland, and the income from the lands made her one of the richest people in the country.[23]

Something of Margaret's character is revealed by a petition she presented probably in 1315, calling herself 'Margarete de Gavastoun, Countess of Cornwall' and addressing her uncle the king as 'my very dear and very honourable lord, your highness'. She stated that some of her Burstwick tenants wanted to be governed by the customs of the manor and others by the common law of England, and that she could not and did not wish to decide the correct course of action without Edward's advice. On 7 November 1315, Edward ordered his chancellor to appoint two men to examine the matter, and to certify him as soon as possible of their findings.[24] Surely no child of Gilbert 'the Red' Clare and Joan of Acre could have been a shrinking violet, though it is hard to imagine that Joan herself would ever have wished to consult the king regarding a matter on one of her manors or would have been unwilling to act without his counsel. Margaret was less sure of herself than her confident mother, and was arguably the quietest of the four Clare siblings. On the other hand, being the widow of a reviled royal favourite, she perhaps felt that she could not exercise her own power and agency as freely as she might have wished, and preferred to place the decision in her uncle's hands to avoid incurring serious criticism of her actions.

The king took care of Gaveston and Margaret's infant daughter Joan, his own great-niece. As Piers Gaveston had been a tenant-in-chief who held land directly from the king, by the law and custom of the time Edward II was now Joan Gaveston's legal guardian, not her mother Margaret. He sent Joan to Amesbury Priory to be raised there. This was not Edward pushing his favourite's child out of the way or cruelly depriving her of her mother's care, but was a privilege for her. Several of Joan's relatives lived at Amesbury, which had been fashionable among royal ladies since Edward's grandmother Eleanor of Provence, Henry III's widow, had retired there in the 1280s. Edward's sister Mary and their niece Joan Monthermer, who was Margaret Gaveston's half-sister and thus Joan Gaveston's aunt, were nuns there, and in later years Isabella of Lancaster, daughter of the Earl of Lancaster's brother Henry, also became a nun at Amesbury. Joan's aunt Elizabeth Burgh lived at Amesbury for a year after her wedding and lived there again during a later pregnancy in 1316/17, and the three Clare sisters may have grown up there, at least partly. In 1312, there is every sign that Edward II was hugely fond of his niece Margaret and keen to look after her and her child, and he went out of his way to ensure that Margaret had lands to provide her with a large income (which was almost seven times higher annually than her elder sister Eleanor Despenser's).

On 18 June 1313, a year almost to the day after Piers Gaveston's execution, Elizabeth Burgh also suffered a great loss. Her husband John Burgh died in his early 20s, leaving her a widow at still only 17 years old with a 9-month-old son, William. Two of the Clare sisters had now become widows while still only in their teens, and both had infant children. Elizabeth had expected to be Countess of Ulster, but as John died in his father's lifetime it was not to be, although her son was heir to his grandfather's earldom. What or who killed John is unknown. He is a shadowy figure, as medieval noblemen who pre-deceased their fathers and never succeeded to their titles and lands generally are. Elizabeth remained in Ireland for the time being, under the protection of her powerful father-in-law Richard, Earl of Ulster. Young though she still was, *c*. 1313 Elizabeth almost certainly founded the Augustinian priory of Ballinrobe, County Mayo, supposedly to celebrate the birth of her son William and perhaps also in memory of her husband. Its origins are lost, but it stood on land which belonged to Elizabeth and John Burgh. Her paternal grandfather Richard Clare, Earl of Gloucester (1222–62), had been the man responsible for bringing the Augustinians or Austin Friars to England in 1248 when he founded Clare Priory in Suffolk, the first Augustinian house in England and the burial place of Elizabeth's mother Joan of Acre.

The Clare sisters' much younger first cousin Edward of Windsor (r. 1327–77), first child of Edward II and Isabella of France, had been born in the meantime, at Windsor Castle on 13 November 1312. The country rejoiced at the birth of their future king, especially in London, where a public holiday was held on 14 November to mark the birth and where the inhabitants celebrated with free wine and feasts. The royal couple, leaving their baby son behind, spent two months in France between May and July 1313 when Isabella's three brothers were knighted. Gilbert Clare, Earl of Gloucester, was left behind in England as regent, and his sisters Eleanor Despenser and Margaret Gaveston probably accompanied the king and queen to Paris. Margaret was with Edward II at Westminster on 28 November 1313 and at Canterbury on 20 February 1314, and was almost certainly with him on numerous other occasions during the five years of her widowhood, but establishing the Clare sisters' itineraries is very difficult.[25] The king was particularly generous to Eleanor Despenser in late 1313 and early 1314: he gave her £10 on 10 October, another £10 five days later, £5 on 27 October and 5 marks (£3 and 33 pence) on 29 October, £10 on 7 November, 10 marks on 19 November, £4 on 11 December and 5 marks on 4 February. The money was paid out to Hugh Despenser as her husband, but was specifically said to be for Eleanor.[26] She was surely often at court with the king and frequently attended her aunt-in-law Queen Isabella, and therefore perhaps spent much time with her sister Margaret. Eleanor may have given birth again in or around 1314, following her three eldest children Huchon, Edward and Isabella Despenser. The birthdates and birth order of the middle five of her Despenser children are very difficult to establish, but she probably bore her second daughter Joan around 1314/15, naming her after her mother Joan of Acre, and perhaps her third son Gilbert Despenser a year or two later, naming him after her father and brother.

Chapter 5

The Earl of Gloucester's Heirs

Edward II marched north with a great army in June 1314 to face Robert Bruce, king of Scotland (r. 1306–29) in battle, and the two forces met near Stirling on 23 and 24 June at the Battle of Bannockburn. Gilbert Clare, Earl of Gloucester, was one of only three English earls who fought, the others being Edward's brother-in-law Humphrey Bohun, Earl of Hereford, and his cousin Aymer Valence, Earl of Pembroke. The king and his nephew Gloucester argued fiercely the evening before the battle and Edward unreasonably taunted the earl as a coward. Come the morning, Gloucester was desperate to prove himself in battle, and argued with the Earl of Hereford over which of them had the right to command the vanguard. Gloucester and his men rode full tilt at the Scottish soldiers without waiting for an order to advance, and the young earl was killed. He had made the horrible mistake of forgetting to put on the surcoat identifying him as an earl; had the Scots known who he was, they would have captured him for a large ransom. The greatest of all English noblemen (excepting Edward II's cousin, Thomas of Lancaster) lay dead on a Scottish battlefield at the age of only 23. Gloucester's second cousin and his wife Maud's brother-in-law Robert Bruce personally kept an overnight vigil over his body in a nearby church, and sent it back to England with full honours. The young earl was buried at Tewkesbury Abbey in Gloucestershire, the mausoleum of the Clares, with his father, grandfather and other family members, though his heart was buried separately at Shelford in Nottinghamshire. Edward II passed through Shelford three years later, and attended Masses and distributed 5 shillings and sixpence in oblations at the conventual church for his nephew's soul.[1] The great Clare family was now extinct in its senior male line.[2] Gilbert's brother-in-law Hugh Despenser the Younger and Despenser's father Hugh the Elder were two of the English noblemen who fought for the king at Bannockburn, and Hugh the Younger must have acquitted himself bravely, as Edward II made him a knight banneret shortly afterwards (a reward for valour on the field of battle). Elizabeth Burgh's future husband Roger Damory also fought well at Bannockburn in Gloucester's retinue, though the battle ended in a humiliating defeat for the English.

The Earl of Gloucester's Inquisition Post Mortem was held in July/August 1314 in the many English counties where he had held lands, and in Wales and Ireland. Dower was granted to his widow Maud on 5 December, amounting to well in excess of £2,000 a year (i.e. more than ten times Eleanor and Hugh Despenser's annual income).[3] On 14 July, Edward II admitted that his nephew had died without an heir of his body.[4] In the absence of any surviving children, Gloucester's heirs were his three full sisters Eleanor, Margaret and Elizabeth, in accordance with contemporary English inheritance law: the system of primogeniture, whereby the eldest son inherited everything, did not apply to female heirs, who inherited equally. Their older half-sisters Isabella and Joan Clare, who had probably been made illegitimate by the annulment of their parents' marriage in 1285, and their younger half-siblings Mary, Joan, Thomas and Edward Monthermer, who were the children of Joan of Acre but not of Gilbert 'the Red', were not Gloucester's heirs.

Unfortunately, the earl's Inquisition Post Mortem was inaccurate and something of a mess. The jurors of five counties (Suffolk, Hertfordshire, Berkshire, Oxfordshire and Devon) called his youngest sister Elizabeth 'Isabella' in error, and the Suffolk jurors also got her late husband John's name wrong and called him 'Thomas Burgh'. The jurors of Suffolk, Worcestershire, Wiltshire and London cautiously added that the earl's three sisters were his heirs only if his widow the countess was not pregnant, and the Gloucestershire, Hampshire and Wales jurors went further and declared that they had heard Maud was indeed expecting a child. Given the huge significance and wealth of the Earl of Gloucester's landholdings and his important political position, it was most unfortunate that his Inquisition Post Mortem left a delicate situation unclear. All the confusion caused a long delay while the matter was clarified, and further inquisitions had to be held in all the counties which wrongly named Elizabeth as Isabella a year later in August 1315.[5] The dowager countess Maud Clare had begun to claim that she was pregnant with her husband's posthumous child, and for a few months it was not clear whether Gloucester's three sisters were his heirs or not.

Isabella Clare, wrongly named as one of Gloucester's heirs in his IPM, was the siblings' decades-older half-sister, born in 1262 as the eldest child of Gilbert 'the Red' Clare from his first marriage to Alice Lusignan. Isabella seems to have been briefly married to Hugh Despenser the Younger's uncle Guy Beauchamp, Earl of Warwick, in 1297, but the marriage must have been annulled, and around 1316 she wed Maurice Berkeley. He was the heir to his elderly father Lord Berkeley, an important nobleman of Gloucestershire, and was a widower about nine years her junior. Maurice Berkeley was trying to force himself into a share of the Clare inheritance, but his plan was doomed to fail as Isabella Clare was not one of her half-brother's rightful heirs, even if the earl's IPM left some room for doubt on the matter by confusing Elizabeth and Isabella. The vast wealth the three sisters would inherit as Gloucester's heirs made Margaret and Elizabeth vulnerable, as they were widows and did not have a husband and protector: in the Middle Ages, abduction and forced marriage of heiresses was sadly all too common. Women could and often did inherit lands in their own right, but if they married, their husbands would control the lands and would swear homage to the king for them. If a married couple had at least one child together who lived long enough to take a breath, the husband would own and control his wife's lands for the rest of his own lifetime even if she died before him, by a custom called 'the courtesy of England'. Eleanor Despenser was safe as she had a husband, though many years later after she had been widowed would be abducted and forcibly married to a second spouse, and Elizabeth Burgh was, at least for the moment, also safe under the protection of her former father-in-law, the Earl of Ulster, in Ireland. Sometime not long after Bannockburn, Edward II took Margaret Gaveston into his own household, partly to protect her, and surely also to keep an eye on her and ensure that she did not marry without his permission; one of his wealthy nieces marrying an enemy of his was a nightmare scenario for the king.

On 24 December 1314, Edward II appointed Elizabeth Burgh's future third husband Sir Roger Damory or d'Amory as the constable of Knaresborough Castle in Yorkshire, an important strategic location and one which had formerly belonged to Piers Gaveston. He repeated the appointment on 5 January 1315, just days after he finally had Gaveston buried two-and-a-half years after his death.[6] Damory had fought bravely with the Earl of Gloucester at Bannockburn: Edward praised him for 'his good service against the Scots at Strivelyn [Stirling, i.e. Bannockburn] and elsewhere', promised him an income of 100 marks a year, and took him into the royal household as a retainer in his eighth regnal year, July 1314 to July 1315.[7] The king also began to give Damory appointments, lands and gifts in 1315, 1316 and 1317, including custody of the castles of Corfe in Dorset and St Briavels in Gloucestershire, and of the Forest of Dean also in Gloucestershire.[8]

The Damory family was neither particularly rich nor influential, though they had a noble pedigree stretching back to the early twelfth century and probably earlier, and Roger's older brother Richard inherited a respectable dozen manors in four counties (Oxfordshire, Buckinghamshire, Northamptonshire and Somerset) from their father Robert (d. 1285).[9] Roger Damory is almost completely obscure for the first few years of Edward II's reign, but Richard was high in the king's favour and received numerous appointments from him, notably on various occasions which make it apparent that Richard loyally supported the king during his many political crises, such as in the aftermath of Gaveston's death. The author of the *Vita* called Roger Damory a 'poor and needy knight' (though also praised his 'industry and valour'), and Roger was landless until he came to Edward II's attention and rose high in his favour, with two exceptions. These were a gift of the Oxfordshire manor of Bletchingdon for life from his brother Richard on 7 August 1312, and a gift of the Somerset manor of Easton-in-Gordano from the Earl of Gloucester.[10] Roger Damory already had enough money in February 1315 to purchase custody of two manors from Edward II for £140 each, and by early September 1315 was owed £200 by a Thomas Stokesby, so was perhaps not quite as poor as the *Vita* assumed.[11] He would later marry Elizabeth Burgh and become a beneficiary of her late brother's wealth as a direct result of her uncle the king's infatuation with him.

Margaret Gaveston attended her husband's funeral at Langley Priory, Hertfordshire (which Edward II had founded in 1308) at the beginning of 1315. Piers Gaveston's embalmed body had remained with the Dominicans of Oxford since his death in June 1312. Margaret's brother-in-law Hugh Despenser the Younger was also present with his father Hugh the Elder and presumably his wife Eleanor, but most of the English nobility pointedly stayed away. Edward II spent the vast sum of £300 on three cloths of gold to dress Gaveston's body, and paid £15 for food and £64 for twenty-three tuns of wine, around 26,500 litres.[12] A few days before the funeral, the king gave the chancellor and scholars of Oxford University £20 to pray for Gaveston's soul, and spent another £15 on the wages of two men guarding Gaveston's body for twenty-eight days in December 1314. Edward also spent almost £150 between 8 July 1312 and 7 July 1313, the sixth year of his reign, which included payment for 5,000lbs of wax for candles to burn around the embalmed body.[13] At the time of the funeral, the king ordered a hundred Dominican friars to say Masses for Gaveston and his ancestors; between October 1315 and October 1316 he ordered every Augustinian house in England and Ireland to celebrate a daily Mass for Gaveston's soul; in 1319 he paid for a Turkish cloth to be placed over the tomb, which was replaced later by gold cloth; in 1324 he sent his confessor to Langley to mark the anniversary of Gaveston's death, and in 1325 he sent a man there with 100 shillings for the friars to keep Gaveston's soul 'more in remembrance'. In 1326, the last year of his reign, he made provision for numerous clerks at numerous houses to pray for the soul of his lost friend, or lover.[14]

Edward II's infatuation with Piers Gaveston and his intense grief at his death is so overwhelming and so blazingly obvious, even more than 700 years later, that it blots out his niece's feelings entirely; the role Margaret played in the story of the man who was her husband for four and a half years and the father of her daughter Joan is lost. One can very easily gain the impression that Edward, not Margaret, was the one burying his spouse in the depths of winter 1314/15, and perhaps that was exactly how the king – and even Margaret herself – felt. Several fourteenth-century chroniclers state that Edward delayed burying Gaveston for years because he wished to take revenge on Gaveston's killers first (though this had proved impossible). Perhaps Margaret had wished to bury her husband much earlier, and on her own lands rather than at her uncle's manor of Langley, but if she was ever consulted on the matter, Edward ignored any wishes she might have expressed. It is difficult to gain much sense of Margaret's feelings and opinions, and nowhere is this more the case than at the funeral of her husband. Whether or to what extent Margaret grieved for Gaveston, and whether she resented her uncle taking control and deciding when, where and how her husband should be buried, can only be matters for speculation.

Chapter 6

The First Abduction

In May 1315, Eleanor's husband Hugh Despenser the Younger seized control of Tonbridge Castle in Kent, which had formerly belonged to the Earl of Gloucester. Hugh must have known by this point that Countess Maud could not possibly be pregnant by the earl eleven months after Bannockburn. The jurors who had erred in his late brother-in-law's Inquisition Post Mortem and wrongly named the earl's half-sister Isabella as one of his heirs still had not met to clarify Gloucester's real heirs, and would not do so until August 1315. Despenser, impatient for his and Eleanor's share of her late brother's inheritance, took matters into his own hands. On 20 May 1315, Edward II at Hadleigh in Essex ordered Hugh 'to surrender without delay to the king's escheator the castle and honour of Tunebrigge [Tonbridge], which he has seized'. Edward told his escheator, John Abel, 'to go in person and take the said castle and honour into the king's hand', and ordered several men who were in Tonbridge Castle with Despenser to surrender possession of it to Abel. Hugh's wife Eleanor is not mentioned as being present, and her sister-in-law Maud, the dowager countess, was not there either.[1]

John Abel returned to the king and his council on the 22nd with the news that Hugh Despenser and his men had refused to hand Tonbridge Castle over to him: Abel tried to take possession of it, but Hugh and his associates 'raised the drawbridge, so that he could not enter the castle'. The incident in fact ended shortly afterwards, when Hugh and his men left the castle on Friday, 23 May, and Hugh rode directly to Edward to explain himself in person.[2] Despenser was not trying to remain in possession of his late brother-in-law's castle, but was making some kind of point; presumably an implicit demand to the king to begin the partition of the Clare inheritance. Hugh and Eleanor, although certainly not impoverished by the standards of most of the population, were poor by the standards of their class, and Hugh at least – and surely Eleanor as well – was desperate for their share of Gloucester's lands and income. Hugh Despenser was never punished for his illegal seizure of Tonbridge Castle, even though in 1315 Edward still distrusted and probably even disliked him.

Eleanor, Margaret and Elizabeth, and Hugh Despenser the Younger, were ordered on 25 June 1315, a year almost to the day after their brother's death at Bannockburn, to appear before Chancery on 21 July 1315 (though Elizabeth was still residing in Ireland). Eleanor and Margaret appointed lawyers to act on their behalf on 13 July.[3] In August 1315, the jurors of all the counties who had given Elizabeth Burgh the wrong name finally admitted their error, and declared that 'there is no Isabella, a sister of the said earl by the same father and mother, who could be co-heir' to Eleanor, Margaret and Elizabeth.

One of the most peculiar stories of the fourteenth century, however, was about to unfold. The dowager countess Maud continued to pretend to be pregnant by her late husband, even long after the nine months had passed and it was obvious to all that she could not possibly be expecting her late husband's child. Maud, Edward II and his lawyers pretended until the end of 1316 that Maud might give birth to the Earl of Gloucester's posthumous child, because the king did not want his late nephew's lands divided. By contemporary inheritance law, as the Earl of Gloucester had held his lands from the king-in-chief, after his death the lands passed into the king's own hands until the earl's heir, his putative child, turned 21 (if male) or 14 or 15 (if female). Edward would enjoy the late earl's enormous income of around £7,000 annually for many years, so it is easy to understand his reluctance to give it up to Gloucester's three sisters and his willingness to pretend that Maud was pregnant. Maud's own motives are unclear. It is not impossible that she was pregnant at some point in 1314 – she and Gloucester apparently did have a son in 1312 who died in infancy, so they were not infertile – but if so, she must have had a miscarriage or stillbirth. Hugh Despenser the Younger again went to see Edward II personally on 16 October 1315 at Impington in the Fens, where the king was taking a month's holiday, swimming and rowing with a large company of his common subjects. There, Hugh demanded his and Eleanor's share of the Clare lands and income.[4] His demand, however, came to nothing: the Dowager Countess of Gloucester's alleged pregnancy was raised again, as though this was in any way plausible sixteen months after her husband's death.

In late 1315, Edward II ordered 20-year-old Elizabeth Burgh to return home from Ireland, which indicates that he knew perfectly well she was one of her brother's three heirs and that he would eventually have to hand over the lands to her and her sisters, regardless of what he was pretending in public. (Elizabeth's 3-year-old son William may have remained in Ireland with his grandfather the Earl of Ulster, and was to spend much of his short life travelling between there and England.) Whatever the king's plans for her may have been at this stage, they went badly awry. Elizabeth arrived in Bristol on Wednesday, 4 February 1316, and was staying at the castle there at both the king's command and at his expense when, almost immediately after her arrival – before she even had a chance to see her uncle and her sisters – she was abducted by the baron Theobald Verdon, Lord of Alton in Staffordshire. The two married.[5] Verdon was born in September 1278 and was seventeen years Elizabeth's senior, and had three daughters, Joan, Elizabeth and Margery, from his first marriage to Maud Mortimer (d. 1312), sister of the influential Marcher baron, Roger Mortimer of Wigmore. He was the second son of Theobald Verdon the elder (d. 1309) and became his father's heir when his elder brother John died. Edward I sent a notably unsympathetic letter to the older Theobald Verdon in July 1297 to say that he was 'much displeased' with him for not coming to him as ordered, owing to the 'feeble' excuse of his infirmity and the loss of his eldest son John. The king told Verdon to send his second son Theobald to him instead, calling him 'strong and able'.[6] Theobald the younger was appointed justiciar of Ireland by Edward II in April 1313, and probably knew Elizabeth Burgh there in some capacity.[7]

Verdon claimed to the parliament held in Lincoln until 22 February 1316 that he and Elizabeth had been betrothed in Ireland, and that Elizabeth voluntarily came outside the castle to meet and marry him and that he did not abduct her.[8] This is a classic fourteenth-century example of 'he would say that, wouldn't he?', and should not be taken too seriously. It seems unlikely that Elizabeth would willingly have married Verdon, or indeed anyone else, without obtaining her uncle the king's permission first. It was forbidden for tenants-in-chief (the men and women who held land directly from the king) to marry without a royal licence, and though they sometimes did, a large fine and seizure of lands and goods was the usual punishment. Although in later years Edward II certainly treated

Elizabeth callously, in early 1316 he had done nothing wrong to her which might have made her wish to defy him, and her uncle was both her closest surviving male relative and the king to whom she owed obedience and allegiance. It is not impossible that Elizabeth's second marriage was not an 'abduction' but was arranged and carried out with her consent. That the marriage took place on her first day back in England, however, as soon as she was no longer under the protection of her powerful father-in-law Ulster and before she had a chance to talk to any of her family, might suggest that it happened against her will. She perhaps travelled to Lincoln with her new husband, which would have been the first time she had seen her uncle and sisters since she went to Ireland in the autumn of 1309.

As for Theobald Verdon, any fine he had to pay for marrying Elizabeth without royal permission would be merely a drop in the ocean compared to the riches he would enjoy annually from her lands. In fact, Verdon never did pay a fine, and the only penalty he suffered for abducting and marrying the king's niece was a removal of some of the liberties he enjoyed in one of his Shropshire manors. Verdon's second daughter Elizabeth and her husband Bartholomew Burghersh later complained somewhat disingenuously that Edward II had done this 'on account of his rancour of mind towards the said Theobald' (they of course knew perfectly well that the king had good reasons for his 'rancour of mind').[9] Verdon was a close ally of Thomas, Earl of Lancaster, whom the king considered his greatest enemy, and Lancaster may well have encouraged him to abduct and marry Elizabeth. One third of the Gloucester estate in the hands of the Lancastrian faction was Edward II's nightmare, and his niece's marriage can only have encouraged him not to allow the partition yet.

The constable of Bristol Castle, who allowed the king's niece and one of the richest and most important women in the country to be snatched from under his nose, was Bartholomew Badlesmere, a baron of Kent married to the Clare sisters' first cousin, who was confusingly also called Margaret Clare.[10] Badlesmere had been in the retinue of their brother the Earl of Gloucester, and a contemporary poem written in Latin states that Badlesmere abandoned his lord to die on the battlefield of Bannockburn and therefore was a vile traitor and 'representative of Judas' who deserved to be 'put to the rack'.[11] Despite allowing the king's niece to be abducted, and despite provoking a large-scale rebellion against himself in Bristol in the 1310s which the king had to put down, and despite allegedly abandoning

The First Abduction 47

his lord to die in battle, Bartholomew Badlesmere was appointed steward of the royal household in 1318 and was an important figure in English politics in the late 1310s. He has a bafflingly excellent reputation among some modern historians.[12] Sometime in 1319, his wife Margaret and her household were besieged overnight in a house in Cheshunt, Hertfordshire by a large group of armed men and women, who demanded a payment of £100 in return for allowing Margaret to walk free. The following morning, she was rescued by Hugh Despenser the Younger, her cousin Eleanor's husband.[13] Fortuitously, Despenser happened to be somewhere in the vicinity when he heard of Margaret's plight.

Despenser went before the Lincoln parliament of early 1316, demanding his and Eleanor's third of the Gloucester inheritance again. The royal justices Gilbert Touthby and Geoffrey Scrope told him that he and Eleanor, and her sisters Margaret and Elizabeth, should not yet receive any of their lands, because:

> the said countess [of Gloucester], after the death of the aforementioned earl her late husband, at the due time according to the course of nature, felt a living boy, and that this was well-known in the parts where she lived, and that although the time for the birth of that child, which nature allows to be delayed and obstructed for various reasons, is still delayed, this ought not to prejudice the aforesaid pregnancy, at least while nature does not suppress the same pregnancy, but supposes a future birth.

On top of pretending that Countess Maud might still be expecting her husband's child twenty months after his death, they added:

> the said Hugh could, and ought to … have sued out a writ of the lord king's chancery to have the belly of the aforesaid countess inspected by knights and discreet matrons, that is to see whether the said countess were pregnant or not: and if so, then when she was expected to give birth. And since the aforementioned countess was always prepared to undergo such an examination, and the said Hugh and Eleanor had not observed that due process, their negligence ought not to prejudice the

said pregnancy, but rather to redound to the harm and prejudice of the same Hugh and Eleanor.

Faced with such an absurd legal defence of an impossible situation, there was nothing more Despenser could do, and his frustration and rage revealed itself when he assaulted a baron called John Ros in the middle of Lincoln Cathedral, in the king's presence, by punching him repeatedly in the face until he drew blood. He was arrested and fined £10,000, of which he never paid a penny, and as with his seizure of Tonbridge Castle nine months before, was never punished. Edward II had much else on his mind. His loathed cousin Thomas, Earl of Lancaster, was made his 'chief counsellor' at the Lincoln parliament against his wishes; a deadly famine was holding his kingdom in its grip and he was doing his best to ease his subjects' suffering. In addition, a rebellion broke out in Glamorgan, South Wales against the harsh governance of the royal officials who ruled it after the death of the Earl of Gloucester, formerly lord of Glamorgan. The king sent his three current court favourites, William Montacute, Hugh Audley and Roger Damory, as well as his brother-in-law the Earl of Hereford, cousin Henry of Lancaster, Bartholomew Badlesmere and Roger Mortimer of Wigmore, to quash the uprising.[14] On a much happier note, Edward learned in February 1316 that Queen Isabella was once again pregnant. They had a healthy 3-year-old son, Edward of Windsor, but it was as well to have more potential heirs to the throne, just in case: all three of Edward II's older brothers had died in childhood.

The Clare sisters' aunt Elizabeth, Countess of Hereford and Dowager Countess of Holland, fifth daughter of Edward I and Leonor of Castile, died on 5 May 1316 at the age of 33 after giving birth to her tenth child, who also died. Edward II attended his sister's funeral at Walden Abbey in Essex, and perhaps Eleanor, Margaret and Elizabeth did too. In 1316, Eleanor and Margaret were among the favoured few who received green cloth lined with miniver (expensive fur) from the king, along with the queen, the Dowager Countess of Warwick, and the sisters' first cousin Edward of Windsor, heir to the throne.[15] Margaret Gaveston now lived in her uncle's household, and in 1315 or 1316, the king began to plan another marriage for his widowed niece.

Chapter 7

Widowed Again

Elizabeth Burgh retained her first husband John's family name throughout her two subsequent marriages and for the rest of her life, but this was usually the case for fourteenth-century noblewomen whose second (and third) husbands were of lower rank than their first, and her choice does not necessarily reveal anything about her personal feelings. Her second marriage to Theobald Verdon lasted less than six months: he died on 27 July 1316 a few weeks before his thirty-eighth birthday, leaving her about one month pregnant.[1] Almost nothing is known about their very short marriage, except that Elizabeth probably lived at Theobald's chief seat of Alton in Staffordshire. Edward II gave custody of all Verdon's lands minus Elizabeth's dower to his latest infatuation Sir Roger Damory on 7 August, to hold until Verdon's children came of age (evidently the Chancery clerks did not know at this point that he had three daughters, as the grant to Damory talks vaguely of him holding the lands 'until the full age of the heir').[2] Verdon never benefited from his marriage to Elizabeth as he died before her late brother's lands were partitioned. His early death seems curiously convenient for Edward II and for Elizabeth's next husband, though in the absence of any evidence or accusations it would seem unfair to accuse the king of foul play. Edward now became determined to marry Elizabeth to Roger Damory, and wrote to her on 12 September 1316, even before Verdon was buried.[3] Probably Edward did not know yet that Elizabeth was pregnant with Verdon's posthumous child.

The letter, in French, ran:

> Edward by the grace of God king of England, lord of Ireland and duke of Aquitaine, to our very dear and beloved niece Elizabeth Burgh, greetings. Very dear and well-beloved niece, because of the special affection we have for you above all our other nieces, we wholeheartedly desire your well-being and your

honour, and we are sending to you our dear bachelor Sir John Charlton, our chamberlain, who is one of our closest confidants and whom we trust most with our personal affairs, to tell you certain things with which we have entrusted him concerning your estate and your honour. And we beseech you that you sincerely give credence to what he tells you from us [the last six words were crossed out and altered to 'give credence to him'] and do willingly what he requests of you on our behalf if you wish to have generous lordship from us and wish us to take to heart all matters which concern you, and [we beseech you] that you send back to us, via him, your will on the aforesaid matters. Given under our privy seal at Beverley the twelfth day of September in the tenth year of our reign [1316].[4]

Edward's statement that Elizabeth was his favourite niece was a blatant lie – her eldest sister Eleanor was – and a transparent attempt to flatter and manipulate her into doing what he wished, though the letter does not explicitly mention Roger Damory or a possible marriage to him. The lack of any closing salutation such as 'Very dear niece, may the Holy Spirit have you in his keeping' or even a more abrupt 'May God keep you', as would have been conventional, polite and friendly, tends to give the lie to Edward's claim that he felt great affection for Elizabeth. The letter contains words which were crossed out and two sentences were added above the line, and it was written in three different hands. This reveals that Edward thought hard about what he wanted to say and edited his text, dictating parts of it to three scribes on three separate occasions. One long addition written above the line was the entire sentence about Elizabeth finding him a generous lord who would take her affairs to heart if she willingly assented to his request, clearly a veiled threat that he would not be a good lord to her if she did not. The more amicable sentence about giving credence to what Charlton told her on Edward's behalf was struck out, and the king's revisions to his letter made it sterner and more menacing. Elizabeth's second marriage to Theobald Verdon had infuriated him, and perhaps he held her responsible for marrying the baron without his consent.

Elizabeth might already have known Roger Damory: he had been in her brother the Earl of Gloucester's retinue since October 1308 or earlier, and was with Gloucester at a jousting tournament held in Dunstable, Bedfordshire *c.* April 1309.[5] She might have seen him at the joint wedding of herself and her brother to the Burgh siblings at the end of September 1308. No doubt Elizabeth and her sisters were told what happened to their brother on the battlefield of Bannockburn, and therefore she would also have been aware of Roger's bravery in Gloucester's service. But whatever she might have felt about Damory, her brother was dead, her parents were dead, her two husbands were dead, and her nearest male relative was her uncle the king, the man who wished to see her married to his close friend, or perhaps lover. As a widow and now in her early 20s, Elizabeth might have expected more control over her own choice of third husband (or to remain a widow, as the case may be), but at some point before April 1317 she agreed to marry Roger Damory.

There is little doubt that her uncle put pressure on her to do so, and he probably made her feel that she had little choice. On the other hand, she may have been happy enough to marry Damory. We do not know for sure, and as she never revealed her feelings on the matter in writing, any opinions on her third marriage (as is the case with her second) can only ever be speculation and assumption. Damory was, as previously noted, from a solid Oxfordshire family with a noble pedigree stretching back centuries, but he was far beneath Elizabeth in rank. She was the granddaughter and niece of kings and daughter and sister of earls, and would have been Countess of Ulster if her first husband had lived longer, whereas Damory was not even his father's heir and was a knight bachelor who spent his career in the service of greater lords. He was set to gain far more advantages from the marriage than Elizabeth would. As well as giving Damory control of Elizabeth's third of the Gloucester inheritance, the marriage would also give him control of the large part of the late Theobald Verdon's lands she held in dower and the dower and jointure lands she held from her first husband John Burgh. Elizabeth Burgh was probably the richest woman in the country after Queen Isabella, and she was being given to a mere knight and younger son; it is hard to imagine that many people were happy about it, and the marriage surely caused much envy and resentment. Whenever Elizabeth agreed to marry Damory – perhaps she sent word back to the king via his chamberlain John Charlton in or soon after September 1316, as Edward had ordered her to – their wedding would have to wait until after she had given birth to Theobald Verdon's posthumous child.

Edward II arrived in York on 16 August 1316, accompanied by his niece Margaret Gaveston, and stayed in the convent of the Franciscans (Greyfriars, or Friars Minor) near the river Ouse. There is every reason to suppose that the king and Margaret enjoyed cordial relations for many years, even if he was perhaps not as fond of her as he was of her older sister Eleanor and even though he was refusing to give the Clare sisters their lands and pretending that their sister-in-law Maud was pregnant. The king stayed in York for five weeks and gave the Franciscans £10 for the expenses of himself and his household – as I have been marking. a sum which only covered a fraction of them—and paid Margaret's chamber valet Walter Dymmok 8 shillings and 10 pence for 'certain work done in the chamber of the said countess [of Cornwall]' at the convent.[6]

The king and queen's second son John was born at the palace of Eltham in Kent on 15 August 1316, and Edward heard the news on 24 August when he asked the Dominicans of York to say prayers for himself, his wife, their elder son and especially the newly born John.[7] Margaret Gaveston was on hand to witness her uncle's joy at the birth of his second son; the St Albans' chronicler makes a point of commenting on the king's delight, and Edward gave the queen's messenger £100 for bringing him the news.[8] Less happily, the king had a furious row with his cousin Thomas, Earl of Lancaster, in York in August 1316, which Margaret might have witnessed first-hand.[9] Lancaster was her grandfather Edward I's nephew and thus closely related to her, but was also the man chiefly responsible for the death of her husband Piers Gaveston. Lancaster's main ally among the English barons and Gaveston's kidnapper had been Guy Beauchamp, Earl of Warwick, uncle of Margaret's brother-in-law Hugh Despenser the Younger, but Warwick died in August 1315, leaving his baby son Thomas as his heir.

Margaret was still with the king at Clipstone in Nottinghamshire just before Christmas 1316, when Edward confirmed numerous grants of land to her and detailed various land exchanges they had made, 'for her sustenance and until the king should see fit to make other provision for her estate'. She had given the royal manor of Burstwick back to him in exchange for other manors sometime after November 1315.[10] Edward surely already had it in mind to marry her to the second of his three current court favourites, Sir Hugh Audley. Hugh had been a member of the royal retinue since late 1311, and surely Margaret almost certainly knew him already. Audley was not as high in the king's favour as Roger Damory, but evidently Edward was very fond of him, and in June 1315 ordered the chancellor to complete some of Audley's business as soon as possible, so that Audley 'can return to us as quickly as we have instructed him to do'.[11] At the beginning of August 1314, a few weeks after the Battle of Bannockburn—at which he, like Hugh Despenser the Younger and Roger Damory, might have fought—Hugh Audley received the lands and marriage rights of Mary, younger of the two daughters and co-heirs of the Scottish nobleman Sir Edmund Comyn.[12] Audley swore an oath sometime in 1317 that he would 'aid him [Edward II] in all things throughout his whole life, and in no wise depart from him come what might, on pain of forfeiture of all his lands', an oath he broke in 1321 after he and Roger Damory became the king's enemies.[13]

Sir William Montacute, from a noble family of Somerset and one of the men knighted with Edward, Piers Gaveston, Hugh Despenser the Younger and the rest in May 1306, was the third of the three influential court favourites of the mid-1310s. He was appointed steward of Edward II's household in 1316, though as he was already married could not be rewarded with the grand prize of a Clare bride. Montacute, Roger Damory and Eleanor Despenser's husband Hugh Despenser the Younger all witnessed royal charters at Nottingham on 27 December 1316 and at Clipstone on 3 January 1317, so apparently Eleanor spent the festive season of 1316/17 with her uncle the king and her sister Margaret (the royal retinue moved from Clipstone to Nottingham on Christmas Eve).[14] The Clare sisters' aunt Mary, nun of Amesbury Priory, also spent Christmas at the royal court and departed afterwards with a gift of fifteen tapestries worth 40 marks from her fond brother the king.[15] It is possible that Elizabeth Burgh travelled to the Christmas court with her aunt and saw her uncle and sisters—and Roger Damory—there, and returned to Amesbury with Mary. She was now more than six months pregnant, and would spend the last trimester in the peace of the convent with her aunt.

Chapter 8

Two Favourites, Two Weddings

The king gave Roger Damory custody of the castle of Alton in Staffordshire, formerly Theobald Verdon's main seat, on 24 January 1317, and later also granted Damory the marriage rights of the younger two of Elizabeth Burgh's three stepdaughters, Elizabeth and Margery Verdon.[1] Edward gave his friend Sir William Montacute the rights to her eldest stepdaughter's marriage, and 14-year-old Joan Verdon married Montacute's eldest son and heir John at Windsor on 28 April 1317, in the king's presence.[2] The teenaged John Montacute died a few months later, to the king's evident sorrow: he paid forty clerks to pray for his soul and thirteen widows to watch over John's body. John was buried in the cathedral church at Lincoln on 14 August 1317, and a few days later the king gave generous alms at the Masses celebrated in the cathedral for the repose of John's soul.[3] After John Montacute's death, his younger brother William, probably born in 1301, became their father's heir, and was later a close friend of Edward II's son Edward III and was made Earl of Salisbury in 1337.

The year 1317 saw a further deterioration in the already dreadful relations between Edward II and the Earl of Lancaster, and the king foolishly allowed Roger Damory, Hugh Audley and William Montacute to encourage him in his hatred and distrust of his cousin. At a meeting of the royal council at Clarendon in early 1317, the three men openly attacked the earl, calling him a traitor.[4] Lancaster sent messengers to the king, claiming that 'he fears the deadly stratagems of certain persons who thrive under the protection of the royal court'.[5] He asked Edward to expel the men from court, but the king refused. Lancaster continued to demand their removal from court, and the lands Edward had granted them taken away. The men had no intention of allowing Lancaster to diminish their vast influence over Edward, and selfishly counselled the king to remain hostile to his cousin and 'intrigued against the earl as best they could'.[6] The king was blind to Damory and Audley's faults and foolish, dangerous behaviour, and wished as much as ever to marry the men to his two younger Clare nieces.

Elizabeth Burgh gave birth to her second child Isabella Verdon at Amesbury Priory, Wiltshire on Monday, 21 March 1317, eight months after Theobald Verdon's death. Edward II sent a silver cup as a christening gift for his great-niece, and Queen Isabella was escorted the few miles from the royal palace of Clarendon near Salisbury by the under-sheriff of Wiltshire, John Harnham, to attend the infant's christening at Amesbury on the day of her birth. Isabella Verdon was named after the queen, who was her chief sponsor or godmother, and one of her other godparents was Elizabeth's aunt Mary. The christening was conducted by the Bishop of Salisbury, Roger Martival.[7] If Elizabeth had borne a boy, he would have become Theobald Verdon's sole heir from the moment of his birth and disinherited Elizabeth's three stepdaughters Joan, Elizabeth and Margery, but Isabella Verdon became her father's joint and equal heir with her older half-sisters. A few years later, the division of the Verdon inheritance into four parts was to cause much ill-tempered legal squabbling among the sisters and their husbands.[8]

Edward II allowed his niece to recover for three weeks after giving birth then visited Elizabeth at Amesbury on 10 April 1317, taking Roger Damory with him. The date of the visit is not recorded, but the king granted a favour to a Robert Scales at Elizabeth's request on 10 April, so she was in his presence on that date. This is the only known instance of Elizabeth successfully interceding with her uncle, which tends also to give the lie to Edward's claim in September 1316 that he felt more affection for her than his other nieces. If he had, she would have been in his presence far more often and would have been able to ask him for favours on behalf of others, as her aunt-in-law the queen often did and her husband-to-be Roger Damory very frequently did.[9] Edward left the royal palace of Clarendon near Salisbury on 10 April and was in Andover on the 11th, and Amesbury was just a short ride off the road between the two places.[10] Presumably the visit was intended to arrange a date for Elizabeth and Roger's wedding.

Elizabeth must have gone through the ceremony of purification (also sometimes called 'churching') on about 30 April 1317 approximately forty days after giving birth, though as she gave birth to a daughter she may have been churched only thirty days afterwards. As soon as this was over, she could be married to Roger Damory. The date of their wedding is, rather oddly, not recorded anywhere, but had already taken place by 3 May 1317 when an entry on the Patent Roll talks of 'Roger Damory and Elizabeth his wife'.[11] A month later, Damory was granted the castle of Knaresborough in Yorkshire (formerly Piers Gaveston's) for life, and on 25 September 1317 Edward gave Damory and Elizabeth the castle of Salmon Leap in Ireland. It was to pass to their future 'first-born son'—though as it turned out, they would not have any sons together—and after the son's death, back to Edward and his heirs.[12] Elizabeth gave birth to Damory's daughter a little under eight months after the date of this grant, so it is not impossible that she, her husband and the king already knew she was pregnant.

It is sometimes assumed that Elizabeth's attitude towards her new husband is revealed by her travelling on pilgrimage to various sites around the country before and after their wedding with her aunt Mary (the nun) and their kinswoman Isabella of Lancaster, second daughter of the Earl of Lancaster's younger brother Henry (and a future nun and prioress of Amesbury).[13] The idea goes that Elizabeth tried to delay married life with Damory, though this is only speculation, and it seems unlikely. Edward II paid all the ladies' expenses, and is hardly likely to have been willing to pay his niece's costs if he thought she was deliberately disrespecting Roger Damory. For all we know, Elizabeth asked Damory's permission to travel and he gave it his full blessing, and she intended her travels to sanctify their marriage, not run away from it. For many years after Damory's death, Elizabeth showed a great interest in pilgrimages and frequently went to Canterbury, Walsingham and Bromholm, and she must have been aware that her mother Joan of Acre had been born in the Holy Land while her grandparents Edward I and Leonor of Castile were on crusade there. In 1343, Elizabeth was absolved by Pope Clement VI from a vow she made 'in her husband's lifetime' (perhaps Damory's) to go on pilgrimage to the Holy Land and Santiago de Compostela, and in her will of 1355 left 100 marks for five men-at-arms to go to the Holy Land in 'the service of God and the destruction of His enemies'.[14] She might also have intended her 1317 journey to give thanks for her safe delivery of her daughter eight months after she lost her second husband.

There seems little reason to assume that her pilgrimage speaks to her distaste for Damory and her marriage to him. Then again, on 1 November

1317, six months after their wedding, Roger Damory founded a chantry at Bindon Abbey in Dorset and requested daily prayers for the 'good estate' of himself and Edward II but, perhaps rather pointedly, not for Elizabeth nor for any children they might have together, though he surely knew by then that she was pregnant with their child.[15] The early months of their marriage may not have been particularly harmonious. Damory is mentioned in the Chancery rolls interceding with Edward II on 18 May 1317, still at Windsor, and it is likely that he remained at the king's side for the weeks and months after his wedding while Elizabeth resumed her pilgrimage with her aunt.[16] Elizabeth gave birth on or a little before 23 May 1318, so Damory had claimed his marital rights by late August 1317. Presumably Elizabeth's pilgrimage had ended by then, and the couple had taken up residence together.

Elizabeth's biographer has called the circumstances of her wedding to Damory 'brutal and unfeeling', though the marriage does not necessarily seem more brutal and unfeeling than most other fourteenth-century noble marriages, which were rarely founded in romance and true love. Her third marriage was surely less brutal and unfeeling than her second husband Theobald Verdon abducting her within hours of her return to England, and at least Damory sought Elizabeth's consent, as Verdon may not have done.[17] Elizabeth, already getting married for the third time and a mother of two, was still only 21 years old in April/May 1317, and Damory (like Theobald Verdon) was much older than she. Roger's date of birth is not known, but his father Sir Robert Damory died in about July 1285, so he must have been at least in his early 30s in 1317 and was possibly a few years older than that. His elder brother Richard was old enough to be summoned for military service in 1297 and acted as keeper of the peace in Oxfordshire in 1300, so cannot have been born later than the mid-1270s or thereabouts.[18] Whether Roger Damory had been married before is unknown, though as he was already in his 30s it is certainly possible. If so, he had no surviving legitimate children, though seems to have had illegitimate ones.

On 28 April 1317, the wedding of Elizabeth's sister Margaret Gaveston and Sir Hugh Audley took place at the chapel in the park of Windsor Castle, in the king's presence. Edward gave £3 in coins to be thrown over the heads of the bride and groom and another mark (two-thirds of a pound) for oblations.[19] It is virtually certain that Elizabeth and Damory's wedding took place within days of Margaret's nuptials, also at Windsor, where the king stayed for much of May. Elizabeth Burgh spent five days at Windsor, so almost certainly attended her sister's wedding as well as her own.[20] Four days after the Audley wedding, Edward II wrote to his chancellor and treasurer to inform them that all the lands which Margaret held of him, providing her with an income of 2,000 marks a year, should be now held by herself and Hugh Audley jointly.[21] Margaret was now 23 or almost, and Audley not much older. His parents married in 1288 or soon afterwards—his mother Isolde was widowed from her first husband in 1287—and he was the second of their three children. He was probably born around 1291 or 1293.[22] Hugh was a nobleman, and his father Hugh Audley Senior of Stratton Audley in Oxfordshire was a former justice of North Wales and acted as steward of Edward II's household for a while in 1312.[23] Like Roger Damory, Hugh Audley was a second son: his elder brother James was their father's heir, and they had a younger sister, Alice, ancestor of the Neville earls of Westmorland. Their father, the elder Hugh, was also a second son. Hugh Audley the younger may have known Roger Damory before they became royal favourites, as his family's seat of Stratton Audley lies just ten miles from the Damorys' seat of Bletchingdon, though Damory was a few years Audley's senior. Whether the two men got along is uncertain, though as they rarely appear on record together while they were prominent at court between 1315 and 1318 (such as witnessing the same royal charters, for instance), perhaps they considered themselves rivals for the king's affections.

Margaret Gaveston, whose name became Margaret Audley, had now married two of her uncle's male favourites, though what kind of relationship Edward II had with Audley is impossible to say for sure: perhaps it was sexual, perhaps not. In the absence of any evidence on the matter, we cannot know how Margaret felt about marrying another man who may have been Edward's lover. She was certainly more compliant than her mother Joan of Acre, who married a second husband of her own choice in 1297 while her father Edward I was pressing ahead with a marriage for her with the Count of Savoy. From other evidence we have, Margaret was arguably a biddable and acquiescent person in general. She could perhaps also have clandestinely married another man in the five years of her widowhood, and braved her uncle's wrath, but she did not. This was probably a result of the king's generous grants of land to her in the aftermath of Gaveston's death, which she held 'provided that she does not marry without the king's licence' (a common and entirely usual condition, not Edward imposing a harsh or unfair restriction on his niece).[24] Hugh Audley seems to have been a rather decent and capable man, so Margaret might not have been at all unwilling to marry him. Their marriage would last for a quarter of a century, and in 1320, when their accounts happen to survive for a few months, they spent most of their time together. After the failed baronial rebellion of 1321/22, Margaret successfully begged the king to spare Audley's life which she would hardly have done if she hated him, and they would be buried together at Tonbridge Priory, which also implies that they had built a happy and successful marriage. Eleanor Despenser buried both her husbands at Tewkesbury Abbey on her own lands and herself chose to be interred there with them, and it is probably also revealing that Elizabeth Burgh, by contrast, chose not to be buried next to any of her three husbands (admittedly, requesting burial next to John Burgh in Ireland would have caused some perhaps insurmountable logistical issues).

Eleanor Despenser and her husband Hugh the Younger probably attended her sisters' weddings, and after the farce of Maud Clare's pretended years-long pregnancy and Despenser's long efforts to claim their lands, they must have been delighted that the inheritance could now be partitioned, though a lot of work remained to do before they were ready. The king finally gave the order for the partition on 12 May 1317, almost three years after the Earl of Gloucester's death, now that his two younger nieces were married to men he trusted. Almost certainly he did not trust Hugh Despenser, but there was nothing he could do about it. On or just before 22 May, the king took the homage of Hugh Despenser, Hugh Audley and Roger Damory for the lands they would now control in right of their wives, though it would take another six months before the lands were ready to be partitioned.[25] Edward II had every right to feel pleased with himself in 1317. One third of the Clare inheritance would fall to his beloved Piers Gaveston's daughter Joan—assuming Margaret and Hugh Audley did not have a son, which would disinherit her—and another would pass to William Burgh, grandson and heir of the king's ally the Earl of Ulster (in 1317, Edward arranged Joan Gaveston's future marriage to John Multon, born 1308, another grandson of the Earl of Ulster). One third of the inheritance falling to Hugh Despenser the Younger, a man he had never liked or trusted, was the one thing Edward was probably not pleased about, though one consolation was that it would ultimately descend to Despenser's son Huchon, Edward's eldest great-nephew.

It may have been Hugh Audley and Roger Damory's marriages to the most eligible women in England which prompted some of Edward's household knights to stage a theatrical protest against the king's promotion of new favourites in May 1317. As Edward dined at Westminster Hall at Pentecost, a woman entered dressed as a stage-player and riding a magnificently caparisoned horse. She rode around the hall, then turned to Edward on the dais, placed a letter in front of him, and rode out. Edward, amused, began to read the letter, but soon stopped, horrified; it was an indictment of the favouritism he showed his friends. Although the woman, when later questioned, denied knowledge of the contents of the letter, the St Albans' chronicler says it was written by established men of Edward's household angry with him for not treating them properly and for promoting worthless men in their place.[26] The letter exhorted him to remember his duty to his nobles. Although Edward released the woman and, impressed with the integrity of the knights who had written the letter, gave them gifts, he failed to take their sage advice. In 1317 and 1318, the pernicious influence of Edward's favourites, now his nephews-in-law, grew ever stronger.

Chapter 9

A Rich Inheritance

In April 1317, Elizabeth Burgh's former father-in-law Richard Burgh, Earl of Ulster, was imprisoned in Dublin Castle, and Edward II ordered Roger Mortimer of Wigmore, 'keeper of Ireland', to determine whether it would be more beneficial to the king to have Ulster sent to him in England or to continue to detain him. By early August 1317, Ulster had been released and was ready to set out from Ireland to England, and was still in England in November 1317.[1] Elizabeth probably had a chance to spend time with her father-in-law, and perhaps he brought her son William, his grandson and heir, with him. Ulster's daughter Elizabeth Bruce had been freed from house arrest in England and returned to Scotland and to her husband King Robert after the Battle of Bannockburn in 1314, and another of the earl's many daughters, Maud the Dowager Countess of Gloucester, lived in complete obscurity after the peculiar and unprecedented situation of her pretended three-year pregnancy. Maud was to die in 1320 at the age of only 30 or so. As for Roger Mortimer of Wigmore, the king's lieutenant of Ireland and a nobleman of Herefordshire and the Welsh Marches, he was a loyal ally of the king until the behaviour of Elizabeth Burgh's brother-in-law Hugh Despenser the Younger drove him into opposition some years later.

The Clare lands were divided at last in November 1317. The Despensers took the rich lordship of Glamorgan in South Wales; the Audleys, many of the estates in the south-east of England including Tonbridge, and the Welsh lordship of Gwynllŵg; the Damorys, the lands in Essex and Suffolk and some in Dorset, and received the rich Welsh lordship of Usk in 1320. Eleanor and Hugh Despenser received far more lands in England in 1320 after Maud Clare née Burgh died, and almost all their lands lay in Wales from 1317 until 1320.[2] The three parts of the Clare lands were not equal (it being impossible to divide lands into exactly equal parts), and the Despensers received lands worth £1,415 a year, the Audleys £1,292, and the Damorys £1,287. On the death in the 1320s of their sister-in-law Maud, Dowager Countess of Gloucester, the reversion of her dower lands gave each couple more lands worth around £900 a year. Hugh Despenser the Younger, as husband of the eldest sister, was given first pick of the divisions, and naturally enough took the largest one and the one which included the great lordship of Glamorgan.[3] Eleanor and her husband now owned Caerphilly Castle, her birthplace, though whether she ever spent time there is unclear. In 1320, the Gloucestershire manor of Tewkesbury, Elizabeth Burgh's birthplace and the burial place of the sisters' father Gilbert 'the Red' and brother the younger Gilbert, also passed to the Despensers. Elizabeth and Roger Damory now owned Clare in Suffolk where the sisters' mother Joan of Acre was buried at the Augustinian priory.

A third each of the Clare inheritance made the three sisters probably the richest women in the country after the queen, with the exception of their second cousin Alice Lacy (b. 1281), who inherited the earldoms of Lincoln and Salisbury from her parents (and who walked out of her unhappy marriage to Thomas, Earl of Lancaster in May 1317).[4] Hugh and Eleanor Despenser also received two manors in Lincolnshire and Northamptonshire which had formerly belonged to Eleanor's much older half-sister Joan MacDuff, Dowager Countess of Fife.[5] Joan, younger of the two daughters of Gilbert 'the Red' from his first marriage to Alice Lusignan, was now married to her second husband Gervase Avenel, and they returned to Scotland sometime after the Battle of Bannockburn in 1314 and took an oath of loyalty to Robert Bruce. Joan's son Duncan MacDuff, Earl of Fife, who was the Clare sisters' half-nephew and married to their younger half-sister Mary née Monthermer, also returned to Scotland and entered Bruce's allegiance in 1315. Mary MacDuff née Monthermer appears to have stayed in England for a few more years: her uncle Edward II gave her permission to go to Scotland in January 1320, ostensibly to rescue a noblewoman called Elena Neville being held captive there. By May 1321 Mary was living in Scotland, but still sent servants to shop for clothes and jewels for her in London.[6]

Edward II's powerful first cousin and enemy, Thomas, Earl of Lancaster, still distrusted the three royal favourites Roger Damory, Hugh Audley and William Montacute immensely, especially Damory. In early October 1317, Lancaster seized Knaresborough Castle in Yorkshire and kept hold of it until January 1318, and by the beginning of November had also forcibly gained possession of Alton Castle in Staffordshire.[7] Roger Damory was the custodian of both.[8] Clearly, Lancaster saw Damory as his chief enemy at court, and determined to attack him. Edward's chief priority was the safety and well-being of his friends, and he took Damory's lands in Yorkshire, Herefordshire and Lincolnshire into his own hands on 18 October 1317 to protect Damory from his cousin's aggression, also ordering a clerk to remove Damory's stud-farm from Knaresborough to Burstwick. He restored Damory's lands to him on 2 December, assuming the danger from Lancaster was past (Damory had in the meantime taken possession of his and Elizabeth's many lands as well).[9] Lancaster did not attack the lands and castles of Hugh Audley or William Montacute, implying that Roger Damory was the foremost man at court, highest in Edward's affections, and thus Lancaster's chief enemy.

Numerous grants and favours recorded in the Chancery rolls in 1317 were made 'on the information of Roger Damory', and the royal favourite was clearly very often at court and had frequent access to the king's ear.[10] The king had a falcon named Damory after his friend or lover which had presumably been a gift from him, and he still owned the bird in 1319.[11] Damory's closeness to the king implies that his wife Elizabeth Burgh was also often at court in 1317 and into 1318, though she mostly disappears from the record during their marriage. Elizabeth probably saw much of her sister Eleanor in 1317/18, as the itinerary of Eleanor's husband Hugh Despenser reveals that he was also far more often at court than previously.[12] As for Hugh Audley, he witnessed none of Edward II's charters after August 1317, so apparently was not as close to the king as he once had been; perhaps he spent most of his time away from court with his new wife Margaret and did his best to build a good relationship with her. Two favours granted, which were made at Audley's request, were recorded on 7 April and 20 May 1318, and on 18 November that year Hugh was commissioned to arrest a group of men who had imprisoned and tortured a woman in Northamptonshire, but otherwise he rarely appears on record (and by 20 May 1319 had still not arrested the torturers).[13]

Roger Damory's frequently malignant influence over Edward II caused much concern among many of the English barons and bishops. In early October 1317, it is likely that Damory came close to persuading the king to attack Thomas of Lancaster at Thomas's stronghold of Pontefract in

Yorkshire. Lancaster, astonishingly, jeered at the king and his retinue as they rode past in a display of appalling manners and *lèse-majesté*, and Edward understandably never forgave him for it, but assaulting the Earl of Lancaster in his own castle would have led to civil war. To restrain Damory, the Earl of Pembroke and Bartholomew Badlesmere signed an indenture with him in London on 24 November 1317, just days after the division of the Clare inheritance had made Damory and his wife Elizabeth Burgh rich. The favourite promised that he would do his best to prevent Edward II from taking action prejudicial to himself or his kingdom—a telling comment which demonstrates what little faith Pembroke and Badlesmere had in Edward—and if he were unable to dissuade him, would inform Pembroke and Badlesmere as soon as possible so that the three of them together could talk Edward out of whatever foolishness he might be planning. Damory swore on the Host to obey the covenant, and pledged the massive sum of £10,000 as a penalty for breaking it. For their part, Pembroke and Badlesmere swore to defend and maintain Damory against all persons except the king, as long as he kept and observed the covenant. This indenture may be unique, or it may be one of a series which Pembroke and Badlesmere signed around this time with Edward's friends, and the only one which happens to survive.[14]

As early as November or the beginning of December 1317, Hugh Despenser the Younger took the homage of some of the lords and tenants of the county of Gwynllŵg in South Wales, which had once been part of his lordship of Glamorgan but had been given to Margaret and Hugh Audley. News of this and of the tenants' refusal to do homage to Audley reached the king's ears at Windsor on or before 12 December 1317.[15] This is the first example, but by no means the last, of Despenser trying to gain control of more lands in South Wales than he was rightfully entitled to. Edward II refused to accept his behaviour and told his council to consider the oaths taken to Despenser 'as of no effect', but Despenser refused to give up, and in September 1318 Hugh and Margaret Audley gave in and exchanged Gwynllŵg, including the castle and manor of Newport, for some of the Despensers' manors in England.[16] These were of much lower value, so Hugh and Eleanor Despenser profited considerably from the deal. There is no evidence of how this affected the relationship between the two sisters, but it must have damaged it, and perhaps the year 1318 saw the beginning of a permanent rift between them.

Hugh Despenser's enemies were to accuse him in 1321, probably correctly, of trying to encroach on the lands of Roger Damory and Elizabeth Burgh as well.[17] The version of the *Flores Historiarum* chronicle written at Tintern Abbey on the border of England and Wales—Damory was the abbey's patron—states that Damory successfully resisted Despenser's encroachments.[18] The *Lanercost* chronicle says that 'being a most avaricious man, he [Despenser] had contrived by different means and tricks that he alone should possess the lands and revenues, and for that reason had devised grave charges against those who had married the other two sisters'. The *Vita* agrees, saying that Despenser 'set traps for his co-heirs; thus, if he could manage it, each would lose his share through false accusations and he alone would obtain the whole earldom [of Gloucester]. But they, relying on the help of the barons, were a match for his wickedness'.[19] The three Clare sisters now stood on opposite sides of a divide where the husband of one was trying his hardest to take lands from the other two, and as the years went on, things only became worse.

The king and queen and their court spent Christmas 1317 at Westminster, and Edward gave rings to his nieces Margaret Audley and Elizabeth Burgh and his sons Edward of Windsor and John of Eltham, although the latter was only 16 months old. Eleanor Despenser is not listed as receiving a gift despite the king's undoubted great affection for her, so perhaps this reveals his annoyance with her husband Hugh, who had only owned Eleanor's lands for a few weeks and was already causing trouble. Margaret Audley's 5-year-old daughter Joan Gaveston received a gold ring with two emeralds and three pearls from her great-uncle the king, worth 32 shillings, and another gold ring with six emeralds, worth 20 marks, went to the Clare sisters' aunt Mary. Queen Isabella's gift from her husband was an enamelled silver-gilt bowl, with foot and cover, worth £17.[20] It is rather interesting to note that on 27 December 1317, Edward II took the custody of all the lands and tenements of the late Theobald Verdon away from Roger Damory, and granted them to Queen Isabella instead.[21] Perhaps this was intended to persuade the turbulent Thomas of Lancaster, Isabella's uncle as well as the king's first cousin, to relinquish control of Alton Castle, though in that case granting the queen custody of Alton alone might have served the intended purpose. Isabella was several months pregnant with the royal couple's third child and first daughter Eleanor of Woodstock, who was born in June 1318.

Damory's wife Elizabeth Burgh was also pregnant, and her child was due a few weeks before the king and queen's. Edward II and his sister Mary attended the funeral of their stepmother Queen Marguerite, Edward I's widow, at the Greyfriars church in London in mid-March 1318, a month after her death. Roger Damory also attended, a sign that he was still high in Edward's favour and spent much or most of his time with him; the king bought Damory two pieces of Lucca cloth to have himself mourning clothes made for the funeral.[22] Roger Damory was still powerful at court, but his ruthlessly ambitious brother-in-law Hugh Despenser the Younger was waiting in the wings for his opportunity, and in 1318 he took it.

Chapter 10

The New Favourite

Edward II stayed with Elizabeth Burgh and Roger Damory at Clare in Suffolk between 23 and 27 March 1318, and presumably took time to visit the tomb in the Augustinian priory there of Elizabeth's mother Joan of Acre, his much older sister. Shortly before his arrival, the king sold the marriage rights of Elizabeth's two younger stepdaughters Elizabeth and Margery Verdon to Damory for £200.[1] Elizabeth Burgh was seven months pregnant at the time of her uncle's visit, and gave birth to a child on or just before 23 May 1318 when an entry in the king's wardrobe accounts records a hugely generous payment of £20 to Roger's messenger John Pyrro for bringing him news of the birth. Sadly, it does not specify the child's name or sex, though it was perhaps a daughter called Margaret (presumably Elizabeth Burgh named her first Damory child after her sister). Roger Damory was with Edward II at Westminster on 20 and 27 May just before and after his child was born, though as he sent a messenger to the king on 23 May he must have returned to be near Elizabeth when she gave birth.[2] This implies that Elizabeth bore their child at one of their manors close to London/Westminster, perhaps Kennington or Vauxhall.

The Damorys had a household of at least fifty people, and their extant accounts of 1318/19 provide a fascinating insight into what they ate and drank in a day: 40 gallons of ale and 8 of wine, 150 eggs, 2 ducks, 6 hens, 13 pullets, half a carcass of salt beef, half a pig, a quantity of mutton, 40 herrings, 2 salt stockfish, 2 ling, salmon, whiting and eels.[3] The year 1318 saw the marriage of the Clare sisters' stepfather Ralph Monthermer, widowed from their mother Joan of Acre since 1307, and Hugh Despenser the Younger's sister Isabella Hastings. Isabella, born around 1290 or 1291, was many years Ralph's junior, and had lost her second husband John, Lord Hastings, father of her three children, in 1313. It is difficult to say much about what kind of relationship Ralph Monthermer had with his

68   Edward II's Nieces: The Clare Sisters

three stepdaughters, though in early May 1320 he sent three minstrels to perform for Margaret and Hugh Audley.[4]

Edward II presided over a meeting of his great council at Northampton in July 1318, and the *Vita Edwardi Secundi* says that Roger Damory, Hugh Audley, William Montacute, Hugh Despenser father and son and the Earl of Surrey arrived at Northampton 'in great strength, so that you would have thought they had not come to parliament, but to battle'. The author gives this as the reason for the non-attendance of Edward's cousin Thomas, Earl of Lancaster, as 'he counted all the aforenamed as his deadly enemies'.[5] Also in July 1318, Lancaster accused Roger Damory and William Montacute of trying to murder him, and claimed that he had intercepted letters at Pontefract, written by Edward II and sent to Scotland, inviting the Scots to help kill him.[6] Since April 1318, a group of barons and prelates had been negotiating with the Earl of Lancaster, and trying to persuade Edward and his unruly cousin to overcome their hostility to each other. On 8 June, they came to a preliminary agreement: Edward would uphold the hated Ordinances (the reforms imposed on him by the Lords Ordainer in 1311), govern by the counsel of his magnates, and conciliate Lancaster, who was threatened with sanctions if he continued to hold armed assemblies. Although Lancaster declared that he did not trust Edward's safe-conducts, he did eventually consent to meet the king on 7 August 1318, and the two men exchanged the kiss of peace in a field between Loughborough and Leicester. A formal agreement, the Treaty of Leake, was signed in the village of East Leake near Loughborough two days later. Hugh Despenser the Younger was one of the men involved in negotiating and drafting the treaty.[7]

Part of the agreement was for Roger Damory, Hugh Audley and William Montacute to be sent away from court. Surprisingly, Edward agreed. He would never have consented to Piers Gaveston's removal from court, and this suggests that he had grown tired of his friends and was not willing to fight for them. On 20 October 1318, Bartholomew Badlesmere replaced William Montacute in the key role of Edward's household steward, while Montacute himself was appointed steward of Gascony a month later.[8] This was technically an honour and even a promotion, though Montacute and everyone else realised he was being removed from the king's side and sent far away. Although Roger Damory's friendship with Edward was certainly not over, without constant access to the king's presence, his influence over him would henceforth be severely limited. Damory, Hugh Audley and William Montacute made their peace with the Earl of Lancaster, and agreed to pay him compensation for their hostility to him, 906 marks on Damory's part, 1,229 marks on Audley's, and 413 on Montacute's.[9] Montacute was to die in Gascony the following year. His heir was his second son William, his eldest John having died in 1317.[10] As for Roger Damory, he was with Edward at Clipstone on 9 September and at York on 20 and 27 November and 18 December 1318, though on 27 December and 19 January 1319 seems to have been at Farnham in Surrey. By early February 1319, he was reunited with the king in York.[11] Presumably his wife Elizabeth accompanied him, though she is rarely mentioned.

At the parliament of October 1318, Margaret and Hugh Audley audaciously presented a petition claiming the earldom of Cornwall as Margaret's dower from her first husband Piers Gaveston, on the basis that the Magna Carta 'wills that her inheritance and marriage shall be rendered to a widow immediately after his death'. The matter was discussed again at parliament in May 1319, but, not surprisingly, their petition failed on the grounds that all grants made by the king to Piers Gaveston had been revoked. Edward II made a deal with the couple that they would relinquish all claims to Cornwall and all other lands Margaret had held jointly with Gaveston in return for lands worth 2,000 marks (£1,333) a year. If Margaret died before Audley, Audley would continue to hold lands to the value of 1,200 marks a year for the rest of his life.[12] Hugh Audley kept his wardrobe in some houses in Ismanghere ('Ironmonger') Lane, London, which had formerly belonged to Piers Gaveston and where Gaveston also kept his wardrobe.[13] He and Margaret sent a clerk called John Dufford to Ireland to take care of their affairs there on 6 June 1319.[14]

In or a little before October 1318, Hugh Despenser the Younger was appointed as Edward II's chamberlain at the request of the English magnates. This appointment would eventually lead to a baronial rebellion against the king during which Elizabeth Burgh and Hugh and Margaret Audley were imprisoned and Roger Damory was killed, and ultimately to the king's downfall, Despenser's grotesque execution and Eleanor Despenser's imprisonment. From 1318 to 1320, there must have been furious jockeying for position and favour as Hugh Despenser worked his way into Edward's affections and began to oust Roger Damory and Hugh Audley. (The third powerful royal favourite of the 1310s, Sir William Montacute, was now in Gascony and out of the picture, and died in 1319.) Hugh Audley was with the king on 28 March and from 20 to 26 May 1319 and was politely acknowledged as the 'king's nephew', but witnessed none of Edward's charters at all after August 1317, so apparently was only rarely at court.[15] He and his brother-in-law Sir Ralph Greystoke (1299–1323), his younger sister Alice's husband, were given letters of protection to go to Scotland on 20 July 1319.[16] Roger Damory witnessed his last-ever royal charters on 4 February, 25 May and 19 July 1319, and the large number of entries in the Chancery rolls made 'on the information of Roger Damory' cease entirely after December 1318; his disappearance from court and from Edward's favour is visible in the records.[17]

Hugh Despenser the Younger was almost always at court with the king—where his itinerary can be established in 1319 it always coincides with Edward's, except on one occasion—and unlike his rivals, he had every right to be at the king's side, as he had been elected by the magnates as royal chamberlain. He witnessed no charters of Edward II's at all until May 1316, but by the end of the reign in 1325/26 was witnessing almost all of them.[18] As with Roger Damory's fall from royal grace, Despenser's rise in Edward's favour is visible in the records. Despenser, ambitious almost beyond description, soon began to use his influential position to benefit himself, and demanded bribes from petitioners to allow them to speak to the king and answered their petitions himself, or whispered to the king what he should say. He very soon became grossly unpopular, and his behaviour as chamberlain became the talk of the kingdom. Edward II, however, became infatuated with him. This in itself is fascinating, as the two men must have known each other most of their lives—Despenser was a high-ranking nobleman whose father, grandfather the Earl of Warwick and great-uncle Sir Walter Beauchamp spent most or all of their time at Edward I's court when Despenser was growing up—but Edward had never shown the slightest interest in or liking for Despenser previously despite his obvious fondness for Despenser's wife Eleanor.

Robert Bruce, king of Scotland, had captured the vital port of Berwick-on-Tweed in 1318, and in September 1319 Edward II finally made his way there to retake it. The siege of Berwick proved an utter failure, and the port remained in Scottish hands until Edward's son Edward III took it back in 1333. Hugh Despenser frequently sent letters to his sheriff of Glamorgan, Sir John Inge, micromanaging the affairs in his and Eleanor's lordship, and the earliest one which survives today was written on 22 September 1319 shortly after the siege of Berwick.[19] It is clear from this letter that Despenser was already confident of his hold on the favour of the king who had disliked him for so many years. He had already persuaded Edward to find a church for Inge's clerical brother, but it had proved to be inadequate, and so, Despenser wrote, he personally would ensure that Edward gave 'the first good church' which fell vacant to Inge's brother.

It seems that Edward II fell in love with his nephew-in-law once the two men began spending almost all their time together. The *Anonimalle* chronicle wrote that 'the king loved [Hugh Despenser] dearly, with all his heart and mind, above all others' and Geoffrey le Baker wrote much later that Despenser had enchanted (or bewitched) Edward's heart. The *Lanercost* chronicle called Despenser Edward's 'right eye' on two occasions, and the *Scalacronica* added that 'the great men had ill will against [Edward] for his cruelty and the debauched life which he led, and on account of the said Hugh, whom at that time he loved and entirely trusted'.[20] An annalist in 1326 called them 'the king and his husband', which strongly implies that their relationship was sexual or at least perceived by outsiders to be.[21] The Liège chronicler Jean le Bel, who was in England in 1327, wrote that Hugh was 'a pervert and a sodomite, above all with the king himself, which was why the king, at his urging, had driven the queen away'.[22] It certainly seems that Edward and Despenser's relationship was intimate, and that Hugh was thought to be the third person in the royal marriage. Piers Gaveston had enjoyed the wealth which came from being the king's favourite, though had little if any interest in ruling via Edward. Hugh Despenser was an entirely different matter, and over the next few years came to dominate the English government. His correspondence from the years 1323 to 1325 makes it apparent that he, not the king, was directing English policy when Edward II went to war against his brother-in-law Charles IV of France (r. 1322–28). Endless complaints were raised about Despenser appropriating and using royal power which did not belong to him, not least by Despenser's sister-in-law Elizabeth Burgh, who in 1326 talked of 'the royal power which is in the hand of the said Sir Hugh'.[23]

What Eleanor Despenser made of this is anyone's guess. Perhaps she was delighted that her husband, now 30 years old and in the political wilderness for the previous dozen years of her uncle's reign, had reached a prominent and highly influential position at last. Where her itinerary can be established after 1318, it reveals that she was almost always at court or at least just a few miles away and in touch with Edward II and Despenser, so she can hardly have failed to be aware of the presumably intimate relationship between her husband and her uncle. Eleanor was one of the king and Despenser's closest allies in the 1320s, so if she knew that the two men were lovers, it did not drive her away from them. At least four or five of the Despensers' many children were born in the late 1310s and 1320s, so she and Hugh certainly continued their intimate marital relationship after he grew extremely close to the king. Eleanor herself would also be said by one chronicler (admittedly, a chronicler outside England) to have had a sexual relationship with her uncle. Whether that is true or not—and some evidence from Edward's household accounts from 1324 to 1326 seems to support the notion (discussed in Chapters 13, 15 and 18)—she was certainly a supporter of her uncle and her husband during their tyrannical regime of the 1320s.

Hugh Despenser the Younger and his current ally Bartholomew, Lord Badlesmere, appointed steward of the royal household when he was elected chamberlain in 1318, were jointly involved in some shady business in 1319 or early 1320 when they unlawfully released one John Lashley from prison in Colchester. Despenser kept Lashley in his own prison until the latter released one of his Essex manors to Despenser, and a few months later Despenser gave Badlesmere the manor.[24] Despenser rescued Badlesmere's wife Margaret, his wife Eleanor's first cousin, while she and her servants were being held captive in a house in Cheshunt, Hertfordshire sometime before 6 December 1319.[25] This was the only known occasion in 1319 when Despenser was not at court with the king, and perhaps he had come south—Edward II spent that whole year in and near York, 180 miles from Cheshunt—specifically to deal with the Lashley situation and to benefit from it. Later evidence demonstrates that Eleanor Despenser was well aware of what her husband was up to, and she surely also knew about the Lashley situation, one of the earliest examples of Hugh Despenser's penchant for false imprisonment and for forcing men and women to hand over manors to him.

Eleanor Despenser was ill sometime in 1319/20 when her uncle Edward bought medicines for her, and the two were linked together in a way which, given the later rumours about their relationship, was perhaps significant: 'for the king and Eleanor Despenser his niece, when ill'.[26]

On 6 March 1320, while she was in Canterbury with her husband and the king and queen, Eleanor sent a letter (in French) to Sir John Inge, sheriff of Glamorgan. Courteous and friendly, it could hardly be more different from the impatient, hectoring, threatening tone her husband generally adopted in his own frequent letters to Inge, and demonstrates that Eleanor took an interest in the affairs of the lordship she had inherited, her birthplace:

> Eleanor Despenser [*Alianore la Despensiere*] to our beloved Sir John Inge, sheriff of Glamorgan, greetings and true love. Because we know well that you would gladly hear good news of us always, we make known to you that at the making of these letters we were in good physical health, thanks to God, and we always wish very much to know the same of you. We thank you very much, and are very grateful to you, that you are so diligent concerning our affairs in those parts [Glamorgan]. And we beseech you as much as we can that you may aid and counsel Sir Lessam d'Avesne, bearer of these letters, in the business he has to attend to there, without any prejudice to our very dear lord [Hugh Despenser], and we will be very grateful to you. And send us news of any happenings where you are as soon as you can, for love of us. May our lord keep you.[27]

The household accounts of Eleanor's sister Margaret and Hugh Audley survive for 183 days in 1320, and reveal that Margaret spent almost all that time that year at their manor of Tonbridge in Kent. Tonbridge was the castle which Hugh Despenser the Younger temporarily seized in 1315, and where Margaret's parents Gilbert 'the Red' Clare and Joan of Acre had retired shortly after their wedding in 1290, to the displeasure of Joan's parents Edward I and Queen Leonor. Audley himself was with his wife most of the time at Tonbridge, though made some journeys away with a small group of attendants. The couple also spent quite a bit of time at their Northamptonshire manor of Whiston in the late 1310s and early 1320s.[28] They had ninety-six people in their household and owned forty-two horses, two of which were destriers called Ferant de Roma and Grisel le Kyng.[29] The latter name implies that Grisel had been a gift to Hugh Audley from Edward II—and it is interesting to note that the name *le Kyng* is half-French and half-English—and both *ferant* and *grisel* meant a grey horse (*ferant* is iron-grey). The king and queen and much of his court travelled to France in June 1320, because Edward owed homage, as Duke of Aquitaine and Count of Ponthieu, to his brother-in-law Philip V, who had succeeded his brother Louis X in 1316. Hugh Despenser the Younger and Roger Damory, presumably with their wives Eleanor and Elizabeth, were among those who accompanied the king overseas.[30] Damory was still just about clinging to royal favour, though was well on the way out and Despenser well on the way in, while Hugh Audley appears to have given up entirely by this stage and did not travel abroad with the king. Roger Damory and his wife Elizabeth Burgh were in Reading on 25 August 1320 when they and Hugh Despenser the Elder, Eleanor's father-in-law, came to an agreement with Elizabeth's former father-in-law, the Earl of Ulster, regarding the Buckinghamshire manor of Steeple Claydon. Roger and Elizabeth were at their manor of Kennington on 26 October 1320, when they arranged with the Augustinian priory of Clare in Suffolk that two friars would celebrate Mass daily in Clare Castle during Roger and Elizabeth's lifetimes in exchange for annual allowances of wheat and malt. Parliament was being held at Westminster on the other side of the River Thames at that time and Damory presumably attended, though, unlike his great rival Hugh Despenser the Younger, did not witness any of the six charters Edward II issued at this time.[31]

The excessive favouritism of the king towards Despenser pushed Hugh Audley and Roger Damory, and other men, into opposition. Despenser had already forced Audley and Margaret to exchange one of their valuable lordships for some of his manors of lower value. He tried to take over some of Damory's lands in South Wales as well, presumably the lordships of Usk and Caerleon which came to them on the death of the Dowager Countess of Gloucester in 1320. Damory successfully resisted him, though after his death his widow Elizabeth Burgh was vulnerable to her brother-in-law Despenser's machinations, and lost Usk and Caerleon to him.[32] There was a widespread, and probably correct, belief in the late 1310s and early 1320s that Hugh Despenser the Younger was trying to claim the entire earldom of Gloucester. At the parliament in August 1321, it was said that 'by other false compassings he [Despenser] compassed to have the lands of Sir Roger Damory in order to attain the whole of the earldom of Gloucester'.[33] If this is true, he perhaps felt entitled to it as the husband of the previous earl's eldest sister, and Despenser certainly did his utmost to increase his control of South Wales, and yearned to possess the Gower peninsula. Edward II had ordered an inquisition into the lordship of Gower, almost certainly to benefit Despenser, on 28 July 1319, which is one of the earliest signs of the royal chamberlain's rise in Edward's favour.[34] The king ordered Gower to be taken into his own hands on 26 October 1320, as a prelude to granting it to Despenser.[35] Gower's lord, William Braose, was still alive, and his son-in-law John Mowbray claimed the lordship and had, according to the king, entered it without a royal licence. This act of confiscation was the final straw for the Marcher lords, and for Roger Damory and Hugh Audley. 'Deeply moved by such abuse, the barons departed [from court] full of indignation, and meeting in Wales, they unanimously decided that Hugh Despenser must be pursued, laid low and utterly destroyed.'[36] Edward II tried to mollify Roger Damory and Hugh Audley on 5 November 1320 by confirming his father's May 1290 regrant of Gilbert 'the Red' Clare's lands to Gilbert, Joan of Acre, and the heirs of their bodies, most probably an attempt to reassure Damory and Audley that Despenser would not try to claim all the lands; but it was too late.[37] The king's former favourites and nephews-in-law were now his enemies, and a war was soon to come in which the three Clare sisters would find themselves on opposite sides.

Chapter 11

The Despenser War

Eleanor Despenser suffered a personal tragedy at the end of 1320 or beginning of 1321 when she lost a child. It was a boy, whose name was never recorded, if he ever even had one; perhaps he was stillborn. Edward II bought a piece of gold and silk tissue to lie over the coffin or tomb of 'the son of Hugh Despenser the son' on about 13 January 1321.[1] By the end of 1320 Eleanor and Hugh Despenser already had many children, though their birthdates and birth order are almost impossible to ascertain. They had three and perhaps four sons already: Hugh or Huchon born sometime before July 1309, Edward born sometime before October 1313, conceivably in 1310, Gilbert born perhaps in the mid- or late 1310s (though not mentioned on record until July 1322), and John, who was already old enough to ride a horse in November 1324 when Edward II bought a saddle for him. John was born in the late 1310s or early 1320s. Their eldest daughter Isabella was probably born in 1312, their second, Joan, in the mid-1310s, and their third, Eleanor, in the late 1310s or early 1320s. Two more daughters, Margaret and Elizabeth, would follow in 1323 and 1325. Nine Despenser children would survive childhood, and possibly there were more miscarriages or stillbirths or early deaths in addition to the one we know about at the beginning of 1321. Like her mother Joan of Acre, Eleanor was very fertile, and given the regular pattern of her pregnancies throughout her twenty-year marriage to Despenser—she gave birth at least every two years—the couple seem to have had significant physical desire for each other and to have spent much time together.

The Despensers attended the wedding of their 8-year-old eldest daughter Isabella Despenser at the royal manor of Havering-atte-Bower in Essex on 9 February 1321. She wed the 7-year-old Richard Fitzalan, son and heir of Edmund, Earl of Arundel, and nephew and heir of John Warenne, Earl of Surrey, the estranged husband of the Clare sisters' cousin

Jeanne de Bar. In theory it was an excellent match for the Despensers' daughter and was intended to make her a countess twice over, but the marriage proved to be an unhappy disaster and was to end in annulment, and although Richard became one of the richest men in England in the entire fourteenth century neither Isabella nor her son benefited from it. Edward II was also present, and paid for a piece of Lucca cloth to make a veil for spreading over the heads of the child couple during their nuptial Mass and gave £2 in pennies to be thrown over them at the chapel door.[2] This was a custom of the era, intended to bring the couple luck, and the money was later distributed to the poor; Edward II had provided over £7 for the same purpose at Margaret Clare and Piers Gaveston's wedding in 1307. Less happily, the king learned shortly after Isabella Despenser's wedding that his hated cousin the Earl of Lancaster and other magnates, not named but presumably some of the Marchers or their representatives, had met five days earlier and decided to 'raise disturbances and begin some mischief' against Hugh Despenser the Younger in Wales. The king was advised to 'command Despenser, the son, that he be prepared and arrayed in his lands that he may be able to counteract these evils'.[3] The king and Despenser left London on 1 March 1321, and travelled slowly towards Gloucester, hoping to reconcile the Marcher lords. Eleanor Despenser's whereabouts are not clear, though perhaps she remained in and around London with the queen, who was pregnant with her fourth and last child.

Sir Henry Spigurnel, a justice of the assize, and Edward II's much younger half-brother Thomas of Brotherton, Earl of Norfolk and Earl marshal of England, were appointed on 2 April 1321 to put Hugh Audley on trial. Hugh was accused of having sworn an oath in writing to 'assist the king in all things all his life' and never to leave Edward's company come what may, but of doing so. The king fumed that he 'has frequently ordered the said Hugh to come to him at certain dates and places to obey the king's orders and pleasure, and Hugh has refused to obey'. (Whether Edward and Audley had had a sexual relationship or not, 'pleasure' in this context certainly does not mean sexual pleasure.) Edward told Norfolk and Spigurnel 'to give judgement and act as the king himself might do, if present'.[4] Hugh Despenser the Younger already knew on 21 March that Spigurnel and Norfolk would be appointed to try Audley when he wrote a letter to Sir John Inge, sheriff of Glamorgan, and did his best to influence Spigurnel to find Audley guilty by sending him letters stating that he could not believe Spigurnel 'would like to be against us nor against any of our friends'.⁵ This was a not very subtle threat that if Spigurnel was too lenient with Audley, he would displease the king and his powerful favourite (and Despenser was prone to ordering his followers to harm and generally harass men who displeased him, or threatening them with execution). Edward sent the sheriff of Gloucestershire to Hugh and Margaret Audley's manor of Thornbury to summon Audley to appear and argue his case as to why his lands and goods should not be confiscated, but Hugh did not do so. On 8 April, therefore, Spigurnel and Norfolk duly pronounced a sentence of forfeiture on him, and on the 9th the king ordered sheriffs all over the country to confiscate all Audley's lands and goods.⁶

The garrison of Hugh and Margaret Audley's castle of Tonbridge refused to surrender it to the sheriff of Kent, so Edward II ordered the sheriff to take all the *posse comitatus* (the county militia) and besiege it and arrest everyone inside. The garrison duly gave in, and the king pardoned them all. He granted custody of Tonbridge to his steward Bartholomew Badlesmere on 17 May 1321.⁷ Edward was considerably less forgiving towards Audley himself than towards the Tonbridge garrison: he was so furious with him that a few months later he fined a merchant of Hereford 20 marks merely for communicating with him. A clerk called Hugh of Leominster felt the need to beg the king's pardon because he had borrowed 50 shillings from Audley.⁸ Much had happened in the four years since a besotted king had married Hugh Audley to his niece Margaret, and Audley had now moved into a position of hostility to Edward thanks to the excessive favouritism the king showed to Hugh Despenser. Confiscating Audley's lands and goods also affected Margaret profoundly, but this did not stop Edward, and where Margaret and Audley lived for the next few months is not clear. They were officially penniless, landless and possession-less, and perhaps had to throw themselves on the mercy of Audley's parents Hugh senior and Isolde, or Margaret's sister Elizabeth and Roger Damory. The man given custody of the Audleys' lands in Devon, however, complained to the king probably in 1322 that 'some people came on behalf of the said Sir Hugh Daudeleye [Audley] and left with the issues of the lands for the use of the said Sir Hugh'.⁹ Hugh and Margaret Audley still had friends and supporters taking care of their welfare. Suffering from one of his usual bouts of over-confidence, Hugh Despenser the Younger told John

Inge, his sheriff of Glamorgan, 'do not doubt that neither [Hugh Audley] nor any of his allies have the power to hurt any of us' on 21 March.[10] A few weeks later, he would be proved badly wrong. Audley and his former rival Roger Damory, now his ally, were not men to sit back and passively accept their fate, and almost certainly with their wives Margaret and Elizabeth egging them on, they decided to take action against their brother-in-law Despenser.

The king, who realised that the disaffected Marcher lords could not be reconciled as long as Hugh Despenser remained at his side but who was determined to keep his beloved with him, removed Roger Damory from his position as keeper of the castle of St Briavels and of the Forest of Dean on 11 April 1321. He replaced him with Hugh Despenser's cousin Sir William Beauchamp, and Damory was also replaced as the keeper of Corfe Castle in Dorset on 8 May.[11] At some point in the next few months, Damory seized the castle of St Briavels, formerly in his custody, and kept more than twenty men imprisoned there; they managed to escape after he left the town of Gloucester, a few miles away.[12]

On 1 May 1321, Edward made one last attempt to prevent the impending violent conflict by ordering his brother-in-law the Earl of Hereford, Roger Mortimer of Wigmore and Hugh Despenser not to attack each other, but his commands fell on deaf ears.[13] The 'Despenser War' began on 4 May, when Hereford, Damory, Audley, Mortimer of Wigmore and his uncle Roger Mortimer of Chirk, John Mowbray, Roger Clifford and their allies including Bartholomew Badlesmere (who had switched sides) attacked Hugh and Eleanor Despenser's castle at Newport in South Wales. It fell three days later.[14] Eighty-eight men-at-arms, 500 hobelars and 10,000 footmen were with them.[15] The Marchers and their men tried to burn down the Despensers' castles, and although they succeeded only in destroying a few outer buildings, they did steal windows, lead and ironwork. They made a special point of burning the charters and documents granting the lands to Eleanor and her husband.[16] Hugh Despenser later claimed that the Marchers had stolen from him and Eleanor, among many other things, 40 destriers, 60 mares, 10,000 sheep, 400 pigs, 400 oxen, 500 cows and 160 plough-cattle, armour for 200 men, siege-engines, crossbows and other military equipment, wagons and carts, wine, honey, corn, rye and other victuals, to a total loss of £14,000 on twenty-three manors. The Marchers also attacked Eleanor and Despenser's lands in England, 'throwing down houses, robbing and spoiling what they could find' to a loss of £10,000, or so Despenser claimed, and 'whatever the barons found of value in the castles, contrary to the laws of war they divided between themselves', according to the *Vita*.[17] They kept for themselves the Despensers' rents and other income, cut down their woods, burned their barns, robbed all their moveable goods, imprisoned Hugh's supporters, and killed quite a few men, including the constable of Neath Castle, Sir John Iweyn. Despenser's father Hugh the Elder and the Despenser retainers Sir Ingelram Berenger and Sir John Haudlo also saw their lands attacked and plundered. Roger Damory's sister Katherine and her husband Sir Walter Poure robbed six manors in Oxfordshire belonging to Haudlo.[18]

Edward II was forced to grant a pardon on 20 August 1321 to the main Contrariants—as he soon took to calling his and Despenser's foes—and their followers for all the crimes they had committed against the Despensers, during a parliament held in London. The Marcher lords sat menacingly with their armies all around the walls of the capital to prevent the king leaving. Over 100 adherents of Roger Damory were pardoned for their actions against the Despensers, including the 50-year-old Maurice, Lord Berkeley, husband of the Clare sisters' much older half-sister Isabella Clare (b. 1262). Damory's former position close to the king and his excellent marriage to the king's rich niece had enabled him to attract a large following, and the fact that such a wealthy and powerful nobleman as Lord Berkeley was classed as his supporter and not vice versa also reveals how influential Damory had become. Around fifty adherents of Hugh Audley were also pardoned, including his sister Alice's husband Ralph Greystoke.[19] The Marchers demanded the permanent exile and disinheritance of Hugh Despenser and his father, and the perpetual disinheritance of their descendants. With no other choice, a furious Edward II was forced to consent, but as he had done with Piers Gaveston years before, immediately began plotting to get them back. Hugh Despenser the Elder took himself off abroad; Hugh the Younger became a pirate in the English Channel with the king's full knowledge and connivance.

Eleanor Despenser was, as her sister Margaret had been a few months previously, deprived of her lands and her income, and had to suffer the knowledge that her children were also permanently disinherited thanks to her husband's actions. How she felt about her husband's foray into piracy is not known, though she must have been furious that he had been expelled from his own homeland with no money and possessions at the instigation of her sisters' husbands and others. Unlike Margaret Audley, however, Edward II was keen to look after Eleanor and protect her interests. Although it is difficult to ascertain her whereabouts while her husband was a 'sea-monster' (the word the *Vita Edwardi Secundi* ascribes to him in 1321), it is highly likely that Edward took Eleanor, her children and her servants into his own household and paid all her expenses. It is also possible, given the regular pattern of Eleanor's childbearing throughout her Despenser marriage, that she was pregnant when her husband was exiled, as her sister Margaret had been when her first husband Piers Gaveston was banished for the third time in late 1311. Eleanor was not included in her husband's exile, and although she may have travelled abroad with Hugh when he took part in jousting tournaments on the continent in 1310, she is unlikely to have participated in his piracy—though must have received some of the goods and money he stole.

On 16 August, 25 September and again on 28 November 1321, the king ordered Roger Damory and Hugh Audley to deliver Eleanor and Hugh Despenser's lands in Glamorgan and Gwynllŵg into his own hands.[20] They failed to do so. Damory wrote to Edward with the lame excuse that if he handed over Glamorgan, this would cause the inhabitants to believe that Despenser had remained in the country and that therefore they would rise in war, 'which answer the king deems altogether insufficient and derisory'. Audley claimed not to have any of Despenser's lands in his custody as Gwynllŵg was part of his wife's inheritance and rightfully belonged to him, 'which answer the king reputes as naught'. Edward seized Damory's lands and goods in Essex, Suffolk and Hertfordshire on 22 November.[21] The king's former favourites were now counted among his deadliest enemies, and their marriages to his nieces would not save them. Over the next few months, Edward regularly ordered sheriffs to arrest Damory and Audley; the fact that he had to keep repeating the order either shows that sheriffs were reluctant to do so, or that the two men were adept at making themselves scarce. Hugh and Margaret Audley had no home and no income after April 1321, and as her uncle the king seems to have washed his hands of her and to have deemed her his enemy, Margaret perhaps stayed with her parents-in-law Hugh the Elder and Isolde. A later petition by Elizabeth Burgh and entries in the Chancery rolls make it apparent that Edward II seized her lands and goods as well on 19 November 1321.[22] All three Clare sisters had now lost their income.

Chapter 12

Contrariants

Edward II recalled Hugh Despenser the Younger and his father from their supposedly perpetual exile in December 1321, and although it was the middle of winter, the king set out on campaign against the Marcher lords, including Audley and Damory, shortly after Christmas. Before Edward's arrival in the west of England, the Marchers had seized Gloucester, and controlled its bridge over the Severn. When they heard that the king was approaching Gloucestershire, they fled from him rather than engage him in battle, burning and devastating the countryside as they went.[1] Edward marched the forty miles to Worcester, where he arrived on New Year's Eve, but was unable to cross the bridge because the Marcher army was on the other side holding it against him. On 7 January 1322, Edward left Worcester and headed farther north, and as soon as he had left, Roger Damory swooped in with an armed force and took the town back for the Marchers. Damory remained at Worcester, other Contrariants headed north, while the Earl of Hereford sacked the Worcestershire castles of Hanley and Elmley which belonged to Eleanor and Hugh Despenser the Younger.[2] Elizabeth Burgh seems to have remained at Usk in Wales while all this was going on, though her sister Margaret Audley's whereabouts are unclear. Evidence suggests that their uncle believed they had joined the rebellion against him and encouraged their husbands to do so, and other evidence suggests that both women may have been pregnant in 1321/22.

The king had most of his earls and a large number of his household knights with him, and the Contrariants' cause was doomed. Hugh Audley's father Hugh the Elder surrendered to the king in January 1322 and was incarcerated; he would die in prison in 1326. Maurice, Lord Berkeley, husband of the Clare sisters' half-sister, also died in prison in 1326 after surrendering to Edward in early 1322. Roger Mortimer of Wigmore and his uncle Roger Mortimer of Chirk submitted to the king at Shrewsbury in late January and were sent to the Tower of London. The remaining

Contrariants fled to Yorkshire to Thomas, Earl of Lancaster, their only hope. Among them was Roger Damory, whom Lancaster had once accused of trying to kill him, and Hugh Audley was another. The men made the terrible error of sending letters to Scotland, inviting its king, Robert Bruce, to send an army to help them fight against their own king.[3] The letters were discovered, and this was clearly treason. Edward II's fury at his former favourites Damory and Audley is apparent, and he called them 'contrariant' whenever he could and continued to order their arrest regularly in the early months of 1322.

Edward, openly joined by Hugh Despenser father and son in or before early March 1322 only five months after their supposedly perpetual exile from England, reached Burton-on-Trent and Tutbury in Staffordshire on 10/11 March. There he ordered the arrest of several leading Contrariants, including Hugh Audley, who had fled from Burton to join the Earl of Lancaster in Pontefract, Yorkshire before the king's arrival.[4] Roger Damory was, however, unable to join his allies' flight: he had been badly wounded in Burton-on-Trent and had to be left behind at Tutbury Priory four miles from Burton. Damory's wounds were sustained either while holding the bridge at Burton against the royal army, or shortly afterwards when Edward and his men managed to cross the river by a ford and faced the Contrariant forces outside the town. According to the king, the rebels 'divided into battles in manner of war in a field', but when they saw his enormous force, they 'turned their backs, set fire to the town, and fled'.[5] Damory's injuries must have been severe as he was soon to die of them, and they prevented him fleeing from Edward; he surely expected little mercy from the king he had betrayed and who had been ordering his arrest for months, and from the powerful brother-in-law, Hugh Despenser the Younger, who was his deadliest rival.

Either with the captured and badly injured Damory present or not, judgement was rendered against him by Sir Fulk FitzWarin as constable of the royal army, Sir John Weston as marshal of the royal household, and Geoffrey Scrope, chief justice of the King's Bench, on Saturday, 13 March 1322. Damory was sentenced to death, but then FitzWarin added surprisingly: 'But, Roger, because our lord the king much loved you in the past and you were of his household and a confidant of his, and married his niece, our said lord the king by his grace and his royalty delays the execution of the said judgement, by his will.'[6] This was a mercy

Damory had perhaps not anticipated, though the stay of execution was to make little difference. Although the two men may well have been lovers, the statement that the king 'much loved' Damory does not automatically imply it; it was common in the early fourteenth century for men to declare love for another man in public. Also in March 1322, Thomas, Earl of Lancaster discovered that his closest ally and friend Sir Robert Holland had joined the king against him, and groaned 'How could he find it in his heart to betray me, when I loved him so much?'[7]

Sir Roger Damory died anyway, presumably of his injuries, still at Tutbury Priory. The date of his death is not entirely clear; chroniclers give 13 or 14 March 1322, but his widow Elizabeth Burgh kept it as the 12th, and she would seem to be in the best position to know.[8] Then again, Elizabeth kept the date of her father Gilbert 'the Red' Clare's death as 6 December (the feast of St Nicholas) when in fact he died on 7 December, and her brother Gilbert's on 23 June when he died on the 24th, so she may have kept Damory's anniversary on a convenient major saint's day—12 March is the feast of St Gregory—rather than on the exact date.[9] Edward II moved from Tutbury to Derby on 12 March and thus seems to have missed Damory's death, and how he felt about a man he had once 'much loved' dying in rebellion against him cannot be known. If Roger did die on 12 March, that was the day before the judgement against him and the respite of the death penalty, so perhaps the judges did not know he was already dead. Eleanor Despenser's husband Hugh was surely triumphant at the demise of his rival.

The author of the *Vita Edwardi Secundi*, although he praised Roger Damory's diligence and valour, condemned him for turning against the king who had done so much for him and stated that many people 'marked him down as ungrateful'.[10] Damory's widow Elizabeth Burgh was to claim in 1326 that her husband was 'pursued and oppressed until he died'.[11] This was a highly disingenuous statement, given that Roger was in control of his own actions and freely decided to join a rebellion against Edward II, and to fight against the royal army at Burton. Elizabeth's biographer has called Roger Damory 'a grasping, reckless mediocrity with a petty crook's mentality', which seems a very harsh value judgement.[12] Damory made the most of the chances which came his way thanks to Edward II's infatuation with him, and none of his contemporaries would have turned down marriage to the king's wealthy niece or refused all the appointments, grants, money and favours on offer. There seems no real reason to suppose that Damory was a thoroughly unpleasant or abusive person, or that he was more of a 'crook' or 'grasping' than any other fourteenth-century nobleman. He was an excellent soldier who first came to the king's attention because of his bravery at Bannockburn, remained high in the king's favour for several years, managed, unlike many others, to resist the ruthless Hugh Despenser the Younger's encroachments on his lands, and in early 1322 captured the town of Worcester for the Contrariants and fought again for his allies at Burton a few weeks later. This all suggests a man who was courageous, competent and charming, and he did at least seek to gain Elizabeth's consent to her marriage with him, rather than abducting and forcibly marrying her as Theobald Verdon had probably done. Damory's influence over Edward II was certainly self-interested and on occasion even malign and dangerous, but not nearly as malign, dangerous and self-interested as that of the man who replaced him in the king's favour, Hugh Despenser the Younger, who was to bring Edward and himself down a few years later.

Elizabeth Burgh had perhaps never wished to marry Roger Damory (though we do not know for sure whether she did or not), but he had been her husband for five years and they had at least two children together. In 1326, Elizabeth called herself 'formerly the consort of Sir Roger Damory', talked about him respectfully as 'my lord, Sir Roger' and complained that he had been oppressed to his death. The evidence we have implies that Elizabeth supported her husband during his rebellion against her uncle, which indicates sympathy with Damory and his aims, and there is much evidence of the way the two co-operated as a couple to further their interests. She fed the poor on the anniversary of his demise and left money in her will for Masses to be sung for his soul, as she did for her other two husbands, and was one of the executors of Damory's will (which does not survive).[14] Even if Damory had been her uncle's lover and she had been pushed into marrying him, relationships are complex, and the couple may have developed an understanding and an affection during their years together. She may have disliked him, but there is no real evidence to suggest she did. Elizabeth was still only 26 years old in March 1322 and had now been widowed for the third time; she outlived Damory by almost forty years, but never married again. Sometime before 1343, she took a vow of chastity.[13] As a widow she controlled her own lands, her own income and her own destiny, and evidently she liked it that way.

Roger Damory's death left Elizabeth alone and vulnerable to her uncle and her brother-in-law Hugh Despenser. She was captured at Usk by the king's men even before Roger's death, and taken the 150 miles to Barking Abbey in Essex with her children. Elizabeth learned of her husband's demise at Barking, and Edward II ordered her not to 'go out of the abbey gates in any wise' on 16 March and not to marry without his consent.[15] As horrible as the command to stay within Barking Abbey might sound, in fairness Elizabeth was now a widow and her enormous lands reverted to her by right on Damory's death, which made her once again very vulnerable to potential abduction and forced marriage. Edward may have been thinking of her safety as well as his own interests, at least partly. Eventually, the king paid £74 for Elizabeth's expenses at Barking, restored her Welsh lands to her on 25 July 1322 and the English and Irish ones on 2 November that year.[16] Elizabeth petitioned her cousin Edward III, Edward II's son, in or after 1327, stating that she had lost £3,000 in income from her lands while they were in Edward II's hands between November 1321 and November 1322, and another £3,000 from the 'great loss of jewels, plate, remembrances and other things' which she kept on her manors.[17]

Unfortunately for Elizabeth, there was a price to pay and a brother-in-law to satisfy in return for receiving her lands, income and freedom, as she would soon find out. Roger Damory was buried at St Mary's church in Ware, Hertfordshire, though by whom and on whose authority is not clear; presumably not on Elizabeth's, as she was incarcerated at Barking Abbey. It seems a little strange that Roger Damory was buried more than 100 miles from the place where he died, in a town which belonged neither to his family nor his wife and which lay 65 miles from the Damorys' main seat of Bletchingdon.[18] His elder brother Richard Damory was arrested on 16 February 1322 and imprisoned at Banbury in Oxfordshire, but was released and restored to his lands on 16 March a few days after Roger's death and was made steward of the king's household in July 1322, a position he held for almost three years.[19]

A battle was fought at Boroughbridge in Yorkshire on 16 March 1322 between the Contrariant army and a royalist army led by Sir Andrew Harclay, sheriff of Cumberland and soon to be made Earl of Carlisle. Edward II's brother-in-law and the Clare sisters' uncle Humphrey Bohun, Earl of Hereford, was killed during the battle fighting for the Contrariants, and Edward's cousin Thomas, Earl of Lancaster captured and taken to his own castle of Pontefract, where the king was waiting for him. Lancaster was sentenced to death and beheaded on 22 March outside the castle; among those who sat in judgement on him were Hugh Despenser father and son and the earls of Kent, Surrey, Arundel, Pembroke, Richmond, Atholl and Angus. The Clare sisters' stepfather Ralph Monthermer, their mother Joan of Acre's widower and now Hugh Despenser the Younger's brother-in-law, was also with Edward II at Pontefract at the time of Lancaster's execution.[20] About twenty other Contrariants were executed in March and April 1322, including the Clare siblings' first cousin John, Lord Mowbray (son of their father's sister Rohese Clare), their first cousin Maud Clifford's son Roger, Lord Clifford, and their first cousin Margaret Badlesmere's husband Bartholomew, the only Contrariant given the full horrors of the traitor's death.

Sir Francis Aldham, an adherent of Hugh Audley, was one of those hanged, as were Sir Henry Wilington and Sir Henry Tyes, adherents of Roger Damory. A petition presented after the men's deaths accused Henry Wilington of threatening to kill a man called Richard Apperley unless Apperley gave him his lands and tenements, and stated that Wilington 'menaced Richard with the great force and power he had from Roger Damory'.[21] Damory had wielded great influence in his years as a royal favourite, but now he was dead, disgraced and disinherited. Hugh Audley was captured after he fought for the Contrariants at the Battle of Boroughbridge and was imprisoned.[22] His brother-in-law Ralph Greystoke, though pardoned as one of his followers in August 1321, fought against him at Boroughbridge, and three days after the battle Greystoke was summoned by Edward II to go on campaign in Scotland with him.[23] Margaret Audley pleaded with her uncle to spare her husband's life, and Edward II did—Audley would be the only one of the king's favourites to survive the reign—but the Contrariant rebellion of 1321/22 marked the end of Margaret's influence with her uncle, and the end of their previously close relationship. Almost nothing is known of Margaret and Elizabeth's actions in 1321/22, but Edward II imprisoned both women and was clearly furiously angry with them, which strongly implies that both had played an active role in events and had supported their husbands against him.

Margaret Audley was, like her sister Elizabeth, incarcerated in a convent in 1322. Unlike Elizabeth, however, Margaret was to remain there until after her uncle and her brother-in-law Despenser's downfall, and her lands remained in the king's hands for the rest of his reign. She was sent to Sempringham Priory in Lincolnshire, where she had the company of her kinswoman Gwenllian ferch Llywelyn (1282–1337), who had been sent there as a baby by Margaret's grandfather Edward I after the death of her father Llywelyn ap Gruffudd, Prince of Wales. Edward II paid Gwenllian, his second cousin, an allowance of £20 a year at Sempringham.[24] Margaret may have recently given birth to her only child with Hugh Audley, a daughter also named Margaret, and she arrived at Sempringham probably with her little daughter on 16 May 1322.[25] She was allowed three attendants and the king paid generous expenses of 5 shillings a day for her and for them, but as with her younger sister Elizabeth, he ordered the prioress not to let her out of the gates.[26] Margaret's elder daughter Joan Gaveston, now 10, presumably remained at Amesbury Priory in the care of Margaret's aunt Mary.

Margaret was still at Sempringham Priory on 24 June 1326, when the king ordered the sheriff of Lincolnshire to continue paying her daily allowance of 5 shillings to her 'without delay'. She still had servants with her, so it was not an overly harsh and onerous imprisonment, at least.[27] This, of course, is not to say that it was not a traumatic experience for Margaret. She was only 28 years old in 1322 and had, as far as she knew, been condemned to lifelong incarceration in a convent by the uncle who had previously shown her only affection and favour. She was released after Edward II's downfall in late 1326, but she could never have imagined that a king might be removed from power (it had never happened in England before) and she might well have believed that she would remain at Sempringham until Edward died. As her uncle was only ten years her senior, her situation from 1322 to 1326 must have seemed as permanent and hopeless as that of her kinswoman Gwenllian.

There is, however, an entry on the Patent Roll in April 1323 which might indicate that Margaret was then visiting court. Edward II, at Westminster, granted a favour to the priory of St Frideswide in Oxford 'at the instance of Margaret, Countess of Cornwall, the king's niece'.[28] It is not clear when Margaret asked Edward to grant this favour and it may have been before she was sent to Sempringham, though the king's calling her by her correct title and acknowledging her as his niece—which he pointedly refused to do with Elizabeth Burgh after the 1322 rebellion—does at least imply some measure of residual affection. But Edward II could be vindictive to the point of cruelty towards anyone he cared about who he believed had betrayed him, and he was not a forgiving man. Apart from this favour in 1323 and the regular payments to her at Sempringham, Margaret disappears from the record after the spring of 1322. Her uncle cut her out of his life entirely, banished her to a convent and refused to have anything more to do with her. Her husband Hugh Audley was also placed in Edward's 'unforgivable' category; the king cared enough about his niece or about Audley himself to grant Margaret's plea to spare Audley's life, but he kept his former beloved companion in prison for years.

Chapter 13

In the King's Favour

While Margaret Audley languished at Sempringham and Elizabeth Burgh at Barking, their sister Eleanor Despenser rose to great prominence. Edward II, implacably spiteful to those he believed had betrayed him, was immensely loyal and generous to people he loved and were faithful to him. Eleanor as well as her husband Hugh benefited from his munificence and his great affection for her. She was so high in the king's favour and so close to him in and after 1322 that one Flemish chronicler even claimed that Hugh Despenser gave her to Edward for sex, and that she was imprisoned after the two men's downfall in 1326 in case she was pregnant by the king.[1] Any relationship between Edward II and Eleanor Despenser would, of course, have been incestuous, and therefore the allegation should be treated very seriously. There is no conclusive evidence to prove that they were lovers, though there are ample instances of closeness between the two in the king's chamber accounts in the 1320s. Between 1322 and 1326 Eleanor spent most of her time at court, Edward frequently gave her large sums of money, and on the rare occasions they were apart they exchanged letters and gifts. In the summer of 1326—when we are fortunate to have the evidence of Edward's last chamber account in its entirety—they spent considerable time together, sometimes with Eleanor's husband there and sometimes not, sailed along the Thames in the king's barge, and dined 'privately' or 'secretly' together. In October 1324, Edward was rowed across the River Thames to a house opposite the Tower of London for a secret assignation with a lover, and it is not impossible that this was Eleanor. There is much evidence of Edward's great regard for his eldest niece early on in his reign, when he paid her expenses and often gave her money. The amounts of cash increased substantially in the 1320s: in the early 1310s Eleanor received between about £3 and £10 regularly, and by the 1320s this had gone up to £100 or 100 marks (£66). On 9 April 1325 and again on 2 December 1325, for example, Edward gave Eleanor 100 marks.[2] Eleanor gave her uncle sets of clothes on 1 November 1324 and 3 December 1325, an oddly wifely thing to do. In June and October 1325 Edward gave Eleanor caged larks, goldfinches and three swans, and on another occasion two gallons of honey to make a sweet called *sucre de plate* when she was pregnant. Eleanor sent him presents every New Year including a palfrey horse in 1326, and during her pregnancy in 1325 he accommodated her at his manor-house of Sheen, where she gave birth.[3]

Hugh Despenser the Younger himself was called the king's 'husband' by an abbey annalist in 1326, chronicler Jean le Bel thought Hugh was executed that year partly because he had been 'a sodomite, above all with the king himself', chronicler Geoffrey le Baker wrote that Despenser bewitched Edward's mind, and the writer of the *Anonimalle* that Edward 'loved [Hugh] dearly, with all his heart and mind, above all others'.[4] It does seem as though something intimate was going on between the Despensers husband and wife, and Edward II. The *Flores Historiarum*, a chronicle written at Westminster Abbey, accused the king of taking pleasure in 'illicit and sinful sexual intercourse', which might mean sex with men, incestuous sex with his niece, or both.[5] The *Flores* author despised Edward II and so may not be a particularly reliable source, though Edward did spend a lot of time in Westminster and London, and perhaps the chronicler picked up information or rumours. Sir Thomas Gray, whose father of the same name served in Hugh Despenser's retinue in the 1320s and who may therefore have been privy to accurate information, wrote in his chronicle called *Scalacronica* that Edward II led a 'debauched life', and added that he 'loved and entirely trusted' Hugh Despenser.[6] There is no evidence at all, however, that Hugh Despenser raped Queen Isabella—an invention of two writers of the early twenty-first century—or that he had sex with her.[7]

In or before 1323, Edward II took possession of a ship which he renamed after his niece, calling it *La Alianore la Despensere*. Originally it was a Spanish ship, which was lost off the coast of the Isle of Wight and taken to Portchester, Hampshire. It is surely highly revealing that Edward decided not to name the ship after any of his children or anyone else—he already had one called *La Isabele* after his wife—but after his niece. This was not only a great honour for Eleanor, it was a very public declaration of the important place she held in the king's life and heart. Edward also spent £130 on another ship which was named *La Despenser* in Hugh Despenser the Younger's honour. It was meant to be a gift from Hugh to Edward, but the king himself paid for it.[8]

It is also perhaps revealing that in Edward's extant chamber accounts, Eleanor Despenser is the only woman besides Queen Isabella herself to be given the honorific title *ma dame*, 'my lady'. Jeanne de Bar, the Countess of Surrey and another niece of the king, was not called *ma dame*, and neither were Edward's sister-in-law the Countess of Norfolk or even his own royal daughters Eleanor of Woodstock and Joan of the Tower. The only sisters of Edward II alive after 1316 were Mary, nun of Amesbury Priory, and Margaret, Duchess of Brabant in the Low Countries, with whom Edward had little contact. He was certainly fond of Mary, and she visited his court on occasion and left with gifts, but he never sent her large sums of money and frequent letters and gifts as he did with their niece Eleanor Despenser. Mary does not appear in Edward's two last chamber accounts of 1324/26, whereas Eleanor and her husband frequently do.

Eleanor's father-in-law Hugh Despenser the Elder, now 61 years old and a loyal ally of Edward I and Edward II ever since he had come of age in the early 1280s, was made Earl of Winchester in May 1322. Under normal circumstances the earldom would have passed to Hugh the Younger and Eleanor one day, but as the situation in the 1320s was anything but normal, it never did. Various contemporary chroniclers say that Hugh the Younger desired his late brother-in-law Gilbert's earldom of Gloucester. Although he never received it, after the Battle of Boroughbridge on 16 March 1322 Edward II gave Hugh alone, and Hugh and Eleanor jointly, dozens of manors confiscated by the Contrariants. Eleanor alone received the Leicestershire town of Melton Mowbray, the Warwickshire village of Shustoke and the Northamptonshire village of Crick, all forfeited by her cousin John Mowbray. The manors were intended to pass after her death to her third son Gilbert Despenser, though again, never did. (These grants to Eleanor and Gilbert are the first time the boy appears on record, though he might have been as old as 6 or so in July 1322.) Eleanor also received the Bedfordshire manor of Sundon which had belonged to her cousin Margaret's executed husband Bartholomew Badlesmere, to pass one day to Gilbert.[9] Eleanor and Hugh Despenser's eldest son Huchon was their heir and was set to receive Eleanor's third of the earldom of Gloucester, his grandfather's earldom of Winchester, and all the other

Despenser lands; Hugh had made arrangements in 1315 for their second son Edward Despenser to receive a number of manors on the death of his (Hugh's) mother's cousin Idonea Cromwell; and now the Despensers were sorting out lands for their third son, thanks to the forfeiture of their enemies. Eleanor appears to have been in Yorkshire with her husband and uncle from May to July 1322 when the king handed out these grants to her and Despenser, though she parted from them out of necessity when they went on an unsuccessful military campaign to Scotland in August 1322. In October 1322, the month she turned 30, and probably in other months that year, Eleanor attended Queen Isabella. She also spent at least some of the period from January to March 1323 in and around London with Isabella.

Hugh Despenser the Younger had huge ambitions in Wales, and by early 1325, with grants of territories from the king to him and Eleanor directly and wardships held during the heirs' minorities, he controlled almost all South Wales. In the summer of 1322, Hugh forced Elizabeth Burgh to exchange her valuable Welsh lordships of Usk and Caerleon for the much less valuable lordship of Gower, which Edward II granted to him and Eleanor on 9 July 1322. This was the price Elizabeth paid to regain her freedom and to be allowed to leave Barking Abbey. In 1324, Despenser forced William Braose, formerly lord of Gower, to take legal action against Elizabeth to recover his land from her, and thus managed to gain control of Gower and Usk and to deprive his sister-in-law of them both. Edward II gave Despenser all the 'corn, hay, grass, animals and goods' in Usk and Gower and other manors recently granted to him and Eleanor, permitting him to keep all his own goods, crops and livestock and also to take Elizabeth's. In the records of this grossly unfair land deal in the Chancery records, Eleanor Despenser was called 'the king's niece' but Elizabeth Burgh was not. Elizabeth was, in fact, called 'late the wife of John Burgh', her two subsequent marriages to Theobald Verdon and Roger Damory being ignored.[10] Edward II gave the Surrey manor of Kennington to Hugh Despenser the Elder on 4 April 1322, and the grant refers to the king's dead favourite incorrectly as 'Robert Damory'.[11] Although this was probably just an error by one of his clerks, it gives the impression that the king was now so dismissive of the man he had once 'much loved' that, three weeks after Roger's death, he struggled to remember his name. Edward also ignored the fact that Elizabeth Burgh and Roger Damory had held Kennington jointly, and that it now rightfully belonged to her.

Edward II had rarely shown much kindness or generosity to Elizabeth, in stark contrast to her eldest sister and despite his pretence in 1316 that he favoured her above his other nieces, and now he made his dislike only too apparent. Edward also lied to Elizabeth, stating that he would make up the difference between the values of Usk and Gower by giving her other lands, but failed to do so. Not only that, he actively menaced her by ordering her to spend Christmas 1322 with him in York, and after her arrival imprisoned her officials and councillors, thus leaving her alone and vulnerable. The king tried to force her to sign documents—documents 'contrary to the law of the land' according to Elizabeth—renouncing all her claims to Usk and the rest of her inheritance in Wales. Elizabeth argued her corner, bravely stood up to her uncle and refused to sign, and eventually fled from court 'in great displeasure'. She had been on the long road back to Clare in Suffolk for five days when Edward sent men after her ordering her to return. He threatened to confiscate all her lands and never again allow her to hold even a foot of land from him if she did not. Elizabeth dictated a text setting out her uncle's appalling treatment of her some years later, and an entry in the Chancery rolls confirms her narrative: on 7 January 1323, Edward seized all her English lands into his own hands again.[12] On that day, the king was at the royal manor of Cowick in Yorkshire with Hugh Despenser and perhaps Eleanor, listening to four musicians playing 'interludes' for them in the hall and playing dice. This sounds like a very pleasant, relaxing occasion, were it not for the king's bullying of his niece to benefit her brother-in-law and his willingness to ride roughshod over the laws of his own kingdom. In contrast to his harsh treatment of Elizabeth, Edward II invited Margaret Audley's brother-in-law James, Hugh Audley's older brother, to court at the beginning of 1323, and gave him two salmon.[13]

At Christmas 1322 and New Year 1323, Eleanor Despenser was some weeks pregnant with her fourth daughter, who was at least her ninth child and who must have been conceived around the second week of November not long after Eleanor had been at Tynemouth Priory with Queen Isabella. Eleanor almost certainly spent the festive season with Edward II and Hugh in York before she headed south to attend Isabella in London. Perhaps she met Elizabeth at this time, and witnessed her uncle and husband bullying her sister. She must at the very least have been aware of what was going on. The only possible sign that Eleanor tried in any way to help Elizabeth comes from a letter written by Hugh Despenser the Younger to the sheriff of Glamorgan, Sir John Inge, in September or October 1322.[14] Despenser told Inge to maximise his profit in the Gower peninsula before he gave it to *la dame de Burgh*, 'the Lady Burgh', a courteous but cold way to refer to his sister-in-law Elizabeth. He also wrote, with reference to Elizabeth, 'regarding the lady's wet-nurses, we have been requested that they be moved from Usk to Gower or elsewhere, and we have permitted this and wish it to be so'.[15] (The haughty, self-important tone Despenser adopted here is entirely typical of his correspondence.) Presumably it was his wife Eleanor who had interceded on behalf of her sister, though Hugh did not clarify.

Besides this letter of Despenser, there is another reference to a wet-nurse of Elizabeth Burgh's at Usk Castle in 1322.[16] In the 1330s and later, Roger Damory's heir was named as his daughter Elizabeth, who married John, Lord Bardolf. By English law, to be his sole heir, Elizabeth Bardolf must have been his only surviving legitimate child then. In 1329, however, there is a reference to two daughters and heirs of Roger Damory: Margaret and Elizabeth. Elizabeth Burgh certainly gave birth on or shortly before 23 May 1318 a little over a year after her wedding to Damory, when the king paid Damory's messenger John Pyrro for bringing him news of the birth. Sadly the sex and name of the infant were not recorded in his account, though perhaps this was Roger and Elizabeth Burgh's daughter Margaret; in the record of 1329, Margaret was named before her sister Elizabeth and would therefore seem to have been the elder.[17] The child who required wet-nurses in the autumn of 1322 was perhaps Elizabeth Damory, later Bardolf, another daughter of Elizabeth Burgh and Roger Damory and apparently born in 1321 or 1322, perhaps even posthumously after Roger died on 12 or 13 March that year and when Elizabeth Burgh was imprisoned at Barking. Elizabeth Bardolf was Roger's only surviving legitimate child by 1337. An agreement Roger and Elizabeth Burgh made with the Earl of Ulster on 25 August 1320 talks of their 'children', plural, though as this was a deal relating to land, it might mean any future children they may have, as well as any existing ones.[18]

If Elizabeth Burgh had given birth not long before her uncle the king and Hugh treated her so appallingly, it makes their behaviour even more atrocious. Her sister Margaret may also have given birth to her only child with Hugh Audley not long before she was incarcerated at Sempringham Priory in May 1322, or perhaps she even gave birth there after the battle of Boroughbridge and after Audley had been imprisoned. When Margaret died in April 1342, her daughter and heir Margaret Stafford was said to be either 18 or 20, placing her date of birth between 1320 and 1322. The young woman was variously said to be either 24, 26 or, improbably, 30 when her father Hugh Audley died in November 1347, which also places her date of birth around 1321 or 1322.[19] As Margaret Audley the younger was not yet married when she was abducted and forcibly married to Ralph Stafford in February 1336, a later date of birth is more likely, i.e. 1322; it would be odd by fourteenth-century standards if a noblewoman and great heiress was as old as 16 and still single, and it makes more sense that she was only 13 or 14. If this is the case, the young Margaret must have been born almost five years after her parents' wedding on 28 April 1317. The older Margaret also took several years to become pregnant in her first marriage to Piers Gaveston, though this is partly explained by her youth at the time of her wedding in 1307—and, perhaps, by Gaveston's preoccupation with Margaret's uncle. Even so, it seems that Margaret Audley was, unlike her older sister Eleanor Despenser, not particularly fertile.

As well as his two daughters with Elizabeth Burgh, Roger Damory may have left illegitimate children. A namesake of his, Roger Damory, lived in Elizabeth Burgh's household from 1331 to 1336 when he was still underage (i.e. under 21), so if this was Roger's illegitimate son the boy must have been born after 1315 and perhaps during Roger's marriage to Elizabeth Burgh. Elizabeth purchased cloth, shoes, candlesticks and other necessities for the young Roger and two other boys living in her household in 1331/32, and Roger remained there for five years.[20] It is not impossible that he was a nephew of Elizabeth's late husband (either legitimate or illegitimate), or a cousin's son, but it seems far more likely that a boy called Roger Damory who lived in the household of Sir Roger Damory's widow was the elder Roger's namesake son. Sir Nichol Damory, an immensely capable knight and lawyer who enjoyed a stellar career covering much of the fourteenth century, was a long-term and important member of Elizabeth's retinue, and was also high in her cousin Edward III's favour. The *Complete Peerage* speculates that Nichol was a first cousin of Roger Damory's nephew Richard Damory (*c.* 1314–75), son and heir of Roger's older brother Richard (d. 1330).[21] If this is the case, Nichol must either have been Roger Damory's illegitimate son, or he was the son of another Damory brother who appears on no known record anywhere and whose existence has never been discovered. Nichol was a king's scholar at Cambridge from 1318 to 1321, was a student of civil law by March 1326, and died in or shortly after February 1381 when he must have been well into his 70s.[22] Going to Cambridge in 1318 probably means he was born in 1304 or a little earlier. Roger Damory's date of birth is not known, but he cannot have been born later than 1286 and was certainly over 30 when he married Elizabeth in the spring of 1317, perhaps many years past 30. He surely, therefore, had previous relationships and perhaps one or several of them resulted in children, and as he would not have been expected to be faithful to Elizabeth, he might have fathered another son during his marriage to her.[23]

Elizabeth Burgh knew Nichol Damory for decades: she spent £2 on a book of civil law for him in March 1326, and he was an executor and beneficiary of her will thirty years later. Nichol was also closely associated with Roger Damory's legitimate daughter Elizabeth and her husband John Bardolf. The couple gave him the manor of Holton in Oxfordshire (which Elizabeth Bardolf inherited from her parents) for life in 1340, John appointed Nichol as his attorney when he went overseas in 1363, and the following year Nichol went to Ireland with Robert Bardolf, a relative of John to whom John gave an annual income of £10 for life from one of his manors.[24] This lends credence to the notion that Nichol was Roger Damory's illegitimate son and the half-brother of Elizabeth Bardolf, and another family link is that Nichol married a woman called Eleanor, widow of Alan Zouche, stepson of Elizabeth Burgh's sister Eleanor Despenser.[25] Sir Nichol Damory was trusted for many years by Elizabeth Burgh, and appears numerous times on record throughout the fourteenth century serving her cousin Edward III. He was appointed steward of the household of Edward III's eldest daughter Isabella of Woodstock in 1359, for example, and in April 1364 was appointed by the king to conduct the funeral cortege of King John II of France, who had died in captivity in England, to Dover. He was also appointed as the king's ambassador to the pope.[26] Nichol Damory made his own way despite the burden of illegitimacy—assuming he was indeed illegitimate—and was a highly capable, respected and renowned knight.[27] Elizabeth Burgh's trust, support and fondness for a man who may well have been her husband's illegitimate son reveals a great deal about her character.

Chapter 14

Unequal Treatment

While Elizabeth Burgh was incarcerated at Barking, her sister Eleanor Despenser was placed in charge of the household of their first cousin John of Eltham, the king and queen's second son, at least on occasion. This arrangement began on 3 July 1322 or earlier.[1] John was born on 15 August 1316 and was twenty-four years Eleanor's junior, and perhaps he spent time with some of his many Despenser cousins: Eleanor and Hugh's third son Gilbert Despenser was probably about John's age. It is often stated in modern books that Edward II and Hugh Despenser the Younger deliberately and cruelly removed Queen Isabella's three younger children from her in 1324 in order to cause her emotional pain. This is nonsense, and merely an invention of the late twentieth century. Certain modern historians have created a narrative that Queen Isabella was a passive victim forced to stand by helplessly while her children were cruelly ripped from her care, which not only does a highly intelligent, able and influential woman a huge disservice, it makes no sense by the familial norms of fourteenth-century royals.

Queen Isabella must have been satisfied with Eleanor's appointment as the guardian of her son in 1322 or before, as she made no complaints about it and there is no reason why she would not have been satisfied with it; Eleanor was of high birth and rank, the king's eldest niece, and Isabella was evidently fond of her as Eleanor spent much time in her company for many years. Medieval queens were not the primary carers of their children, and it was entirely normal for royal offspring to live in their own household with a noblewoman appointed to look after them, and for the children of the nobility to be placed in a noblewoman's household. The king and queen's daughters Eleanor of Woodstock (b. 1318) and Joan of the Tower (b. 1321) had their own household, under the command of Isabella Hastings and later Joan Jermy. Both women were members of the king's extended family: Isabella Hastings was Hugh Despenser the Younger's sister and was married to Eleanor's stepfather Ralph Monthermer, formerly the king's brother-in-law; and Joan Jermy was the sister of Edward II's sister-in-law Alice, Countess of Norfolk (his half-brother Thomas of Brotherton's wife). Eleanor Despenser was apparently on good terms with Joan Jermy, as Joan's chamberlain John was said to have 'remained in her company' in August 1326.[2] One of Edward II and Isabella of France's daughters, though which one is not clear, spent some time living at the priory of Ankerwick (or Ankerwycke) in Buckinghamshire in or before May 1325; a period of residency at a religious house was also entirely normal.[3]

Eleanor Despenser spent a few weeks with the queen in London in early 1323. They sent almost identical letters on 17 February on behalf of the imprisoned Contrariant Roger Mortimer of Wigmore's wife Joan, who was being held under house arrest with eight attendants and who was struggling to receive the allowance allocated to her from the exchequer promptly and regularly.[4] On 5 March, Eleanor's uncle the king ordered 'various horses' of hers to be transported from Knaresborough in Yorkshire (where he and Hugh Despenser were) to London, so presumably she was still with Isabella.[5] To the queen's credit, she did not hold Eleanor responsible for her husband's misdeeds such as the Tynemouth Priory affair. There, Isabella accused Hugh Despenser of abandoning her in October 1322 and allowing her to come close to capture by a Scottish army. Eleanor was with her at Tynemouth Priory, however, which makes the queen's claim that Hugh Despenser deliberately left her in danger extremely dubious.[6] If it was indeed the case that Eleanor had an incestuous affair with her uncle the king, Isabella seems not to have heard about it in early 1323 when she spent much time with Eleanor. The two women were also together at Kenilworth Castle at the beginning of 1325 just weeks before the queen departed for her native France, and seem still to have been on excellent terms then.

At the beginning of 1327, however, not long after having Hugh Despenser executed, Isabella would show a measure of spite and cruelty to Eleanor by having three of her five daughters forcibly veiled as nuns, by having her eldest son besieged at Caerphilly Castle and threatening him with execution, and by imprisoning Eleanor herself in the Tower of

London for fifteen months. In February 1330, Isabella would confiscate all Eleanor's lands, use most of them to benefit her (Isabella's) daughter-in-law and help herself to the rest, and imprison Eleanor again. Eleanor's closeness to the queen for many years did not spare her children, or herself. It is possible, though this is only speculation, that while Isabella was overseas between March 1325 and September 1326 someone made her aware of rumours of a sexual relationship between her husband the king and his own niece, or perhaps even provided her with stronger evidence of such than mere rumours. One modern historian has suggested that the Flemish chronicle which states that Eleanor had a relationship with her uncle Edward II picked up the information from members of Isabella's entourage when the queen was in Hainault in the summer of 1326.[7] It is even possible that in her famous speech of late 1325 decrying the 'Pharisee' and 'intruder' who had come between herself and her husband and destroyed their marriage, Isabella was not referring to Hugh Despenser the Younger as generally assumed, but to his wife Eleanor.[8] The Leicester chronicler Henry Knighton, writing decades later, stated that while Isabella was overseas in 1325/26, Eleanor Despenser behaved as though she were Edward II's queen.[9] Possibly this rather cryptic comment is a hint that Edward and Eleanor had a relationship which went beyond the usual uncle/niece connection, and if Isabella believed that Eleanor had usurped her position in some way—perhaps in Edward's bed or because of the influence she wielded with the king or both—this would explain her anger towards her. Isabella was a woman with a profound sense of her own royalty, intensely proud of her birth and her position as the anointed queen of England, and may have felt that Eleanor's behaviour detracted from her own unique and special status. Isabella would never, as a royal woman of the fourteenth century, have expected her husband to remain faithful to her, but an incestuous affair with his own niece, her own long-term companion, went far beyond what she would have been able to tolerate.

If Isabella had ever been hostile to her husband's previous male favourites and perhaps lovers Roger Damory, Hugh Audley, William Montacute and even Piers Gaveston, there is no evidence of it, and indeed on one occasion she gave Damory splendid gifts for his chapel and seems to have aided Gaveston financially during his third exile in late 1311.[10] She was also to grant Hugh Audley favours and appointments in and after late 1326 during her period of power early in her son's reign, so evidently bore him no grudge for his close and perhaps intimate relationship with her husband years before. Hugh Despenser the Younger was, however, an entirely different proposition, and the queen loathed and feared him and was to claim in 1325/26 that her life was in danger because of him.

Both Hugh and Eleanor Despenser were almost always in the king's company between 1322 and 1326, and were the dominant influence at court. The queen's own influence was on the wane. Until 1322, she had often interceded with her husband on behalf of others and therefore obviously had frequent access to him, successfully mediated between the king and his barons on several occasions, and lobbied for the promotion of her clerks to bishoprics in opposition to Edward's own choices. The king allowed his wife to have a say in politics and even to contradict his wishes in public. This all ended abruptly after the Contrariant rebellion, and Edward and Isabella appear to have had a serious quarrel in late 1322 when the king announced that his wife was going on a long pilgrimage around the country—probably a diplomatic excuse to explain her absence from court.[11] In the context of the queen's once frequent intercessions with her husband ceasing entirely in and after 1322 and of her possible belief that his niece usurped her position with Edward in some way, it is surely significant that while Isabella was in France in 1325/26, various grants by the king made 'at the request of Eleanor Despenser' appear in the Chancery rolls.[12] Edward gave none of the Contrariants' confiscated lands to his queen in and after 1322. He did give some of them to Eleanor personally, more to herself and her husband jointly, and even more to Hugh Despenser alone.[13]

One of the leading Contrariants of 1321/22, Roger Mortimer of Wigmore, escaped from the Tower of London on 1 August 1323, and fled to the continent. A panicked Edward II sent out numerous orders demanding his recapture when he heard the news of the escape five days later, but it was too late. Some modern historians have speculated that Queen Isabella helped him escape and was secretly supporting him against her husband, but there is no evidence of this besides the letter she had sent six months earlier in support of Mortimer's wife Joan. As Eleanor Despenser sent the exact same letter, if this is proof that the queen of England aided and supported Roger Mortimer, it must also be proof that Eleanor did the same thing. This seems incredibly unlikely, especially as Mortimer sent assassins into England to kill her husband Hugh Despenser the Younger, her father-in-law the Earl of Winchester, and Mortimer's cousin Edmund Fitzalan, Earl of Arundel later that year.[14]

On or just before 2 August 1323, perhaps even on the day of Mortimer's escape, Eleanor gave birth to her fourth daughter Margaret Despenser at the royal manor of Cowick in Yorkshire. The king gave her a generous gift of £100 on that day for the expenses related to 'her childbed'.[15] Margaret may have been named after her Clare aunt—which is interesting, given that Margaret Audley was currently in disgrace at Sempringham and there is no record of her sister pleading for her—or perhaps after her father's sister, Margaret St Amand née Despenser. Not long after her birth, little Margaret Despenser was sent to live in the household of the Yorkshire knight Sir Thomas Houk or Hook, whose manor of Hook lay eight miles from Cowick. Houk stated on 1 March 1327 that he had looked after the little girl for more than three years with a large retinue.[16] This gives some insight into how the Despensers, and probably other noble families of the era, raised their children, or rather, sent them elsewhere to be raised. In June 1323, the Despensers' second daughter Joan, who was born around the mid-1310s, was betrothed to John FitzGerald, born in 1314 and the son and heir of the Anglo-Irish nobleman the Earl of Kildare. John FitzGerald, who was one of the many grandsons of the Earl of Ulster and thus Elizabeth Burgh's nephew, died mere months after his betrothal, and Joan Despenser ultimately never married but joined the Church. The Despensers' eldest daughter Isabella was 11 in 1323, and had been married since early 1321. Edward II paid some of her expenses.[17]

Eleanor was with Edward II and Queen Isabella at Kenilworth on 1 January 1324, and gave the king a cup as his New Year gift; the queen also gave her husband a cup on 1 January. Edward reciprocated by giving Eleanor two silver-gilt cups, and gave the queen one, more valuable, cup.[18] The king and perhaps the queen were guests of Hugh and Eleanor Despenser at Hanley Castle in Worcestershire from about 9 to 15 January 1324. Hanley had been sacked and badly damaged in early 1322 by Eleanor's uncle-in-law the Earl of Hereford (killed at the Battle of Boroughbridge in March 1322), and the king paid for the repairs. Edward II, with his niece and nephew-in-law apparently with him, moved on the eight miles to Hugh and Eleanor's manor of Tewkesbury in Gloucestershire, where he visited the tomb of Eleanor's late brother Gilbert, Earl of Gloucester, and laid an expensive cloth on it. Eleanor was still with the king and her husband at Berkeley Castle in Gloucestershire—where a deposed Edward II would be incarcerated three years later—on 6 February 1324. She sent a letter from there to John Stonor, justice of the King's Bench, on behalf of her chaplain John Sadington, whose affairs, she said, she had 'much at heart' (*mout a cuer*). Her name at the start of the letter was spelt Alianor la Despensiere and the letter is full of her usual courtesy, and she asked Stonor to act in such a 'gracious manner' that Sadington the chaplain would be pleased with her. Eleanor's husband Hugh, prone to threatening even his faithful adherents with dire punishment if they failed him, was the last person on earth to care whether anyone besides Edward II was pleased with him or to take anyone's affairs but his own to heart, and this letter reveals that although the couple got on very well, their personalities were completely different. Queen Isabella had also sent letters to John Stonor on John Sadington's behalf, and Eleanor acknowledged her in her letter as 'our very dear lady the queen'.[19] This is yet more evidence that Eleanor and Isabella were still on perfectly good terms, despite the queen's fear and loathing of Eleanor's husband which, Isabella admitted later, she did her utmost to conceal for a long time to keep herself safe. Eleanor was probably also with her uncle and husband at Westminster on 10 May 1324, when Edward granted her the Bedfordshire manor of Bramingham, forfeited by a Contrariant called William FitzWarin, on top of the four forfeited manors he had given her in 1322.[20]

Whatever was going on between Eleanor and Hugh Despenser and Edward II, Eleanor spent most of her time at court with the two men, so if the king and his chamberlain had a sexual relationship (and it seems almost certain that they did), it is hard to see how Eleanor could have been unaware of it. It is also hard to see how she could have been unaware of her husband's penchant for extortion, false imprisonment and forced acknowledgement of large debts. One abbey petitioned Edward II's son Edward III years later, claiming that they had been forced to accept two new monks 'by the procurement of Hugh Despenser the younger, whom the petitioners dared not gainsay'.[21] 'Whom they dared not gainsay' was a common theme during the regime of the 1320s; even the great English magnates were frightened of Hugh Despenser the Younger and Queen Isabella certainly was. Despenser's own letters reveal that he threatened to have men executed or imprisoned or to harm them if they did not do what he wished. The king himself was certainly completely aware of what Despenser was doing, and often actively participated in his favourite's blackmail and coercion of his own subjects. In March 1323, for example, Despenser took the manor of Iselhampstead (now called Chenies) in Buckinghamshire from John and Maud Botetourt. Despenser's letter to John Botetourt still exists, and reveals that the king supported and aided him in the matter and wished him to have the manor. Despenser wrote confidently that the king would have John Botetourt hanged and drawn if he did not hand over his manor to Despenser. Despenser extorted the sum of £100 from one Thomas of Bishopstone in the summer of 1324, and Edward II's itinerary and an order to one of his sergeants to arrest Bishopstone reveal that he was deeply implicated in the whole underhanded affair.[22] Probably in 1323, Hugh Despenser imprisoned Sir John Inge, sheriff of Glamorgan—one of his most faithful and capable allies—in Southwark prison until Inge and some of his friends acknowledged a debt of £300 to him. Despenser had previously declared 'we are very worried about having some reason for which we might be prepared to harm you' in a letter to Inge of *c*. October 1322, and he duly found some reason to do so.[23] One of Inge's councillors, also imprisoned by Despenser, died in captivity. Eleanor Despenser had written to John Inge at least twice between 1318 and 1321 and knew him well, and must have been aware that her husband had imprisoned him and the members of his council.

Two days after her sister Eleanor Despenser wrote her letter on behalf of her chaplain in February 1324, Elizabeth Burgh was finally restored to her manor of Holton in Oxfordshire, and the king ordered the custodian of the Contrariants' lands in Oxfordshire to allow her the income from the manor backdated to 2 November 1322 when he had granted her English lands back to her. The custodian had kept Holton in his own hands in the belief that it belonged solely to the late Roger Damory, when in fact it had been granted to Damory and Elizabeth jointly.[24] Also in 1324, Elizabeth petitioned for the restoration of five other manors which she had held jointly with Damory and had been confiscated—Vauxhall in Surrey, Kennington in Middlesex, Sandford in Oxfordshire, Caythorpe in Lincolnshire and Sandal in Yorkshire. She was told to come before Chancery with the relevant documents. One of the five, Sandal, was in the king's hands in June 1324 even though Edward had supposedly restored all Elizabeth's English lands to her in November 1322, and Kennington had been granted to Eleanor Despenser's father-in-law Hugh the Elder, Earl of Winchester, in April 1322.[25] Elizabeth had also made one of her rare appearances on record during the period of her brother-in-law Despenser's period of ascendancy in November 1323, when her uncle appointed commissioners of *oyer et terminer* ('to hear and determine') to investigate a theft on one of her manors in Essex. Her servants John Crowe and John Freberne were assaulted.[26]

Otherwise, it is difficult to say much at all about what Elizabeth did in and after 1322. Unlike her sister Margaret Audley, she at least had a generous income from her own lands, even though her rich lordship of Usk and the manors she had held jointly with Roger Damory had been taken from her, and she had freedom of movement. Margaret had nothing, except the 5 shillings a day her uncle granted to her for her expenses at Sempringham Priory in May 1322 and which he continued to pay her until the end of his reign. Elizabeth seems to have spent much or most of her time at her castle of Clare in Suffolk. She was certainly there in May 1326, and most probably in 1324/25 when she spent over £14 having the castle repaired. She had a room called 'the lady's Great Chamber' off the hall which had another chamber below it and had its own porch outside. Her son William Burgh had his own chamber at Clare, though spent much of his time in Ireland with his grandfather the Earl of Ulster, and Margaret Courtenay née Bohun also had her own chamber; she was one of Elizabeth's first cousins and another niece of Edward II, daughter of the late Elizabeth (d. 1316) and Humphrey, Earl of Hereford, killed at the Battle of Boroughbridge in March 1322 fighting against the king. There was a cloister between the hall and the chapel at Clare and another, smaller chapel, and a 'herber' or herb garden with tiled paths.[27] Clare Castle sounds as though it must have been a very pleasant residence for Elizabeth: as well as the herb garden she had her own private garden for which 120 stones were purchased in 1325, with a fountain and an aviary, securely within the castle walls.[28] She often called herself 'lady of Clare'. Even tucked away within the walls of Clare, however, Elizabeth cannot have felt safe from her uncle and brother-in-law.

Edward II, presumably with Hugh and Eleanor Despenser, stayed at Tonbridge Castle in Kent in late June 1324, and the Clare sisters' cousin Jeanne de Bar, Countess of Surrey, also visited her uncle in early July 1324. Jeanne's estranged husband John Warenne, Earl of Surrey, had supported the king during the Contrariant rebellion and was one of his most loyal allies for much of the reign, and sent Edward some salted venison at this time. The king was at Tonbridge again in late August 1324 and borrowed a boat from a local fisherman to go fishing (he also went fishing at Beaulieu Abbey in Hampshire the following May).[29] Tonbridge rightfully belonged to Eleanor Despenser's sister Margaret and brother-in-law Hugh Audley, but was currently in the king's hands thanks to Audley's forfeiture and imprisonment and Margaret's ongoing captivity at Sempringham Priory. Elizabeth Burgh was to claim in 1326 that the king had also seized the woodland in the chase of Tonbridge which belonged by right to her.[30] Eleanor staying at a castle forfeited by Margaret with nearby woodland which belonged to Elizabeth and had been taken from her—Eleanor was most probably at Tonbridge in June and August 1324 and certainly spent several weeks there with her husband in the autumn of 1325—does not seem to indicate any sympathy for her sisters' plight. It is impossible to know Eleanor's private thoughts, but appearances indicate that she was perfectly happy to ride high in her uncle's favour while her two sisters languished in disgrace, and that she had no mind to try to change the situation.

Chapter 15

A Secret Lover

Edward II went to war against his brother-in-law Charles IV of France, Queen Isabella's third and only surviving brother, in the summer of 1324. The king failed to travel to France to pay homage to Charles as his overlord for his lands in Gascony and Ponthieu, and the exasperated Charles invaded Gascony. It was not Edward himself who directed the war effort but Hugh Despenser the Younger, who reached the zenith of his power in and after 1324. For the first eleven years of Edward II's reign, Despenser had wielded no influence whatsoever, and was now making up for lost time by controlling the government and foreign policy. Edward unkindly and unjustly confiscated Queen Isabella's lands on 18 September 1324, as though his wife and the mother of his children were an enemy alien who would willingly aid and support a French invasion of his country, and gave her an income from the exchequer instead. The income was barely half of what Isabella received from her lands, and made her dependent on her husband's goodwill and took away her ability to act as a great magnate in her own right. Not surprisingly, the queen was furious, and blamed Hugh Despenser the Younger. Although it is often claimed that Edward II failed to exempt Isabella's French servants from the general order to arrest all French people living in England, he did in fact exempt eight.[1] He certainly did not cruelly remove his and Isabella's three younger children from her at this time as a means of inflicting further emotional pain on her as the popular modern narrative claims.

A most intriguing entry in Edward II's chamber account of 26 October 1324, while he was staying at the Tower of London, reveals that he crossed the River Thames and 'secretly took his pleasure' (or 'secretly made love') opposite the Tower. The Anglo-Norman words used certainly mean sexual pleasure or lovemaking, and as it was done 'secretly', Queen Isabella cannot have been the lover in question. Afterwards, Edward's chamber clerks William of Langley and Peter Pulford bought a quantity of fish and seafood—eels, lampreys, stockfish, unsmoked herring, oysters, roach, smelt—from three Thames fishermen plus butter and onions for him and his unnamed lover, as well as items which seem to indicate that the king himself made a fire on which to cook the food.[2] His clerks simply called the location 'this place', but in October 1324 Edward purchased land opposite the Tower on which a house called La Rosere stood and on 21 February 1325 bought two further houses next to it, one called La Cage and another unnamed. A man called Robin Carter was paid 2 shillings because he 'came promptly to the Tower of London with his boat to bring the king across the Thames to the place which the king bought there'.[3] The location where Edward met his lover must have been La Rosere, where the king had his own chamber on an upper floor.

Hugh Despenser the Younger was certainly in Edward's company around this time as he and his father Hugh the Elder both witnessed a royal charter in London on 22 October, and parliament which he attended was currently in session there.[4] Eleanor Despenser's whereabouts in late October 1324 are difficult to ascertain (as are the queen's), but when her itinerary can be established in the 1320s she was almost always with the king and her husband, and her fourth son John Despenser was at court on 22 November 1324 when the king paid 13 shillings and 4 pence for a saddle for him.[5] It is possible, of course, that the lover was neither of the two Despensers and someone else entirely, though the reference to the king making love 'secretly' and his leaving the Tower of London to do so strongly implies that he did not wish his lover's identity to become known to anyone bar his two trusted clerks William of Langley and Peter Pulford. The king's enormous household of around 500 people, including the bodyguard of archers who remained close to him at all times, his chamber valets, ushers, pages, clerks, squires and knights, and untold others, must normally have made privacy all but impossible, and many of Edward's servants must have known exactly when, where and with whom he had intimate relations. It is revealing that the king felt the need to cross the Thames away from his household on this occasion to keep the matter private, and surely significant that the Tower of London and the bank of the river opposite it lie only a couple of miles from Westminster Abbey. A monk of Westminster thundered in the *Flores Historiarum* chronicle under the year 1324 that the king delighted in 'illicit and sinful sexual intercourse'.[6] Given Edward's very public and obvious infatuation with

Hugh Despenser the Younger which had begun in 1319, it seems unlikely that he would have gone to such lengths more than five years later just to have sex with him, whereas if he was involved in an incestuous affair with his own niece, it makes more sense that he would have tried to keep it as quiet and discreet as possible. Hugh Despenser, as chamberlain, was in charge of all the chamber staff including the two clerks who bought the fish and recorded the incident in the chamber account, and if he had been in the boat crossing the Thames with the king, his name would have been mentioned as well.

Eleanor Despenser gave her uncle a 'robe of four garments' made of medley cloth with expensive miniver fur shortly after the king's assignation, on or soon before 1 November 1324, and Edward gave her wardrobe servant, who brought it to him, a large gift of 40 shillings or at least half a year's wages.[7] A 'robe of/with garments' meant a complete set of clothes; Elizabeth Burgh left 'robes with the garments' to five female servants in her will of 1355. One 'robe with three garments' she bequeathed consisted of a tunic (*cote*), a *surcote* or overtunic (an outer garment, sometimes sleeveless or with short sleeves), and a cloak (*mantel*).[8] Thirteen months after the private meeting at La Rosere, on 2 December 1325, Edward II visited a heavily pregnant Eleanor Despenser at his manor-house of Sheen, west of London, where she was staying at his expense and gave her a gift of 100 marks. The day after, she again sent him 'a robe of four garments'.[9] On both occasions, the four garments she gave Edward were probably a tunic, an overtunic, a cloak and a shirt, though the fourth item might have been *chaus*, hose, i.e. a kind of leggings that everyone wore.

In July 1322, Edward had granted Eleanor Despenser the manors of Melton Mowbray and Crick forfeited by her cousin John, Lord Mowbray, and Eleanor was sometimes addressed as 'lady of Melton Mowbray'.[10] A John Deyville owned £20 of rent in Melton and Crick for life as a gift of John Mowbray, and at Nottingham on 26 December 1324, released those rents to Eleanor and her third son Gilbert Despenser.[11] Deyville stated later that he had been imprisoned at the Tower of London by Eleanor's husband Hugh until he agreed to do this, and indeed he is mentioned as a prisoner there on 27 June 1324.[12] This is an example of Despenser's extortions benefiting his wife and one of their children directly. Despenser's numerous other exactions also benefited Eleanor indirectly as they made her husband wealthier, and by 1324 or so Despenser was the richest man in the country after Edward II himself. Eleanor was at Nottingham with her husband and uncle at this time, and clearly knew about Deyville's rents being granted to her and her third son. She must also have known that her husband had imprisoned him in the Tower until he agreed to do so, but there is no record of her refusing the rents so apparently she was perfectly happy with the way she and her son had come by them. Historian T. B. Pugh wrote in the 1970s that Eleanor was 'deeply involved in Hugh Despenser's schemes', a judgement with which it is hard to disagree.[13]

The Despensers, husband and wife, spent Christmas 1324 with the king and queen at Nottingham. On Christmas Day, Edward II gave a gift of 40 shillings to Eleanor's damsels, the mother and daughter pair Emma or 'Emmote' and Joan or 'Jonette' Prior. He also sent 20 marks to Sir Thomas Houk, the knight of Yorkshire who had the care of Eleanor and Hugh Despenser's fourth daughter Margaret, then 17 months old.[14] Another person present with the king that Christmas was young William Montacute, son and heir of the William Montacute who had been so prominent at Edward's court some years before, and he and Edward played a game of dice called raffle with the king's chamber squires Burgeys Tilh, Giles of Spain and Garsy Pomit on Christmas Eve and Christmas night. Montacute also received a gift of 40 marks from Edward, and the king did not forget his charitable obligations, giving 20 marks to his almoner John Denton to distribute among the poor.[15] The late Roger Damory's brother Sir Richard Damory, steward of the king's household and Elizabeth Burgh's brother-in-law, was also at Nottingham, as was Eleanor Despenser's father-in-law, the Earl of Winchester.[16] Queen Isabella sent her husband a gift via her servant Adam the blacksmith on 1 January 1325, as was the custom at his court on that date, and Eleanor Despenser sent a man called Robynet to the king for the same purpose on the same date. Edward generously rewarded Adam with 40 shillings and Robynet with 30.

The queen and Eleanor Despenser left court sometime after Christmas and by the New Year were together at Kenilworth Castle in Warwickshire—which had been forfeited by Isabella's uncle Thomas of Lancaster in 1322 and was now in the king's hands—while Edward and Hugh Despenser went to Ravensdale in Derbyshire. Well over two years after Isabella had, or so she believed, deliberately been left in danger at Tynemouth Priory by

Hugh Despenser, she still voluntarily spent much time with Despenser's wife. This suggests that she was genuinely fond of Eleanor and enjoyed her company, as did the king, which further suggests that Eleanor was a charming and pleasant person, and good fun to be around. The few extant letters we have of hers reveal that she was polite and amicable, and although Eleanor was well aware of her own prominence and high status and surely revelled in it—she was a powerful person at Edward II's court in the 1320s—her surviving correspondence reveals none of the haughty self-importance apparent in her husband Despenser's many letters. The closeness between Queen Isabella and Eleanor Despenser is further implied by Eleanor's praising of Isabella's household squire Matthew Berenal to the king: she 'talked great good of him' in or before June 1325, and Edward gave him a gift of 20 shillings.[17]

There is no real reason to believe that Eleanor was appointed as a kind of spy or jailer over the queen, authorised by the king and Despenser to monitor all her correspondence and watch over her, as two chroniclers—*Lanercost* in the far north-west of England and the *Flores Historiarum* of Westminster—claimed.[18] (Two chroniclers also reported a rumour that Edward II was trying to annul his marriage to the queen around this time, which is untrue.) The idea that Isabella was forced to spend time with the niece-in-law who was her jailer and who caused her emotional pain by removing her second son John of Eltham from her custody against her will, paints the queen as a helpless victim, something she assuredly was not. Eleanor had had the charge of John of Eltham's household, at least on occasion, since July 1322 or earlier, and Isabella had plenty of opportunity to complain if she was unhappy about it, but there is no record that she or anyone else ever did. Nor has it ever been explained how Eleanor somehow managed both to spy on the queen constantly so that Isabella had no privacy from her, and at the same time look after Isabella's son away from court where the queen was seldom, if ever, able to see him. The two chroniclers who claimed that Eleanor was appointed as the queen's guardian seem unaware that she had been attending Isabella regularly since at least 1310 and probably 1308, and that the two women had long been on excellent terms. Chroniclers writing about Edward II's reign often tended to interpret events with hindsight after the king's downfall and Hugh Despenser's execution, and this seems to be another example. Isabella refused to return to England from France *c.* late October 1325, and although her elder son Edward of Windsor was with her, she voluntarily stayed away from her three younger children for almost a year. She was therefore hardly in a position to complain that other people looked after them during her absence, and indeed, there is no reason to suppose that she did complain.

During the festive season of 1324/25, Isabella was attended by her damsels Isabelle del Helde, Alisour Donand and Cecily Chaucomb, who received a total of 200 shillings from the king as their Christmas gifts. Edward II was always very careful to give his wife and her servants larger sums of money, a larger number of items, or more valuable items than he gave his niece Eleanor and her servants: in October 1322, for example, he gave Isabella twenty pieces of sturgeon and Eleanor thirteen pieces.[19] Cecily Chaucomb was married to a John Chaucomb, who may be the man of this name whom Eleanor Despenser had sent to Edward II with news of herself in 1310; if so, this is yet another link between the queen and her niece-in-law.[20] Queen Isabella sent her husband letters on 11 January 1325 and again on the 16th and 18th, from Kenilworth.[21] Whatever was going on in the royal marriage, and although Isabella was surely angry with the king for her predicament at Tynemouth in October 1322 and especially for confiscating her lands in September 1324, the couple still spent time together, kept in touch and sent gifts. In 1325/26, Isabella wrote of her husband as her 'very sweet heart' and her 'very dear and very sweet lord and friend'.[22] The latter style especially is highly unconventional and reveals Isabella's enormous affection for her husband.

Margaret Audley's elder daughter Joan Gaveston died at Amesbury Priory on 13 January 1325, of an unspecified illness.[23] Mother and daughter had probably not seen each other for some years, and if Edward II had any contact with the girl who was both his great-niece and the daughter and heir of his beloved Piers Gaveston, there is no known record of it. Nor is it known whether the king paid for the girl's burial, nor whether he had any contact with Piers' other daughter, who was illegitimate. It seems that Edward's decades-long infatuation with Gaveston did not extend to any particular interest in Gaveston's children, even though one of them was his own close relative. Edward did, however, send 100 shillings on 31 January 1325 to the Dominican friars of Langley in Hertfordshire, where Gaveston had been buried ten years previously, for them to keep Gaveston's soul 'more in remembrance'.[24] Joan Gaveston had been betrothed to the Earl of Ulster's grandson John Multon (b. 1308) in 1317, and in March 1332, seven years after her death, an inquisition was held in Wiltshire to determine what had happened to her. Thomas Multon had promised Edward II a payment of £10,000 if the marriage between his son John and Joan did not go ahead, which would have been a huge windfall for the young king Edward III had he been entitled to it (which he was not, as Joan's death and not any default on the Multons' part prevented the marriage taking place).[25]

The jurors of the 1332 inquisition stated that Joan was 15 when she died. If she was the child born to Margaret in York in January 1312, she actually died just after her thirteenth birthday. Inquisitions were often very vague and inaccurate on people's ages, so it is entirely possible that Joan was indeed the child born in January 1312, which is the only recorded birth of a child to Piers and Margaret, and that the jurors seven years after her death miscalculated her age by two years. As we have only one record of a child born to Margaret's sister Elizabeth and Roger Damory, however, yet two daughters of Damory are mentioned in 1329, it is not impossible that Margaret gave birth to another child as well. Perhaps the infant born to Piers and Margaret in York in January 1312 died young, and Joan was born in 1309/10. If this is the case, her birth was not recorded in any known document, but this is not surprising: the births of most of Eleanor Despenser's children were not recorded, the dates of Elizabeth and Roger Damory's wedding in 1317 and the birth of their child in 1321/22 were not recorded, the birth of Margaret's daughter Margaret from her second marriage to Hugh Audley was not recorded, nor those of any of Margaret's six grandchildren. If Joan Gaveston was born when her parents were in Ireland until June 1309, there would have been no payments in Edward II's accounts to celebrate her birth or her mother's purification forty days afterwards. The balance of probabilities, however, would suggest that Joan was indeed the child born to Margaret in York in early 1312, and that twenty years later the jurors sitting on the inquisition estimated her age wrongly by two years. Joan Gaveston died unmarried and childless, and left her much younger half-sister Margaret Audley (later Stafford) as sole heir to their mother's Clare fortune.

Joan left another half-sister: Amie, her father's illegitimate daughter, whom Piers named after his own younger sister. Little is known of Amie Gaveston, except that she worked as a damsel in the household of Edward III's queen Philippa in the 1330s, and married an archer called John Driby. Presumably the older Margaret knew of the existence of her first husband's illegitimate daughter, though how Amie came to work in the household of Queen Philippa is not clear; she does not appear on known record until 1332. She used her father's name, so Piers must have acknowledged her as his child. Edward II also fathered an illegitimate child, whom he called Adam and who died in the early autumn of 1322 aged somewhere between 12 and 17. So, apparently, did Hugh Despenser the Younger; an abbot of Westminster called Nicholas Litlington (*c.* 1312/15–86) is likely to have been his son. Roger Damory also appears to have had at least one or two illegitimate sons, and one of them was perhaps born during his marriage to Elizabeth Burgh. All the Clare sisters, therefore, had husbands who were unfaithful to them, but although they themselves would have had it impressed upon them from the earliest childhood that they must remain virgins until marriage and subsequently to be strictly monogamous, they would not have been raised to expect that their husbands had to follow the same rules.

In 1325 and perhaps before, Eleanor and Hugh Despenser's third daughter Eleanor, born in the late 1310s or beginning of the 1320s, was in the official care of her paternal aunt Isabella née Despenser, Lady Hastings. Isabella's damsel Margaret Costantyn looked after the girl, and in April 1325 received a gift of 50 shillings from Edward II, taken to her by the elder Eleanor's damsel Emma 'Emmote' Prior, for taking good care of her.[26] Isabella Hastings was also in charge of the household of Edward II's daughters Eleanor of Woodstock (b. 1318) and Joan of the Tower (b. 1321) until February 1326, so it seems that the young Eleanor Despenser was raised with her royal cousins. Young Eleanor, no more than about 7 years old in 1325 and perhaps only 3 or 4, was betrothed by 27 July that year to her father's ward Laurence Hastings, born in 1321 and the future Earl of Pembroke.[27] The Despensers' fourth daughter Margaret lived in Yorkshire in the household of Sir Thomas Houk, and their eldest, Isabella, was married to the Earl of Arundel's son and heir Richard so perhaps lived in the Arundel household, at least sometimes. Hugh and Eleanor's eldest son Huchon was often at court with his parents and Edward II and also spent time with his mother's first cousin Edward of Windsor, the king's elder son and the heir to the throne: in July 1324 the king sent letters to his son and Huchon at Shoreham. The boy was referred to in

Edward's accounts on this occasion as Huchoun, an alternative spelling of his nickname.[28] Huchon was about four years Edward of Windsor's senior. Hugh Despenser must have hired a man to oversee his eldest son's military training, and by December 1325 Huchon's weapons needed to be repaired. That month, his great-uncle paid for an *aketon*, a padded or quilted jerkin worn under armour, to be made for him; he was then probably 17.[29] The whereabouts of the three younger Despenser sons Edward, Gilbert and John are unclear, though Edward II bought John a saddle in November 1324, which suggests that the Despensers' fourth son was at court then, at least.[30] In July 1322, the king talked of his 'affection' for the Despensers' third son Gilbert, and perhaps all the Despenser boys were brought up at court.[31] In 1324 the second Despenser son Edward was at least 11 and perhaps 14, Gilbert perhaps between 6 and 8, and John perhaps about 3 or 5.

England and France were still in a state of war in early 1325, and Edward II made the fateful decision to send his queen to her native land to negotiate a peace settlement with her brother Charles IV. Isabella sailed from Dover on 9 March 1325 with a large retinue and plenty of money, though later accused Hugh Despenser the Younger, rather unfairly, of sending her to France 'meanly, against the dignity of her estate'. Isabella was with her husband at the Tower of London in late February and early March before she set off for Dover.[32] As far as the evidence from English sources goes, this was the last time the king and queen ever saw each other, though one Flemish chronicle says that they met after Edward's capture in November 1326 following Isabella's invasion of Edward's kingdom. The king, Hugh Despenser and probably Eleanor Despenser did not travel to the coast to see Isabella off, but remained at the Tower of London and at La Rosere and La Cage, the king's houses opposite the Tower.[33] Eleanor Despenser gave birth to another child sometime soon before 14 December 1325, perhaps on 1 or 2 December, and a full-term pregnancy of thirty-eight weeks from conception would mean that she conceived around 11 March, just days after Queen Isabella left England. This was during Lent, a period when intercourse was forbidden by the Church, something which seems not to have bothered Eleanor. She was with Edward II and her husband at Henley-on-Thames in Oxfordshire on 25 March when one of the king's servants gave her a sack of animal skins which Edward had bought for her in London, and her father-in-law

Hugh Despenser the Elder, Earl of Winchester, was also with them. An entry in Edward's chamber account records a generous payment on 22 March to one 'Katherine of Langley, who talked privately with the king and Sir Hugh [Despenser the Younger]', which sounds as if it might have been a rather intimate meeting.[34]

Another entry in the king's accounts dated 3 April 1325, when the king and Hugh Despenser and presumably Eleanor were at Eling near Southampton on their way to Beaulieu Abbey, describes Eling as 'the place where the king frightened Sir Hugh'. Presumably this refers to a practical joke of some kind rather than the king genuinely terrifying Despenser. The 3rd of April 1325 was Holy Wednesday just before Easter, and in the Middle Ages there was a widespread belief that Judas Iscariot accepted 30 shillings on this day in exchange for betraying Jesus Christ. Perhaps Edward II thought it was a suitable day for a prank of some kind, and he was a particularly playful person who loved to laugh. Hugh Despenser, by contrast, although he was sarcastic and witty, did not have such a slapstick sense of humour. Then again, another entry in the king's accounts on 22 April calls Eling 'where the king and Sir Hugh were frightened', so apparently he got his own back.[35]

Eleanor and her sisters lost their stepfather Ralph Monthermer on 5 April 1325. Ralph's heir was his elder son Thomas Monthermer, the Clare sisters' half-brother, who was now well into his 20s but rarely appears on record during his uncle Edward II's reign. Ralph also left his widow Isabella Hastings, Eleanor Despenser's sister-in-law and the woman in charge of the household of the king's two daughters Eleanor of Woodstock and Joan of the Tower and of the Despensers' third daughter, Eleanor. Edward II gave the elder Eleanor Despenser a generous gift of 100 marks on 9 April 1325.[36] As Eleanor gave birth eight months later, perhaps she had already discovered that she was pregnant and this was the king's reaction to the news (it was at least her tenth pregnancy, so she had surely grown accustomed to recognising the signs early). Beaulieu Abbey in Hampshire, where the king and Hugh Despenser stayed for more than three weeks in April 1325, belonged to the austere Cistercian order. It was prohibited for women to spend the night there, so Eleanor must have been staying somewhere else close by, and the money was given to her by the hands of Edward's chamber squire John Harsik. Eleanor was almost certainly also at court on 28 May 1325 when Edward gave her a house

118   Edward II's Nieces: The Clare Sisters

and some land in Melton Mowbray, the Leicestershire town forfeited by her cousin John Mowbray in 1322 which Edward had granted to her.[37] She was also with the king on 22 and 23 June 1325 when he gave her a gift of larks in an iron cage and she 'talked great good' of one of the queen's squires to him, and on 8 July when he spent 3 shillings on two gallons of honey for her to make a sweet called *sucre de plate*. Perhaps the pregnant Eleanor craved something sweet.[38]

Chapter 16

Intruder and Pharisee

In France, meanwhile, Queen Isabella was involved in long and intense negotiations with her brother Charles IV. She wrote to Edward II on 31 March, addressing him five times as 'my very sweet heart' and telling him how difficult her brother was being.[1] The queen finally managed to arrange a peace settlement between England and France in June 1325. Although its terms were catastrophic for Edward II (through no fault of Isabella), he had no other choice but to ratify it. There remained, however, the awkward situation of the homage owed to Charles IV for Edward's lands in Gascony and Ponthieu which he absolutely had to travel to France to perform. For various reasons, Edward did not wish to leave England. After prevaricating for many weeks and changing his mind regarding the correct course of action almost daily, Edward sent his son Edward of Windsor, not yet 13 years old, to France in September 1325 in his place. Hugh Despenser the Younger had pleaded with the king not to leave him behind in England, as his life would be in severe danger in Edward's absence. His life was also in danger in France: the *Vita Edwardi Secundi* says that if Despenser and his father 'are found within the kingdom of France [they] will assuredly not lack bad quarters', a reference to a punishment (*mala mansio*) where the victim was stretched out and tied to a board. It adds that Despenser and his father 'realised that in the absence of the king they would not know where to live safely' in England and Wales. Adam Murimuth, royal clerk and chronicler, agrees that the whole country hated the two Hugh Despensers and that therefore they did not wish Edward to go abroad and leave them behind.[2] The king, therefore, could neither leave his beloved behind or take him with him.

That Hugh Despenser the Younger genuinely did feel in physical danger because of the loathing he had brought upon himself by his extortions and general despotism is demonstrated by his being guarded by eight *hobelars*, armed men on horseback, all the time: the eight were paid by the king for 'following Sir Hugh at all times wherever he went'.[3] There is no doubt whatsoever that Eleanor Despenser's husband and father-in-law were widely hated in England and Wales, and the younger Despenser was surely correct that someone, or indeed many people, would wish to assassinate him if they got the chance. He had spent the previous few years as cosseted royal favourite taking lands and manors from others, forcing them to acknowledge huge debts to him, and even imprisoning people until they agreed to do what he wished. His sister-in-law Elizabeth Burgh was only one of his many victims. Another, whom he imprisoned for eighteen months in 1324/25 until she signed over three manors to him, his father and the king, was the Scottish noblewoman Elizabeth Comyn. Others included the barons John Botetourt and his wife Maud, John Sutton and his wife Margaret, Despenser's own sheriff of Glamorgan Sir John Inge, and his wife's second cousin Alice Lacy, Countess of Lincoln. Other victims were considerably lower down the social scale, and Despenser was an equal opportunities extortionist who preyed on both women and men.

Eleanor Despenser stayed at Tonbridge Castle in Kent, which by right belonged to her sister Margaret Audley, from mid-September 1325 or earlier until about 9 October. Her husband joined her there on or just after 23 September, eleven days after he and the king watched Edward of Windsor sail to France from Dover; Hugh would next see his wife's first cousin fourteen months later when the boy attended his execution. Eleanor sent her page John Dalby with letters to Edward II from Tonbridge shortly before 16 September, and the king sent letters to Hugh and perhaps Eleanor on or before the 28th.[4] She joined her uncle at Banstead in Surrey on or just after 9 October; he had bought her a present of forty-seven goldfinches (an oddly random number, so perhaps three had died) which waited there for her arrival. Hugh Despenser, meanwhile, may have made a flying visit to their castle of Caerphilly, Eleanor's birthplace, 150 miles away, and might also have been present at Westminster on 12 October when Sir John Sutton handed over eight of his and his wife Margaret's manors to him and Eleanor after being imprisoned for three weeks and coerced.[5] Over the next few days, Eleanor and her household moved into her uncle's manor-house of Sheen west of London, where she would stay for the next few months; she was now about seven months pregnant,

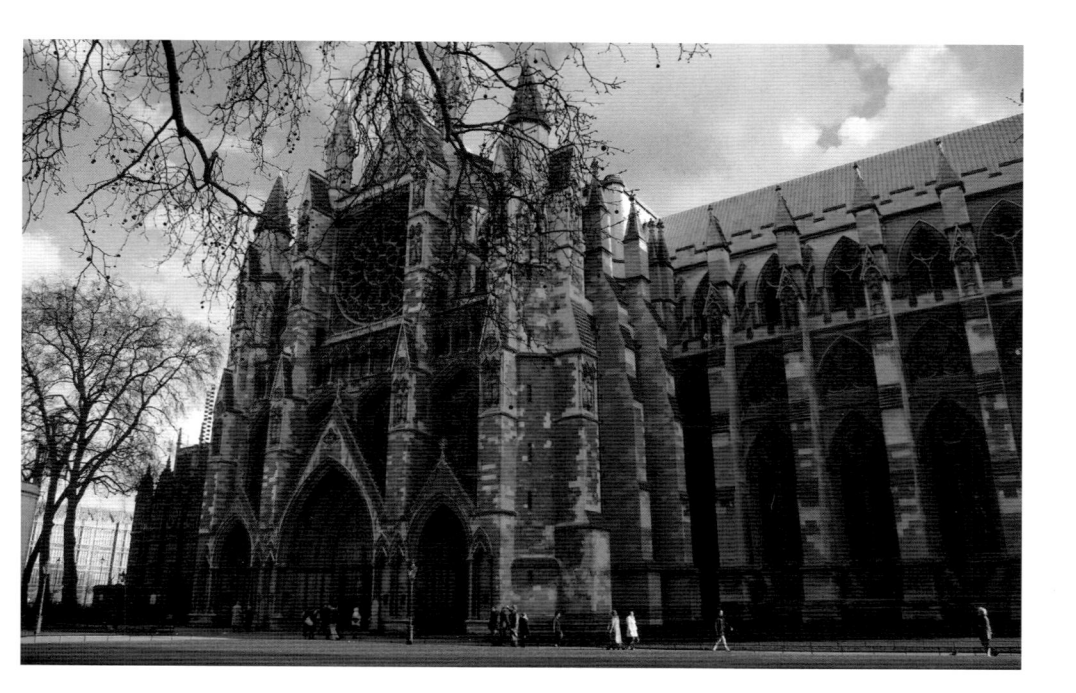

Above: Westminster Abbey, where the sisters' parents Joan of Acre and Gilbert 'the Red' Clare married on 30 April 1290.

Right: Tewkesbury Abbey, Gloucestershire, burial place of Eleanor Despenser née Clare, her two husbands, her eldest son and other descendants, and the Clare sisters' grandfather Richard, father Gilbert 'the Red' and brother Gilbert. (Courtesy of Craig Robinson)

Above left: A stained-glass image of a naked woman representing humility inside Tewkesbury Abbey, probably intended to be Eleanor Despenser née Clare. (Courtesy of Craig Robinson; used with the permission of the Vicar and Churchwardens of Tewkesbury Abbey)

Above right: The tomb of Eleanor's husband Hugh Despenser the Younger in Tewkesbury Abbey. Hugh was executed in November 1326 and Eleanor was given permission to bury him in December 1330. (Courtesy of Craig Robinson; used with the permission of the Vicar and Churchwardens of Tewkesbury Abbey)

Left: The effigy of Eleanor's eldest son Hugh 'Huchon' Despenser, lord of Glamorgan (1308/09-49) and his wife Elizabeth Montacute (d. 1359) in Tewkesbury Abbey. (Courtesy of Craig Robinson; used with the permission of the Vicar and Churchwardens of Tewkesbury Abbey)

Below: The ruins of Berkhamsted Castle, Hertfordshire, where Margaret Clare married Piers Gaveston, earl of Cornwall, on 1 November 1307.

The church of Waltham Abbey in Essex, where Elizabeth Clare married John Burgh, son and heir of the earl of Ulster, and her brother the earl of Gloucester married John's sister Maud, on 29 and 30 September 1308.

The ruins of Tonbridge Castle in Kent, seized by Eleanor's husband Hugh Despenser in May 1315, and later owned by Margaret and Hugh Audley; the Clare sisters' parents Gilbert 'the Red' and Joan of Acre left court without the king's permission after their April 1290 wedding and stayed here.

The Houses of Parliament, London, still officially known as the Palace of Westminster; Eleanor Clare married Hugh Despenser the Younger in a chapel at the palace on 26 May 1306.

Richmond Palace in London, formerly Sheen, where Eleanor lived in late 1325 and early 1326 and where she gave birth to one of her many children in December 1325. It was pulled down by Richard II in 1395 and rebuilt in the early 1400s, and then again in Tudor times.

View from Stirling Castle near the battlefield of Bannockburn, where the Clare sisters' brother the earl of Gloucester fell on 24 June 1314. At least two of the sisters' seven husbands, Hugh Despenser and Roger Damory, fought at Bannockburn.

Caerphilly Castle, South Wales, built by the sisters' father Gilbert 'the Red', and Eleanor's birthplace in October 1292. It passed to Eleanor and her husband Hugh in 1317, and her eldest son Huchon was besieged here between November 1326 and March 1327.

Wallingford Castle, Oxfordshire, which belonged to Margaret's first husband Piers Gaveston and where she lived after his third exile in late 1311.

Above: Ballinrobe Priory, County Mayo, Ireland; an Augustinian house probably founded by Elizabeth Burgh *c.* 1313.

Below: Clare College, Cambridge, formerly Clare Hall, founded 1326, endowed and renamed by Elizabeth Burgh in 1338.

Above: Windsor Castle, where Margaret married Hugh Audley and Elizabeth married Roger Damory in the spring of 1317. The Clare sisters' first cousin Edward III was born here in 1312.

Right: Seal of Eleanor Despenser, 1329.

Below: Usk Castle, which belonged to Elizabeth Burgh and was taken from her by her brother-in-law Hugh Despenser.

The remains of the Franciscan friary in Walsingham, Norfolk, founded in 1347 by Elizabeth Burgh.

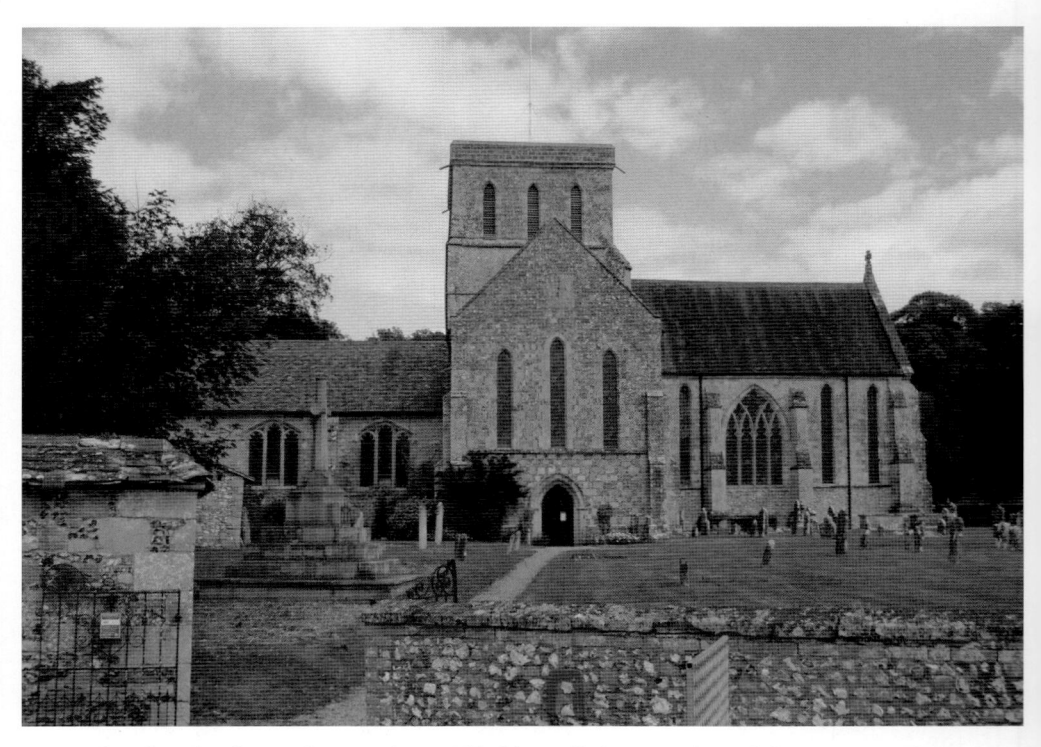

The church of Amesbury Priory, Wiltshire, all that remains of the convent where Elizabeth Burgh gave birth to her daughter Isabella Verdon in March 1317. (Matthew Black via Wikimedia Commons)

and would give birth at Sheen. Edward II visited her there from 12 to 17 October, paid her expenses, bought extra firewood for her chamber, and a month later purchased two lanterns for her. Hugh Despenser was also at Sheen with Eleanor and the king on 16 October, and withdrew £60 from his Italian bankers for his wife's further expenses in November 1325.[6] Given that Hugh and Eleanor owned extensive lands across southern England and South Wales and she could have lived at and given birth at any of them, it is perhaps rather odd, and revealing, that Edward II accommodated her at one of his own manors in the last two months of her pregnancy.

While she was living at Sheen in early November 1325, Eleanor lent £40 to a London merchant called Hugh Madefrey. Her uncle, who doted on her but who never forgave people he thought had betrayed him, ordered her sister Margaret's husband Hugh Audley to be moved from prison at Berkhamsted Castle to Nottingham at this time.[7] Audley had now been in prison for more than three-and-a-half years, and had Edward II and Hugh Despenser not fallen from power a year later, the king's former companion and perhaps lover might have stayed in prison for the rest of his life (and Audley was still only in his early 30s in 1325). The same applies to Margaret Audley at Sempringham Priory. Whether her conscience troubled her over her sister and brother-in-law's fate or not, Eleanor Despenser was surely very comfortable and living very well at the royal manor-house, but things were about to go terribly wrong for her husband, her uncle and herself. Around late October or early November 1325, her aunt-in-law Queen Isabella made a speech to the French court:

> I feel that marriage is a joining together of man and woman, maintaining the undivided habit of life, and that someone has come between my husband and myself trying to break this bond; I protest that I will not return until this intruder is removed, but, discarding my marriage garment, shall assume the robes of widowhood and mourning until I am avenged of this Pharisee.[8]

This has always been assumed to be a reference to Hugh Despenser the Younger. The queen also threatened to destroy Hugh with the help of her brother Charles IV and other Frenchmen; her letter or speech to this effect does not survive, but is known about from a letter which King Edward ordered all the English bishops to write to her during a parliament held in London in November/December 1325: 'But as for what you [Isabella] have written, that what your brother the king of France and your other friends of France intend to do on your behalf, will turn out not to the prejudice of the lord king [Edward] or anyone else, but to the destruction of Hugh [Despenser] alone'.[9]

Rumours reached Edward II near London in about the middle of November 1325 that Hugh Despenser, then in Wales while his wife remained at Sheen, had been killed. The king hastily sent three men to Wales to see what was going on and to return to him as quickly as possible with news of Despenser's welfare (he was in fact perfectly well).[10] It is not impossible that the king—and others, including Eleanor—believed that the queen had had Despenser assassinated. She had not, and Despenser had not been harmed in any way, though the rumour that he had been killed gives an impression of the fevered atmosphere and accusations and counter-accusations at the English and French courts which began in late 1325. Pope John XXII (r. 1316–34) assured Edward II a few months later that the messengers of the king's half-brother the Earl of Kent had not spoken ill of Hugh Despenser to the pope, and assured Isabella herself that no messengers from England had spoken against her honour to him either. Emotions ran high. Isabella claimed on other occasions, though not in this speech to the French court, to be so frightened of Hugh Despenser that she feared for her life from him, and refused to return to Edward or allow her son to do so until the king removed Despenser from his side. The queen stated that she wanted above all else to be in her husband's company, but dared not while Despenser was there, and seems genuinely to have been terrified of him. Whether she had cause to be, whether Despenser had hurt her or threatened to do so, is not clear. In a letter of February 1326, Isabella referred to Despenser as *nostre mauvoillant*, literally 'our evil-wisher', though the word can also mean 'devil'.[11]

Although Queen Isabella threatened on other occasions to destroy Hugh Despenser and he may well have been the person she meant when she spoke of the 'Pharisee' and 'intruder' who had come between her husband and herself and tried to break their marriage, she did not name the person involved, and it is not impossible that she did not mean Hugh but Eleanor Despenser. The word 'Pharisee' is usually used to mean a hypocritical, self-righteous and insincere person or someone who claims to be religious but behaves in an immoral way, and whatever Hugh Despenser's faults, he was not a hypocrite. He certainly did immoral things, but by the standards of the day was not particularly pious and did not claim to be, and openly admitted his ambitions to be rich and powerful. The queen's description might fit Eleanor Despenser better; someone who for years had acted as Isabella's companion and even her friend and confidante, but who, Isabella may have come to believe, betrayed her by usurping her position with Edward II.

Isabella did not name the 'Pharisee' and 'intruder', either because she loathed Hugh Despenser so much she could not bring herself to utter his name, or perhaps because she meant Eleanor Despenser and did not wish, despite her rage and grief at the breakdown of her marriage, to cause too much embarrassment to a noble and partly royal woman in public. Perhaps the rather cryptic comment of the later chronicler Henry Knighton that Eleanor Despenser behaved as though she were Edward's queen during Isabella's absence in France is an oblique reference to Isabella's belief that her husband's niece was the third person in her marriage. It may also be significant that Isabella made her speech just weeks after her husband accommodated the pregnant Eleanor at his manor-house of Sheen and treated her with the utmost solicitousness there. There was a rumour in 1326/27 reported by a Flemish chronicler that Eleanor might be pregnant by the king, and the Westminster chronicler declared in its account of events in England in 1324 that Edward II enjoyed forbidden and sinful sex (and incest was certainly deemed forbidden and sinful). If the lover with whom Edward had a secret and intimate meeting opposite the Tower of London in October 1324 was indeed Eleanor, this was months before Isabella left England, and she and Eleanor spent much time in each other's company at Christmas and New Year 1324/25 two months after that meeting. If Isabella subsequently learned that Eleanor had had sex with her own uncle, Isabella's husband, before the two women were together in Nottingham and Kenilworth, it can only have disgusted and angered her, and made her feel intensely betrayed by them both. Whether the queen meant Hugh or Eleanor Despenser in her speech, it seems beyond doubt that she knew the person was having a sexual and romantic relationship with her husband, and took to wearing widow's clothes to symbolise the destruction of her marriage by a third party.

Edward II wrote a letter to his wife on 1 December 1325, ordering her to come home from France.[12] He told Isabella that he was suffering greatly from her absence, but devoted much of the letter to defending Hugh Despenser from Isabella's complaint that she was frightened of him to the point of fearing for her life. The king made no reference to Isabella's complaint about a third person destroying her marriage, either in his letter to the queen or in another letter he sent to her brother Charles IV. Edward also wrote to his son Edward of Windsor on 2 December to tell him to come home, and later that day went to visit the heavily pregnant Eleanor Despenser at his manor-house of Sheen. The king rowed himself along the River Thames from Westminster with eight of his chamber valets as attendants, who all received 'boots for the water'. He gave his niece yet another generous gift of 100 marks 'with his own hands', dined on fresh roach, dace and loach (kinds of fish) with her, and returned to Westminster that night. The king had bought Eleanor larks and forty-seven goldfinches a few weeks previously and now had thirty of the goldfinches taken to her at Sheen, with three swans for good measure. Her chambers must have rung pleasantly with the sound of birdsong, and presumably she kept the swans on the River Thames outside—unless they were intended for her to eat. And the gift-giving was not one-sided: Eleanor sent a valet of her chamber called Thomas to the king with 'a robe of four garments' (i.e. a set of clothes) for him the day after his visit, as she had also done thirteen months previously, days after Edward's clandestine meeting with a lover at La Rosere opposite the Tower of London.[13] Hugh Despenser may have been with his wife at Sheen; he had returned from Wales and was at Westminster on 28 and 30 November and 3 December, and at the Tower of London on 5 and 9 December.[14] Hugh and Eleanor's eldest son Huchon, now probably 17, was at court with his father and his great-uncle the king in December 1325.[15]

Eleanor Despenser gave birth to another child at the royal residence of Sheen shortly before 14 December 1325, when an offering by the king of 30 shillings to the Virgin Mary in gratitude for her prompt delivery was recorded in his accounts.[16] She may, in fact, have given birth on or just before 2 December, and perhaps this was the reason for her uncle's visit that day and for the large gift of cash. He had also given her 100 marks in April 1325 perhaps on hearing the news of her pregnancy. Little is known about noblewomen's experience of childbirth in the early fourteenth century, but in the fifteenth and sixteenth centuries they went into seclusion with female attendants a month or so before their due date. From this perspective, it seems strange for a man who was not even the child's father to visit the expectant mother only days before she gave birth, or perhaps just afterwards. Eleanor would have been purified after childbirth in late December 1325 at the earliest, and the third week of January 1326 at the latest.

The child, at least Eleanor's tenth, was not named or given a sex in the king's accounts, but was most probably the Despensers' fifth daughter Elizabeth, future Lady Berkeley. Perhaps Eleanor—who was now 33 years old—somewhat defiantly named her daughter after the sister her husband had persecuted, or perhaps Hugh himself chose the name and intended it to honour his own youngest sister Elizabeth Camoys née Despenser. It is also not impossible that Despenser, who was prone to malicious sarcasm, chose his daughter's name as a mocking tribute to his victim of earlier in the year, Elizabeth Comyn. The infant would be the Despensers' youngest child, unless the Flemish chronicler who speculated that Eleanor was pregnant when she was imprisoned at the Tower of London in and after late 1326 was correct.

Chapter 17

A Protest Against the Regime

Edward II and Hugh Despenser the Younger spent Christmas 1325 and New Year 1326 in Suffolk, while Eleanor Despenser remained at Sheen presumably with her new-born child and the infant's wet-nurse and other attendants, unless the girl had already been sent out to a foster family as her older sister Margaret Despenser had been in 1323. Eleanor sent her servant John Mot with letters for her uncle the king on 30 December, and sent Edward a gift of a dappled palfrey horse with saddle and equipment on 1 January 1326 (she might also have sent her husband a gift, but his accounts do not survive). Her carter Richard atte Grene led the horse to the king and was rewarded with a generous 20 shillings by Edward, and was accompanied to Suffolk by another servant of Eleanor's called Walter 'Watte' Somery.[1] Hugh Despenser continued his exactions. At the end of 1325 and beginning of 1326, he demanded an acknowledgement of a huge debt of 1,000 marks or £666 from the townspeople of Sudbury in Suffolk, one of his sister-in-law Elizabeth Burgh's manors and only ten miles from her manor of Clare, where she spent much or most of her time. Many dozens of men and women of Sudbury including the mayor and two bailiffs acknowledged the joint debt to Despenser, and it was cancelled in Edward III's reign because it had been made 'under duress.'[2] Despenser and Edward II were in Haughley, twenty miles from Sudbury, on this date, and the forced debt was another attack on Elizabeth.

Some of the men of Sudbury had been named as Roger Damory's adherents in August 1321 when the king was forced to grant a pardon to the Marcher lords and their followers for their terrible destruction during the Despenser War.[3] Edward II withdrew the sentence of outlawry on four of the Sudbury men on 3 January 1326 as 'the king wills for certain reasons that no further proceedings shall be taken against' them, presumably because three days earlier they had satisfied Despenser by acknowledging the huge debt to him.[4] Despenser also ordered four of his men to 'have the body of Robert Chedworth brought before him at a certain day', and made the four acknowledge that they owed him £200 as his security that they would do so.[5] Chedworth was a knight of Essex who acted as Elizabeth Burgh's attorney, and was pardoned as a Contrariant and adherent of Roger Damory in July 1322.[6] In October 1326, after the queen's invasion, Elizabeth Burgh paid Robert Chedworth for taking her letters to the queen and 'reporting rumours from the king's court'.[7] In May 1326 Elizabeth was certainly living at her castle of Clare, and it is possible that she was also there a few months earlier and thus was very near her uncle and brother-in-law while they were persecuting some of her people.

Edward II sent letters to Eleanor Despenser at Sheen on 10 February 1326 and to her husband Hugh in London on the 11th and 12th. On 12 February, Edward gave his niece custody of the Framland hundred, one of the six divisions of the county of Leicestershire.[8] Since early February, the king had known that Queen Isabella had made an alliance in France with the remnant of the Contrariant faction who escaped and fled abroad in and after 1322, including Roger Mortimer of Wigmore, whom the exiles considered their leader. Hugh Despenser made a public disturbance with weapons ('made a small affray') of some kind in Rothwell, Northamptonshire in late February 1326, perhaps a sign of the stress he was under as a result of the queen making an alliance with his enemies and threatening to destroy him.[9] The Despensers, husband and wife, were with the king at Kenilworth Castle on 28 March 1326, and Edward gave Eleanor a silver goblet with foot and cover.[10] Eleanor was still, or again, with her uncle at Kenilworth on 28 April, when he gave her all the goods formerly belonging to a man called Alan Newenham who had been indicted 'of diverse felonies'.[11] On one of her trips to Kenilworth, Eleanor travelled with her 9-year-old first cousin, the king's second son John of Eltham: she received £12 for her expenses in travelling from Sheen to Kenilworth and staying there with the boy for eighteen days, and the possessions of the two cousins required nine carts and fifty-two horses to transport them the 110 miles. John stayed at Kenilworth from 22 May to 20 July 1326, and in total, the cousins spent about 120 days together in 1325/26.[12]

On 22 May 1326, in her private chapel next to her chamber at Clare Castle in Suffolk, Elizabeth Burgh bravely dictated a protest document detailing what her uncle and her brother-in-law Despenser had done to her, in the presence of her close advisers and clerks Thomas Chedworth and John Diccus and a notary called John Radenhale. If the king or Despenser had found out about it, Elizabeth would have been in serious trouble, and she must have known that her brother-in-law had informants and spies everywhere, so she took a great risk. She was surely aware that Edward II and Despenser—with Elizabeth's sister Eleanor in tow—were currently in Wiltshire/Gloucestershire 125 miles from Clare, so perhaps this made her feel somewhat safer. Her clerk Thomas Chedworth was the brother of Sir Robert Chedworth, whom Despenser had ordered to be arrested and brought to him earlier in 1326, and perhaps these latest threats by Despenser—Chedworth's arrest and the massive debt Despenser forced Elizabeth's townspeople of Sudbury to acknowledge to him—were among the factors which prompted her to write the document.

Elizabeth wrote of Hugh as 'Sir Hugh Despenser the son' and Edward II as 'our lord, Lord Edward, king of England, son of King Edward' with more courtesy than they perhaps deserved, and without acknowledging her close familial relationships to both men. She described herself as 'formerly the consort of Sir Roger Damory' and claimed that her husband had been 'pursued and oppressed until he died', and went on to describe in detail how the king had threatened her in York at Christmas 1322. She claimed that Despenser was now 'seeing the great calumny of the wrongs' he had done to her, and to deceive and damage her and to mislead the people was offering her lands of much lower value in compensation for Gower; but it was far too little and far too late. There is no record of this offer in any extant document, so presumably Despenser had sent men to Elizabeth to discuss the matter orally, or even visited her in person: he and the king were in Suffolk/Norfolk from the end of 1325 until early February 1326. It is not impossible that Elizabeth had already regained her lordship of Usk from Despenser and her sister Eleanor in 1325 or 1326, but if so she was still obviously, and understandably, furious about its seizure from her in 1322.[13] In France, Queen Isabella was refusing to return to her husband because she loathed and feared Hugh Despenser, and Elizabeth Burgh's hatred of her sister's husband and her anger towards her own uncle could hardly be more apparent. She wrote that she would never accept any lands in recompense for the lordship of Gower in South Wales except under duress because she feared the king and the malice of Hugh

Despenser, and because of 'the royal power which is in the hand of the said Sir Hugh'. Furthermore, she wrote, she was frightened to become one of 'those whom the king deems his enemies', of the loss of her children and all her lands and goods, and the disgrace of being humiliated and even physically harmed. Her last sentence declared that she would make her protest publicly but that the possibility of 'peril' prevented her.

Eleanor Despenser was in Wiltshire with her husband and uncle when her sister wrote this text, and on 18 May 1326 Edward II granted her custody of the Goscote hundred, another of the six divisions of Leicestershire.[14] While Elizabeth talked of 'the oppressions done by the king' and the 'great evil' Edward had done to her at Christmas 1322 by threatening to take all her lands from her, Edward continued to dote on her sister. The day after the grant of Goscote, Eleanor's teenage niece-in-law Margaret Martin née Hastings married her second husband, Hugh Despenser the Younger's retainer Sir Robert Wateville, in Marlborough, Wiltshire. Eleanor's sister-in-law Isabella Hastings also attended her daughter's wedding, and Eleanor may have seen her third daughter Eleanor the younger, who had been in Lady Hastings' custody in 1325 and perhaps still was. Edward II's young daughters, Eleanor's first cousins Eleanor of Woodstock and Joan of the Tower, also lived in Marlborough under the care of Joan Jermy, and the king sent them letters there two months later.[15] The 26 May 1326 marked Eleanor and Hugh Despenser's twentieth wedding anniversary. No direct evidence, such as private letters between the couple, exists to tell us what their intimate relationship was like, but seemingly they formed a solid and contented partnership over the years and certainly spent a lot of time together. Despenser had a knack for making women including Eleanor's sisters and aunt-in-law the queen loathe him, but clearly his wife did not. There is every reason to suppose that Eleanor supported Despenser in his schemes and extortions, and no evidence that she ever tried to protect her sisters (or indeed anyone else) from her husband, possibly excepting Despenser's comment *c*. October 1322 that he had been requested to allow Elizabeth's wet-nurses to move with her. Eleanor was one of her husband and her uncle's most loyal supporters.

Eleanor and Hugh Despenser, who were still only 33 and about 37 years old respectively, became grandparents sometime in 1326 when their eldest daughter Isabella's son Edmund Fitzalan was born. Edmund was said to be 18 in December 1344 and 20 in early 1347, so was born in or before late 1326 and was only a few months younger than his aunt Elizabeth Despenser, born in December 1325 and the Despensers' youngest child.[16] Isabella was only 14 and her husband Richard Fitzalan probably even younger when they became parents, and Richard claimed in 1344 that they had been 'forced by fear and blows to cohabit' when they reached puberty, resulting in Edmund. He also said that they had been married against their will as children and renounced their vows on coming to puberty, but were made to sleep together anyway.[17] This is likely to be a fake story invented by Richard when he wanted to rid himself of an inconvenient wife and marry Eleanor of Lancaster, daughter of the powerful Henry, Earl of Lancaster, instead. The unfortunate Edmund was made illegitimate by the annulment of his parents' marriage, and his father sneeringly referred to him as 'that certain Edmund who claims himself to be my son'.[18] Both of the boy's grandfathers would be executed within days of each other when he was only a few weeks or months old.

Chapter 18

The End of Hugh Despenser

Eleanor Despenser was staying at Leeds Castle in Kent on 4 June 1326 while Hugh and Edward II were at Saltwood Castle thirty miles away. Here they met the archbishop of Vienne and the bishop of Orange, envoys sent to England by Pope John XXII as part of his attempts to reconcile Edward and Queen Isabella. The envoys' journey proved fruitless as the king refused to send Hugh Despenser away from him, as Isabella had demanded as the condition for her return to her husband. At some point in the summer of 1326, the queen moved to the county of Hainault on France's northern border, which was ruled by Willem, husband of her first cousin Jeanne de Valois. Isabella betrothed her son Edward of Windsor to Philippa of Hainault (c. 1314–69), one of Willem and Jeanne's daughters, at the end of August 1326 in return for their aid in raising an army and providing ships so that she could invade Edward II's kingdom and bring down the loathed Hugh Despenser. Edward, so dependent on Hugh in some way that he would not remove him from his side even in the face of his wife's impending invasion, also continued to show great affection for his niece Eleanor Despenser. He sent her a gift of 20 marks via his sergeant John Mildenhale while she was at Leeds Castle. Eleanor was taken to Edward at the Tower of London by twenty-five sailors of the ship *La Despenser* on 17 June, and was at the Tower with him and her husband on the 20th and still at court on the 25th, when her uncle gave her 'one piece of white worsted' cloth. Her eldest son Huchon was also with his parents and the king in late June and early July 1326.[1] Edward II continued to make unsuccessful attempts to persuade his wife and son to return from France. Although he wrote to Edward of Windsor on 19 June 1326 (as he was surely aware, it was the fourteenth anniversary of the death of his beloved Piers Gaveston, Margaret Audley's first husband), the boy was not acting under his own agency but his mother's, and Isabella was set on Hugh Despenser the

Younger's destruction. She was not willing to return to her husband's side or permit her son to do so until she had achieved it.

Edward II and Eleanor Despenser 'ate privately' together in the park of Windsor Castle on 11 July 1326. Their cook, Will Balsham, was given 40 shillings to buy himself a hackney horse on which to follow them there, the money given to him by the king in person 'between two silver dishes'. A hackney was a riding horse, so the animal was not intended for Balsham to carry whatever food he had prepared for the two or for his equipment, implying that Edward and his niece went to a remote corner of the park, too far for Balsham to follow them on foot. The king had a personal bodyguard of eight archers who presumably stayed somewhere near him on this occasion, though there is no specific record of anyone other than Will Balsham attending the pair during their alfresco meal. Whether this says anything about the nature of Edward and Eleanor's relationship is unclear, though the word in the king's account which describes their dining can be translated as 'secretly', 'discreetly', or 'covertly', as well as 'privately'. Will Balsham had been in France with the queen and was one of her many servants who returned to England after Isabella refused to come back, and after Edward II's downfall, he went to work for her again. Balsham might, therefore, have been able to inform the queen if he had seen anything untoward in her husband's behaviour towards his niece.[2] The summer of 1326 was terribly hot: two chroniclers comment that there was a drought in England, rivers dried up and 'conflagrations' burst out spontaneously, so perhaps Edward and Eleanor sat in the shade. In June, Edward gave linen cloth to his eight archers for hose which, he said, was a gift in return for their hard work in running fast and well with him in the hot weather (the archers were on foot and ran alongside and in front of the king when he rode from place to place).[3]

Two weeks after their Windsor picnic, on 25 and 26 July 1326, Edward and Eleanor sailed along the Thames together in Surrey in a flat-bottomed boat or barge called a *shoute*, and Edward spent 18 pence on roach and dace for Eleanor from a fisherman in Byfleet. The king paid a man in Walton-on-Thames 6 pence to bring them fresh water from a well, perhaps another indication of the heat, and ordered a servant to give 3 shillings in alms to seven women fishing in the Thames. This entry in Edward's account states that the alms were given to the women 'in the presence of the king and my lady'. This means Eleanor, who was not named, and otherwise in documents of Edward II's reign the words 'my lady' (*ma dame*) without a name referred to Queen Isabella. The same applies in Edward III's reign: his queen, Philippa of Hainault, was often simply called *ma dame* in his accounts without her name.[4] It is most unusual for the king to be linked in such a way with a woman who was not Isabella, and this entry gives the curious impression that Eleanor was Edward II's wife and queen. They could not, of course, truly have married, given the close family relationship between them and given that they had both been married to other people for many years, but perhaps the descriptions of Eleanor in the king's accounts reveal that he thought of her as his real queen, at least in some ways. Eleanor was still with her uncle at Henley-on-Thames, Oxfordshire on 28 July when he granted a favour to the priory of Wix in Essex at her request. Her husband Hugh made a quick visit to Wales—where exactly in Wales was not specified—in late July and early August 1326, though soon returned to the south-east of England, and just before his departure had received a rather poignant gift from the king: a large and expensive manuscript of the doomed love story of Tristan and Isolde. The king sent his 'runner' John Stretton with letters to Despenser in Wales on 25 July while he and Eleanor were in his boat near the bridge at Kingston-on-Thames, and sent him more letters on the 30th.[5] Various extant petitions of *c.* 1322 to 1326 complain about Hugh Despenser taking people's manors from them with the aid of a man called William Horwode, said to be a member of 'the household of the king and Sir Hugh Despenser the son'.[6] This description of their joint household also tends to give the impression that Edward and Hugh were a married couple and reveals the two men's extraordinary closeness. It is easy to understand why a chronicler thought that Eleanor Despenser was treated as though she were Edward II's queen during Isabella's absence abroad, and also why an abbey annalist referred to Edward and Hugh Despenser as 'the king and his husband'.

On 29 July 1326, while Eleanor was with the king in Oxfordshire, Elizabeth Burgh's former father-in-law Richard Burgh, Earl of Ulster, died in Ireland at the age of about 67. His heir to the earldom was Elizabeth's son William 'Donn' Burgh, born in September 1312 and not yet 14, who was also heir to her third of the Clare inheritance. As heir to Ulster, William lived some of the time in Ireland as he grew up. He was in his grandfather the earl's company in July 1322 and April 1323, when he and Richard were given safe-conducts for 'coming to the king [Edward II] on the king's affairs'. William was also in Ireland in August 1323 shortly before his eleventh birthday, when he and Richard Burgh were two of the people ordered to search for the recently-escaped Roger Mortimer in Ireland.[7] He must have spent at least some of his time with his mother, however, as in 1324/25 there is a reference to his chamber at Clare Castle.[8] William was in England with his mother in the summer and autumn of 1326, and one of Elizabeth's servants purchased black cloth for him in Ipswich after his grandfather's death. Elizabeth spent 15 shillings on a saddle for William's courser on 30 September, and gave him 4 pence on 13 October for mending a sheepskin for his basinet (a kind of helmet) and 2 shillings for leather to line the basinet. He had joined his mother in June 1326 or earlier, as that month Elizabeth spent £1, 4 shillings on a 'German saddle' for him.[9] Elizabeth's daughters Isabella Verdon and Margaret and Elizabeth Damory appear to have lived with her for most of the 1320s. She had to travel to Wales in 1327/28 and left her daughters behind at Clare in Suffolk on that occasion, and left them in the care of Isabella, Lady Hastings while she travelled to Gloucester in December 1327.[10] Elizabeth's statement in her protest document of May 1326 that she feared to lose her children also strongly implies that her daughters lived with her, whereas her sister Eleanor Despenser appears to have sent her own daughters, or at least some of them, to foster families. In 1326, Isabella Verdon turned 9 and Margaret Damory was probably 8, Elizabeth Damory perhaps only 4 or 5.

Unfortunately for Elizabeth Burgh, her father-in-law Richard had been too far away to help her or to offer much support against Edward II and Hugh Despenser, and her son was too young. Elizabeth's sister Margaret Audley was still incarcerated at Sempringham Priory in 1326 by their vindictive uncle, but sometime that year or at the end of 1325, Margaret's husband Hugh Audley escaped from captivity in Nottingham Castle. After Edward II's downfall, the castle's constable Richard, Lord Grey of Codnor was pardoned for having allowed him to do so.[11] Grey was appointed constable of Nottingham Castle on 14 December 1325, so Hugh must have escaped after that date.[12] Where he subsequently went is not known, though he may well have joined the Contrariant exiles on the continent (Roger Mortimer of Wigmore, John Maltravers and other men who had fled abroad after the Battle of Boroughbridge in March 1322), and perhaps travelled to Sempringham Priory in Lincolnshire in a bid to see his wife and child. As Audley had had no income at all since April 1321 and was a penniless fugitive, someone must have aided him financially and given him shelter, and perhaps his mother Isolde was one of those who did. In October 1337, Hugh was finally pardoned by Edward III 'for all homicides, robberies, larcenies and trespasses against the peace of Edward II'.[13] Many or most of these felonies probably relate to the Despenser War and the Contrariant rebellion in 1321/22, though the pardon might also suggest that Audley went on a one-man crime rampage after his escape. His father Hugh Audley senior died still in prison on or before 9 March 1326, leaving his widow Isolde and his elder son James as his heir.[14] James Audley is rather obscure, and did not play any part in the rebellion of his father and brother in 1321/22; he seems to have been in the king's favour after the Contrariants' defeat and was with Edward in Yorkshire in early 1323.

Elizabeth Burgh carefully and diplomatically kept in regular contact with her uncle the king, despite her understandable anger with him. She sent him letters in late August, mid-September and late September 1326, and almost certainly earlier that year as well, though her accounts do not survive. There is no direct evidence that he reciprocated, though the messengers Elizabeth sent to him carrying her letters might have returned with Edward's messages to her. Although Elizabeth was surely aware that her sister Eleanor was almost always in Edward's company, there is no record of her sending any letters to her, or indeed vice versa. Elizabeth did, however, keep in touch with their aunt Mary at Amesbury Priory: Mary is almost certainly the 'Lady Maria' of Elizabeth's accounts.[15]

Neither Elizabeth Burgh nor Margaret Audley are mentioned at all in Edward II's two chamber accounts of 1324/26. He did send letters to their cousin Jeanne de Bar, Countess of Surrey (the only daughter of Edward's eldest sister Eleanor, d. 1298) in France where she was attending Queen Isabella, and Jeanne visited him in 1324. Their aunt Mary had been close to her brother for much of his reign, and often visited him and went away with presents, but she also does not appear in Edward II's last two chamber accounts, nor in the Chancery rolls of those years. Edward spent part of May 1326 in Wiltshire and was therefore near his sister at Amesbury, but does not seem to have visited her there or to have invited her to court, or even sent letters. This all perhaps reveals something of

Mary's attitude towards her younger brother in the last years of his reign and her displeasure at his shabby treatment of their two younger Clare nieces, and may indicate that the royal siblings had fallen out.[16] Edward's relationship with Hugh Despenser the Younger had alienated him from his wife Isabella, his son Edward of Windsor, his half-brothers Thomas and Edmund, his cousins Henry of Lancaster and John of Brittany (Earl of Richmond) and his Clare nieces Margaret and Elizabeth, and perhaps the king had now also become estranged from the sister he had formerly been very close to. This surely reveals something sinister about Hugh Despenser's dominance over Edward and about Eleanor Despenser's own relationship with the king. Edward II, so close to Eleanor and Hugh that one can easily gain the impression they were involved in a *ménage à trois*, had become isolated from almost all his family and everyone else.

Queen Isabella's invasion force, consisting of around 1,500 mercenaries and the Contrariants who had fled abroad years before, landed at the River Orwell in Suffolk on 24 September 1326. She and her allies, including the Clare sisters' half-uncle Edmund of Woodstock, Earl of Kent, were determined to rid the country of the hated Hugh Despenser and his father. Elizabeth Burgh cautiously sent letters to both Edward II and Isabella, doing her best to remain studiedly neutral for now though she must have been delighted that at last someone was taking forceful action against her brother-in-law Despenser with the aim of destroying him and his hold over the king. Her manor of Clare lay under forty miles from where the force landed, and she heard the news of the queen's arrival on the same day: on 24 September, she sent a messenger called Thomas Ryot to her manor of Cranborne in Dorset 'in haste' to inform her retinue there. She carefully also sent a messenger to the king on 26 September.[17] Her kinsman Henry of Lancaster, Earl of Leicester (b. *c*. 1280/81), nephew of her grandfather Edward I, who had been deprived by his cousin the king of much of his rightful inheritance from his executed brother Thomas, joined his niece, the queen, by early October though like Elizabeth took the precaution of sending letters to Edward II as well.[18] The Clare sisters' other half-uncle Thomas of Brotherton, Earl of Norfolk, who owned the lands where the queen and her allies arrived, immediately went to join them. The king had tried to conciliate Thomas in 1325 and 1326, but his efforts failed; Thomas had been forced to give up his lands between the rivers Severn and Wye in Wales to Hugh Despenser the Younger for far less than their true value, and both he and his brother Edmund had been edged out of their rightful position by Despenser.

The king was at the Tower of London with his second son John of Eltham, Eleanor Despenser, her husband Hugh, her father-in-law Hugh the Elder and probably her son Huchon, when he received the news of his wife's arrival. At the beginning of October 1326, the king and the two Hugh Despensers realised that they could not hold London—the city tended to be anti-royalist and was hostile to them—and decided to head for South Wales which was controlled by Hugh and where the king was more popular than in England. They left the Tower under Eleanor's command. She would never see her husband or her uncle again. The queen sent a letter to London on 6 October, urging the mayor and citizens to help her 'destroy Sir Hugh Despenser [the Younger], our enemy and the enemy of the whole realm, as you well know', for the common good of the whole country, and told them to capture Hugh and keep him under strict guard 'on the faith which you owe to our lord the king and to us'.[19] At this point, the queen seems not to have known that Hugh and Edward had departed from London three days earlier, and had left the city under the nominal control of her 10-year-old son John of Eltham and the Tower under Eleanor Despenser's. Isabella and her allies followed the king and the two Hugh Despensers west, towards Wales. The *Anonimalle* chronicle says 'the king would not leave the company of his enemies', and that Isabella pursued him to make him leave the Despensers and because she wanted 'to rejoin her lord [husband] if she could'.[20] Thousands of people flocked to the banner of the queen and her son, their future king, and few were willing to defend their present king, at least when he had the hated Hugh Despenser and his father in his company. Even at this desperate stage, Edward II still would not abandon Despenser.

Hugh Audley was said in 1331 to have joined Queen Isabella and her son in pursuing the Despensers, so after his escape from prison in late 1325 or 1326 he must have made his way to Isabella and Edward of Windsor, either on the continent or after their return to England.[21] His wife Margaret remained in captivity at Sempringham Priory for a few more weeks. Audley would be the only one of Edward II's male favourites to survive the reign, and outlived his brother-in-law and great enemy Hugh Despenser the Younger by more than twenty years. Later in life he was to become something of a respected elder statesman, and his career in the 1330s and 1340s was so entirely different from the 1310s as to give the impression that he had become almost another person entirely, no longer the frivolous knight who may have been Edward II's lover and who was called 'worse than [Piers] Gaveston' by one chronicler. Audley was not, however, one of the chief barons and bishops named as the queen's most important allies on 26 October 1326, when Isabella's son Edward of Windsor was appointed *custos regni* or 'keeper of the realm' on the pretext that his father had left his kingdom.[22] Edward II and Hugh Despenser sailed from Chepstow on 20 October probably in a desperate, and futile, attempt to reach Ireland and launch a counter-invasion.

Eleanor Despenser's father-in-law Hugh Despenser the Elder, Earl of Winchester, was hanged in Bristol on 27 October, the day the city fell to the queen and her allies. He was 65. Winchester's body was fed to dogs, and his head was sent to the town of Winchester for public display. Some days before, his son and the king had been forced to put in at Cardiff after contrary winds prevented them leaving the south coast of Wales. They moved on to Eleanor Despenser's birthplace, the great stronghold of Caerphilly, accompanied by Eleanor's eldest son Huchon. Everything was going the queen's way; Edward II's disastrous rule of the previous few years and his encouragement of Hugh Despenser's despotism and extortion ensured that the king found little support, and soon became little more than a fugitive in his own kingdom. Edward and Despenser left Caerphilly on or about 2 November for reasons that remain mysterious, leaving Huchon Despenser and most of their remaining households inside, and a large amount of cash and treasure. They headed for Neath Abbey with a handful of attendants, and were captured on 16 November on their way back to Caerphilly Castle, by a group of men who included Queen Isabella's uncle Henry of Lancaster and a baron named William Zouche.

Elizabeth Burgh, who cannot have been anything but delighted at the turn of events—any affection she might once have felt for her uncle had surely evaporated after he shouted threats at her and allowed Despenser to persecute her—returned to her Welsh lordship of Usk by mid-November 1326, possibly even before the king and Despenser were captured, and spent Christmas there. Her officials had arrived there as early as mid-October.[23] Usk had been taken from her by her brother-in-law and sister in 1322, and she returned there as soon as she could, though officially

Usk was not regranted to her until late February 1327. Elizabeth seems to have made some financial arrangement with her sister Eleanor regarding the lordship, and in the year 1329/30 paid her 500 marks for 'the fine of Usk'. It is even possible that Despenser had given Usk back to her in 1325 or earlier in 1326, as in 1329/30 Elizabeth paid the money to her sister 'for the preceding four years'.[24] Keen to know what was going on, in mid-October 1326 Elizabeth sent a man to 'report rumours from the king's court' to her, and on the same day sent another man to Queen Isabella, perhaps to assure her of her support.[25]

The Clare sisters' wheel of fortune turned; now it was Eleanor Despenser's turn to be imprisoned, while her sisters Margaret and Elizabeth were freed. Eleanor was incarcerated in the Tower of London with some of her children and a few servants on 17 November 1326.[26] She would remain there for more than fifteen months. Her husband and uncle had been captured in South Wales the day before her arrest, though of course this news had not yet reached her in London. Her cousin John of Eltham, who had been left in nominal command of the city of London although he was only a child, was removed from her custody and taken to his mother Isabella at Wallingford just before Christmas. Also on 17 November, the king and the Despensers' ally Edmund Fitzalan, Earl of Arundel, was beheaded in Hereford without a trial on the orders of his cousin Roger Mortimer. Arundel was the father-in-law of Eleanor's eldest daughter Isabella and they had a mutual grandson in the infant Edmund Fitzalan, and his son Richard was disinherited by his execution and would not regain his entitlement to his patrimony for years to come.

Hugh Despenser the Younger was led slowly to Hereford and treated with every possible disrespect, and was pelted with filth by the populace, who hurled abuse at him. In front of the queen, her uncle Henry of Lancaster and her brothers-in-law the earls of Norfolk and Kent, and Roger Mortimer and other barons, Hugh was hanged on a fifty-foot gallows, cut down before he was dead, disembowelled and castrated, and finally beheaded. His long-term rival Hugh Audley probably also witnessed his execution.[27] The four quarters of Despenser's body were sent to be publicly displayed in York, Carlisle, Bristol and Dover, and on 4 December 1326 his head was carried down Cheapside in London to the sound of trumpets and set on a spike on London Bridge. This was barely half a mile from where his widow Eleanor and some of his children were incarcerated in the Tower. Hugh and Eleanor's eldest child Huchon was besieged at Caerphilly Castle from November 1326 until March 1327, and Queen Isabella was determined to execute him, even though he was only 17 or 18 years old and had committed no crime except to be his father's heir. The siege was led by William Zouche, lord of Ashby in Leicestershire, one of the men who had captured the king and Hugh Despenser the Younger on 16 November. Fortunately for the teenaged Despenser, the garrison inside Caerphilly refused to give him up for execution and bravely held out against the besieging force, even though there were only two knights within the castle and most of the garrison were not military men but carpenters, blacksmiths and a few of Edward II's chamber valets and ushers.

And thus so easily did the king and his powerful chamberlain fall. Yet although Edward II's reign was now over in all but name, its aftermath was to prove every bit as turbulent for the three Clare sisters as the previous two decades had been.

Chapter 19

Deposition

Edward II, still the king of England though now in name only, spent a sad and lonely Christmas 1326 at Kenilworth Castle in Warwickshire under the protection of Henry of Lancaster, Earl of Leicester, while the queen and her allies spent the festive season at Wallingford debating what should be done with him. Whether Isabella had sought her husband's downfall or just Hugh Despenser's is not clear, but it had become apparent to all that Edward's support had simply vanished and that he could no longer continue as king. Elizabeth Burgh, meanwhile, spent a lavish Christmas at Usk, which had until so recently been in the hands of her sister Eleanor and brother-in-law Despenser. Her household, officials and guests consumed 800 eggs on Christmas Day alone, plus 230 gallons (over 1,000 litres) of ale, 2 boars' heads, 3 swans, 13 partridges, beef, bacon, pork, mutton and venison.[1] After the persecution of the Despenser years, Elizabeth was back where she belonged, in her element as a great and wealthy noblewoman enjoying her status, being generous and being seen to be generous to her followers. As for her sister Margaret Audley, she was finally released from captivity at Sempringham Priory on 11 December 1326 after spending more than four-and-a-half years there, and spent her first festive season at liberty since 1321. One young woman held at Sempringham with her since 1324 was Joan Mortimer, one of Roger Mortimer's eight daughters, who was released on 2 November.[2]

On 1 January 1327, Eleanor Despenser's daughters Eleanor and Margaret, and perhaps Joan as well, were forcibly veiled as nuns in three separate convents far apart.[3] Margaret, the youngest of the three, was only 3 years old and living with Sir Thomas Houk and his family in the Yorkshire village of Hook, about eight miles from her birthplace of Cowick. She was taken to Watton Priory thirty miles away. Eleanor Despenser the younger, aged somewhere between 5 and 9, was perhaps still in the care of her aunt Isabella Hastings in 1326/27, and was taken to Sempringham Priory in Lincolnshire. Joan the eldest of the three, Eleanor and Hugh's second daughter and about 10 or 12 years old, was taken to Shaftesbury Abbey in Dorset, though the order for Joan's forced veiling is missing and it is possible that she entered the Church voluntarily and was already at Shaftesbury. The abbey was a most prestigious and wealthy religious house, founded in about 888 by King Alfred the Great, who installed his daughter Aethelgifu as the first abbess. It was the wealthiest Benedictine nunnery in England and the second wealthiest nunnery overall, and many of the medieval kings lavished gifts on it. Shaftesbury Abbey was often chosen by the medieval nobility as a suitable location for their daughters to be veiled. This suggests that Eleanor and Hugh Despenser, not Queen Isabella, may have chosen it for their second daughter after her betrothal to the Earl of Kildare's son fell through in 1323 when the boy died aged 9.

Elizabeth, the fifth Despenser daughter, was only a year old and thus was spared, as was the eldest daughter Isabella, 14 years old and married, and already a mother or pregnant. It was almost certainly Queen Isabella who personally gave the order for the Despenser girls to be sent to separate convents, and perhaps she chose Sempringham because the elder Eleanor Despenser's sister Margaret Audley had so recently been incarcerated there. It was not uncommon for members of the nobility to join the Church, as the Clare siblings' half-sister Joan Monthermer, aunt Mary and cousin Isabella of Lancaster did, but it is hard to discern anything except spite and vindictiveness in the queen's actions. The Despenser girls' parents had not intended them for the Church but to marry; the younger Eleanor was betrothed to the future Earl of Pembroke, Laurence Hastings, in 1325, but in 1329 he married one of Roger Mortimer's many daughters instead. Edward II had sent three of Mortimer's daughters to convents in early 1324 after their father escaped and fled the country, but they were not forcibly veiled as nuns and were later released.

His daughters' fate was yet another consequence of Hugh Despenser the Younger's greed and tyranny; he had made his two sisters-in-law, the queen and numerous other men and women suffer, and now his wife and children suffered in return. The forced veiling of her daughters was probably also a consequence of Eleanor Despenser's own behaviour. In and after 1326, there is not the slightest hint of any residual affection for

Eleanor on Queen Isabella's part despite their many years of friendship, and Isabella seemed determined to make Eleanor pay for whatever wrongs she believed the other woman had committed.

Margaret Audley must have resumed her married life with Hugh Audley, and Hugh was also reunited with their daughter Margaret the younger. In early 1327 the little girl was about 5 or 6 years old and, unless Edward II had sent her to be raised elsewhere, had spent almost all her young life with her mother at Sempringham Priory. It is even possible that Hugh had never seen his daughter before. Margaret, the elder, was still only in her early 30s, but no more children would be born to the couple, and the younger Margaret was thus sole heir to one-third of the Clare inheritance. Hugh Audley was high in Queen Isabella's favour in early 1327: on 22 February, he was one of the men appointed to make a truce with her brother Charles IV of France, with the bishops of Winchester and Norwich and the Count of Hainault's brother John Beaumont. Hugh was at Montreuil-sur-Mer, capital of the county of Ponthieu (which had passed to Edward II from his mother and now belonged to his son) on 16 March 1327; perhaps Margaret travelled with him.[4] Audley also asked Queen Isabella for permission for his sister Alice, widow of Ralph, Lord Greystoke, to marry her second husband Ralph Neville, lord of Raby, and this was duly granted.[5] (Alice and Neville were to have many children; their son Alexander became archbishop of York, and their grandson Ralph Neville, the first Earl of Westmorland.) This demonstrates that Hugh Audley had access to the queen and that she was happy to grant him favours and appointments, and if Isabella knew or believed that Audley had been her husband's lover years before, she did not hold it against him. Hugh was also pardoned the forfeiture of his lands and goods in 1321 for breaking his oath to remain with Edward II, and he and Margaret were restored to their lands.[6] Another man close to the queen at the end of 1326 and start of 1327 was Sir Richard Damory, brother of the late Roger, Elizabeth Burgh's third husband. Isabella appointed Richard as justice of North Wales on 12 December 1326, which suggests she had no doubts about his loyalty to herself and her son.[7]

A parliament was held in London at the beginning of 1327, and Edward II was forced to abdicate his throne in favour of his 14-year-old son. This act, unprecedented in England, was presented in public as the king deciding to do so entirely voluntarily, and his subjects accepting his decision. The king's support had collapsed catastrophically, and his tyranny, greed and support of Hugh Despenser the Younger's extortions meant that his most powerful subjects, and even members of his own family, felt they had to take drastic measures to rid themselves of their failed ruler. Edward of Windsor would have become king eventually anyway when his father died, but Edward II was only 42 years old in early 1327 and might live for another twenty to twenty-five years. Nobody could wait that long, and so the succession was, in effect, sped up by forcing Edward II to give up his throne to his son. The coronation of the young King Edward III took place at Westminster Abbey on 1 February 1327, possibly attended by his first cousins Elizabeth Burgh and Margaret Audley, though Elizabeth had still not paid homage for her lands to the new king by 12 April 1327 and thus may not have been present.[8] Her uncle Sir Edward of Caernarfon, formerly King Edward II, was removed from the custody of his cousin Henry of Lancaster at Kenilworth Castle on 3 April 1327 and taken to Berkeley Castle in Gloucestershire. Nobody was entirely sure what to do with Edward of Caernarfon and about the unprecedented and embarrassing situation of a king being alive in the reign of his successor. Contrary to the fabrications of the chronicler Geoffrey le Baker writing in the 1350s, which have all too often been repeated as certain fact by later writers—although Baker was not writing an accurate narrative but pushing the idea of Edward of Caernarfon as an abused and patient saint in the interests of his canonisation—Edward was not mistreated at Berkeley Castle but had access to a chapel, good food and wine, and servants. His custodians at Berkeley were Thomas, Lord Berkeley (b. *c.* 1295), stepson of the Clare sisters' much older half-sister Isabella Clare, and Thomas Berkeley's brother-in-law Sir John Maltravers of Dorset, who in August 1321, at the parliament which exiled Hugh Despenser and his father, had been pardoned as an adherent of Roger Damory.[9]

Elizabeth Burgh's lordship of Usk, along with Caerleon and other manors which Hugh Despenser had taken from her, were formally restored to her on 26 February 1327 on the grounds that Despenser had 'flagrantly usurped royal power' and acquired the lands by force and duress.[10] Meanwhile in the Tower of London, Eleanor Despenser was believed to be in possession of some of the goods and chattels of the late Thomas, Earl of Lancaster, and in March 1327 was ordered to give them up to his executors.[11] Queen Isabella, who had wished to execute Eleanor's eldest son Huchon, finally gave up on 20 March 1327 after the garrison of Caerphilly Castle refused to surrender the young man to her. The siege of Caerphilly had dragged on for more than four months and had become too expensive. She pardoned Huchon 'of the forfeiture of his life', but he was to spend more than four years in prison.[12] Although Huchon was still heir to his mother's inheritance, or at least would be when he was finally pardoned and when Eleanor's Clare lands were restored to her, the Despenser lands of his father and grandfather were forfeit to the Crown. Hugh the Younger and his father the Earl of Winchester would not be pardoned for their treason until 1397, late in the reign of Edward II's great-grandson Richard II (r. 1377–99). Eleanor Despenser's half-uncle Edmund of Woodstock, Earl of Kent—who, curiously, was only about seven years older than his great-nephew Huchon Despenser—received many of the Despenser lands in 1327.

Sometime between 1 May and 16 November 1327 when he was 14 or 15 and she the same age or a little older, Elizabeth Burgh's son and heir William Burgh married Maud of Lancaster, third of the six daughters of Henry of Lancaster, Earl of Leicester and Lancaster.[13] Maud was a niece of the late Hugh Despenser the Younger via her late mother Maud Chaworth, Despenser's half-sister, though this was surely not a connection the Lancasters boasted about in and after 1327. Elizabeth Burgh herself probably had little choice in the matter of her son's bride—William's marriage was in the king's hands and was granted to Henry of Lancaster on 3 February 1327, presumably by Queen Isabella—but she may well have been consulted, and was surely happy about the match. Henry of Lancaster was the greatest nobleman in the country, the nephew of Elizabeth's grandfather Edward I, and was equally royal on his French mother Blanche of Artois's side; she had been a niece of King Louis IX of France (r. 1226–70) and was queen of Navarre (r. 1270–74) by her first marriage, and was Queen Isabella's grandmother. William's bride Maud was not an heiress as she had a brother, Henry of Grosmont, but was a member of the most prestigious family in England, and being Henry of Lancaster's son-in-law would be a huge advantage for William. At Lancaster's request, William was granted custody of his lands in England at the beginning of 1327, despite being well under age, and was already addressed as 'Earl of Ulster' by May 1328 when he was still only 15 years old.[14] The Lancasters were a very affectionate and close family, and William spent much time with them: in February 1328 he attended a jousting tournament with his brother-in-law Henry of Grosmont, and was with the Lancasters again in June 1328, the month after he was knighted.[15] Elizabeth Burgh showed her willingness to be allied to the Lancastrian faction in the late 1320s. Her first daughter Isabella Verdon married Earl Henry of Lancaster's close ally Henry, Lord Ferrers of Groby in Leicestershire, and her youngest stepdaughter Margery Verdon married Sir William Blount, Earl Henry's attorney.

Elizabeth Damory, Elizabeth Burgh's youngest child, also married in 1327 when she was still only a child (she was probably about 5 years old). Her husband was John Bardolf, heir to his father Thomas, Lord Bardolf of Wormegay in Norfolk, and they married sometime before 25 December 1327.[16] John was born in January 1312, so was a few years his wife's senior and almost 16 when they married. His father died in December 1329 and he inherited manors in eleven counties with the bulk of his inheritance in Norfolk, and his mother Agnes was said to be 'by birth of the parts of Almain', which meant Germany or somewhere close to it.[17] Young though his daughter-in-law Elizabeth was, before his death Thomas Bardolf settled three of his manors on her and his son jointly, perhaps at her mother's request.[18] Elizabeth Bardolf née Damory would inherit only half a dozen manors from her late father Roger, and Roger had held them jointly with his wife so that his daughter could only expect to receive them on her mother's death. Roger was not the Damory heir, and the family's dozen manors passed to his nephew Richard Damory (b. *c.* 1314), his elder brother Richard's son. Elizabeth Bardolf was therefore not as great a matrimonial catch as a more significant heiress would be, but she did bring her husband the huge benefit of close kinship to the king of England and was the half-sister of the Earl of Ulster, the greatest nobleman in Ireland. She probably remained in her mother's care for a few years after her wedding, being still a child, and her only son was born in 1349 (her two daughters may have been older). If Elizabeth Burgh's other Damory daughter, Margaret, ever married, there is no known record of it. Elizabeth's eldest daughter Isabella Verdon was heir to one-quarter of the sizeable Verdon inheritance, and hence made a rather better marriage than her half-sister Elizabeth Bardolf when she wed Henry, Lord Ferrers of Groby. As well as arranging a good match for her eldest daughter, in October 1333 four months after the death of her son and heir William, Elizabeth Burgh left almost all her Welsh lands including Usk and Caerleon, and her manor of Bardfield in Essex, to Isabella and her Ferrers husband.[19] Ultimately, however, neither Isabella nor Henry Ferrers benefited from this deal as they both died before Elizabeth.

Elizabeth Burgh's uncle Sir Edward of Caernarfon reportedly died at Berkeley Castle, Gloucestershire on 21 September 1327, though huge question marks were soon raised as to whether he was truly dead or not. He was buried at St Peter's Abbey in Gloucester, now Gloucester Cathedral, on 20 December. Elizabeth attended her uncle's funeral, leaving her young daughters in the care of Isabella Hastings, sister of the late Hugh Despenser the Younger.[20] Elizabeth was not a woman to bear a grudge, and evidently held no ill-will against Lady Hastings for what her brother had done to her. Little is known about Edward II's funeral, except that apart from his niece Elizabeth, his widow Isabella, his son Edward III, his half-brother the Earl of Kent, and Roger Mortimer attended. Before too long, Kent became convinced that Edward was still alive, and indeed it does appear that the former king's family had little if any chance to view his body. Margaret Audley was perhaps also there along with the late king's three younger children and his other half-brother the Earl of Norfolk, though the other Clare sister Eleanor Despenser was still imprisoned in the Tower. A royal wedding followed hard upon the royal funeral when the 15-year-old Edward III wed Philippa of Hainault in York Minster on 25 January 1328. As with his father's funeral, few details are known about the young king's wedding, but most probably his cousins Elizabeth Burgh and Margaret Audley were invited.

Eleanor Despenser was released from the Tower in or shortly before late February 1328, and on 26 February a month after his wedding to Philippa, Edward III ordered her to come to him in York. Her lands were still in the king's hands on 14 May that year, though on 22 April Edward III (or rather, someone acting in his name) had ordered all her lands in Wales, England and Ireland to be restored to her as it was 'not consonant with reason that her lands should be deemed forfeited by Hugh [Despenser]'s forfeiture'.[21] Eleanor's lands belonged to her by right and reverted to her after Hugh's death. They included the great lordship of Glamorgan,

Tewkesbury in Gloucestershire, Hanley in Worcestershire and Burford in Oxfordshire. Eleanor went to live at Hanley Castle, at least some of the time. Edward II had stayed there with Hugh and Eleanor herself in January 1324 and paid to rebuild the castle after the Despenser War, and perhaps Eleanor went to Hanley because it reminded her of both men. The castle had a great chamber called 'Grystenchambres' with rooms below, a hall with two stone towers attached to it, at least three other great chambers one of which was next to the hall, and four other towers to the south.[22] Sadly, Hanley Castle was already ruinous by the middle of the sixteenth century and not a stone of it exists today.

Eleanor had lost her husband, who was subjected to the most grotesque death imaginable, and the uncle with whom she had been extremely close and who may, though we will never know for sure, also have been her lover. Her eldest son Huchon was in prison and her middle three daughters Joan, Eleanor and Margaret were all now nuns whether they wished it or not, but she had her youngest sons Gilbert and John, her youngest daughter Elizabeth, and her eldest daughter Isabella and Isabella's infant son Edmund Fitzalan. Her second son Edward Despenser was perhaps as old as 16 when his father was executed in 1326 and was certainly at least 13, and therefore he was lucky, unlike Huchon, to avoid imprisonment at the hands of the new regime. Perhaps after his father and grandfather's downfall, a Despenser adherent such as Ingelram Berenger or John Haudlo kept Edward Despenser well out of sight and mind of Queen Isabella and Roger Mortimer.[23]

Chapter 20

Rebellion and Abduction

In 1328, it became increasingly obvious that the revolution of 1326/27 had merely replaced one greedy, despotic regime with another. Edward III's mother Isabella ruled the country during her son's minority with Roger Mortimer as her chief counsellor, though neither had been appointed to the regency council and hence appropriated royal power that was not theirs in the same way Hugh Despenser had. Isabella took the opportunity to grant herself an astonishingly large income and to take whatever lands she fancied, and Roger Mortimer also enriched himself hugely and treated the young king himself with increasing disrespect, remaining seated in his presence and walking ahead of him. Mortimer's creation of the grandiose earldom of March for himself in October 1328, on top of the 'shameful peace' the pair and their allies made with Scotland that summer, proved the final straw for many. Henry, Earl of Lancaster, emerged as the leader of the opposition. Most of the men who joined him were already members of his affinity, such as his son-in-law Thomas, Lord Wake (who had, however, played an important role in Edward II's deposition and was Roger Mortimer's first cousin); David Strathbogie, Earl of Atholl; Henry, Lord Beaumont; Henry, Lord Ferrers of Groby; Sir William Blount; and Sir Thomas Wyther. A surprising addition to Lancaster's circle of allies was Hugh Audley.[1] He had played a part in the downfall of the Despensers and Edward II who had imprisoned him and his wife Margaret for years, but like many others, Audley had grown sick of Isabella and Mortimer's unlawful wielding of power and endless greed.

Henry of Lancaster refused to attend the Salisbury parliament in October 1328 when Mortimer awarded himself the unprecedented earldom of March, and made a series of criticisms of the current state of the English government. Lancaster and his allies, including Audley, met at Winchester at the end of October 1328, and came close to clashing with the royal retinue as the king and his mother the dowager queen left Salisbury.

Margaret Audley looked on as her husband joined another rebellion against the rulers of the kingdom, and her sister Elizabeth must also have found events alarming: her son William Burgh was Henry of Lancaster's son-in-law, and her daughter Isabella Verdon and stepdaughter Margery Verdon were betrothed or already married to two of Lancaster's important followers, Henry Ferrers of Groby and William Blount. In early 1329, Lancaster and his allies including Hugh Audley went to Bedford 'armed to the terror of the people', and on 16 January their lands and goods were seized.[2]

Edward II's half-brothers, the earls of Norfolk and Kent, abandoned the Earl of Lancaster at the last moment, and Roger Mortimer went to Lancaster's town of Leicester and sacked it. The rebellion failed, and the chief rebels were forced to acknowledge liability for massive debts to the Crown and to swear humiliating oaths of future good behaviour. Henry of Lancaster's liability was £30,000, and Hugh Audley's £10,000, though they never paid any of it. (On 12 December 1330 after Edward III took over his own realm, the debts were cancelled, and soon afterwards he pardoned all the rebels.)[3] Hugh Audley was given protection to go overseas on 3 March 1329 and appointed attorneys on 12 April to act in his absence; he perhaps judged it politic to leave England for a while. He and Margaret might have gone to Ireland, as a year later when Audley was back in England, he appointed another attorney to act for him there.[4] Elizabeth Burgh, despite her strong connections to the Lancastrian faction, managed to remain in her aunt-in-law Queen Isabella's favour: in October 1329 she was pardoned a debt of 2,000 marks which her late husband Roger Damory had owed to the Exchequer.[5]

Eleanor Despenser was staying at her castle of Hanley in Worcestershire in early 1329 when she was abducted by the baron who had captured her uncle and husband in November 1326 and led the four-month siege of her son Huchon inside Caerphilly Castle: William Zouche, lord of Ashby in Leicestershire. The abduction took place shortly before 26 January 1329, when news of it reached the royal clerks who recorded it on the Patent Roll.[6] The two married, though as with Theobald Verdon and Eleanor's sister Elizabeth thirteen years before, it is unclear whether Eleanor consented to the marriage or not. Zouche had been appointed keeper of Eleanor's lordship of Glamorgan in May 1327, and through his marriage to her would become the outright owner of it and of the rest of her large inheritance, so it is hard to imagine there was much romance involved in his wish to marry her.[7] Somewhat bizarrely, the young nobleman Sir John Grey of Rotherfield (Oxfordshire) also began claiming to be married to Eleanor in early 1329, and the royal clerks recorded the abduction of his supposed wife from Hanley at the same time as recording the abduction of Hugh Despenser the Younger's widow Eleanor also from Hanley, evidently without realising they were the same person. Almost as bizarrely, Eleanor and her new husband William Zouche immediately rode the sixty-five miles to her castle of Caerphilly and began besieging it, presumably because it had not been released to her a few months earlier as it should have been, or because Eleanor believed her son Huchon was being held prisoner inside. Huchon had in fact been sent to Bristol Castle in December 1328, but the location of his incarceration prior to that is unknown, and Eleanor might not have been informed where he was. The siege reached the ears of the ruling regime on 5 February 1329, and a man called John Gynes was sent to arrest Eleanor. Roger Mortimer appointed himself to defend Caerphilly. It was still under siege by Eleanor and William on 8 March.[8]

William Zouche was the widower of Alice Toeni, Dowager Countess of Warwick, who had previously been married to Hugh Despenser the Younger's uncle Guy Beauchamp (d. 1315). Alice, who died in 1324, was the mother of William's children Alan and Joyce Zouche, half-siblings of the heir to the earldom of Warwick, Thomas Beauchamp. Marriage to the Dowager Countess of Warwick had been an excellent match for Zouche given that he was (like Eleanor's brothers-in-law Roger Damory and Hugh Audley before him) a second son and not an heir, and now he had made an even better one with a woman who was granddaughter, niece and first cousin of kings and one of the richest women in the country. 'Zouche' was the family name of William's mother Joyce, and he used it in preference to his father Robert's name, Mortimer; in documents of the era, he is usually called 'William la Zouche de Mortimer', though he was only distantly related to Roger Mortimer of Wigmore. He was much older than Eleanor; his date of birth is not known but was probably sometime in the 1270s, and his elder brother Hugh Mortimer of Richard's Castle in Herefordshire—who was apparently poisoned by his wife Maud in 1304— had two daughters the same age as William's new wife. As 'Sir William de Mortimer of Richard's Castle' before he adopted his mother's name, he fought for Edward I at the Battle of Falkirk in July 1298 when Eleanor was not yet 6 years old, and by the autumn of 1304 had begun calling himself 'William la Zouche'.[9]

Eleanor Despenser's marriage to William Zouche produced a son, the tenth and youngest of her children to survive into adulthood. He was named William after his father, and must have been born around 1330 when Eleanor was in her late 30s and her husband over 50. In the 1350s, William the younger rented the Oxfordshire manor of Bletchingdon from his aunt Elizabeth Burgh, and became a monk at Glastonbury Abbey in Somerset sometime before February 1361 when his kinsman Edward III granted the abbot of Glastonbury 10 marks a year during William's lifetime. One of the Despensers, either Eleanor's son Huchon or her grandson Edward (b. 1336), gave William an annual gift of 100 shillings. William Zouche the monk was still alive and a monk of Glastonbury— and still receiving the 100 shillings from his Despenser kin annually—on 6 December 1390 when he must have been about 60 years old; otherwise, he is entirely obscure, and nothing is known of him. The chronicle of Tewkesbury Abbey states that Eleanor had a son called Hugh Zouche, and although it would be fascinating if Eleanor defiantly named a child from her second marriage after her disgraced first husband, the chronicler's statement seems to be a mix-up; her second husband's son and heir Alan from his first marriage to Alice Toeni had a son called Hugh Zouche born in 1338.[10]

Sir John Grey of Rotherfield began claiming Eleanor as his wife in early 1329, and continued to maintain for four-and-a-half years that they were married. Why he did so is not known; perhaps they had made an informal arrangement to wed, or had been having an affair. Born on 29 October 1300, Grey was eight years Eleanor's junior, and was already a widower with one son. He first appears on record as an adult when he took part in Edward II's last and disastrous campaign to Scotland in August 1322.[11] Grey was determined to be the husband of Eleanor the wealthy and well-connected widow, even though she was now married to William Zouche. Bad feeling persisted between the two men. Early in 1332 they were involved in an altercation so acrimonious that Grey came close to drawing a dagger on Zouche in front of Edward III, whereupon he was imprisoned and his lands taken into Edward's hands because of 'grave excesses which he feared not to commit in the presence of the king'.

In October 1331, Zouche accused Grey and his men of stealing his goods and six of his horses at Lechlade in Gloucestershire.[12] In the middle of May 1333, more than four years after Eleanor's marriage to Zouche, John Grey persisted in his claim that Eleanor was his rightful wife, and took the matter to Pope John XXII in Avignon. The bishop of Coventry and Lichfield found in William Zouche's favour, and confirmed his marriage to Eleanor Despenser.[13] Grey did marry again and had two more children with his second wife Avice, was a founder member of Edward III's great chivalric order the Knights of the Garter in 1348, and was made steward of the king's household in or before 1349, so in the end did not do too badly, despite losing out on marriage to the wealthy Eleanor Despenser.

Eleanor's abduction and forced marriage, assuming that is what it was, was not the end of her woes. Sometime after 24 June 1329 when she was addressed as lady of Glamorgan and was seemingly in royal favour, and before 30 December 1329, she was arrested again. She was charged with removing cash, jewels, and other high-value goods from the Tower of London.[14] This situation is somewhat mysterious. It may be that Eleanor had taken some of her late husband's possessions, which belonged to Queen Isabella, out of the Tower; it may be that the matter had something to do with the late Thomas of Lancaster's goods in her possession there, as in March 1327 she had been ordered to give them up to his executors; it may even be that the charge was fabricated as an excuse to deprive her of her lands again. It had become increasingly scandalous by late 1329 that Edward III's wife Philippa of Hainault did not have any lands of her own—the young queen was deprived of her rightful position by her mother-in-law Isabella and had not even been crowned yet—and Eleanor's lands were used to provide Philippa with a dower. Eleanor's lordship of Glamorgan was confiscated again and given to Philippa on 12 February 1330, six days before Philippa's belated coronation as queen of England when she was already five months pregnant with her first child, and more than two years after her wedding. Philippa also received the castle and town of Pontefract in Yorkshire which should have gone to Henry, Earl of Lancaster in 1327 but which was taken by his niece Queen Isabella. Isabella helped herself to Eleanor Despenser's manors of Tewkesbury and Hanley in February 1330 as compensation for losing Pontefract to her daughter-in-law. Later in 1330, the dowager queen and her son Edward III stayed at various manors forfeited by Eleanor.[15]

Eleanor did not only lose lands to Queen Philippa (not, in fairness, by any doing of the young queen herself), her former damsel Emma Prior had entered Philippa's household by 24 June 1328, and was joined there by Piers Gaveston's illegitimate daughter Amie by 28 January 1332.[16] Emma had, rather curiously, already retired and been sent to a convent (as was usually the case with retired royal servants) in 1325, but must have decided to come out of retirement and serve the new queen.[17]

According to a petition Eleanor presented to Edward III after he overthrew his mother, she was imprisoned for a while at Devizes Castle in Wiltshire, though was free and at court—whether voluntarily or not— at Guildford in Surrey around mid or late February 1330 shortly after her lands were confiscated. Two servants accompanying her were named as Thomas Tyverton and Hugh Dalby.[18] It may not be a coincidence, given the accusation of theft from the Tower of London, that her new husband William Zouche was constable of the Tower until 31 January 1329, when he was replaced by Sir John Cromwell a few days after the government found out that he had abducted and married Eleanor.[19] Perhaps Zouche helped her remove the jewels and other items from the Tower, though he was only officially appointed to the position on 9 May 1328, a few weeks after her release.[20]

Eleanor, who had been so safe for so long as King Edward II's cosseted niece and as the wife of his despotic favourite, and who had certainly been a willing participant in Despenser's crimes, was now experiencing what her younger sisters had gone through at the hands of her husband and uncle and realising how vulnerable wealthy women could be without a powerful male protector. Queen Isabella, her former close companion for so many years, not only did not lift a finger to help Eleanor but took two of her manors for herself and deprived her of her lordship of Glamorgan. Between 1322 and 1325 Isabella still voluntarily spent much time with Eleanor after Eleanor's husband Hugh had, so Isabella believed, deliberately left her in danger at Tynemouth Priory and persuaded the king to confiscate her lands. This seems to demonstrate that she did not hold Eleanor responsible for her husband's misdeeds. The actions of the dowager queen against Eleanor in 1326/27 and again in 1329/30, and her absolute refusal to protect her, were not, therefore, a consequence of Isabella's loathing for the late Hugh Despenser the Younger but were based on something Eleanor herself had done which roused Isabella's ire. Eleanor was pardoned for the theft of the goods from the Tower on 22 February 1330, ten days after her lands were given to Queen Philippa, and it was promised that the lands would be restored to her as soon as she and William Zouche or her heirs paid £50,000 in one instalment.[21] This was, of course, completely impossible even for a woman of Eleanor's means, the equivalent of asking someone in modern times to pay hundreds of millions or even billions in cash in one sum.

Chapter 21

The King Lives

How much contact the Clare sisters had with their younger Monthermer half-siblings at this stage of their lives is not known, but good news came in the late 1320s: their niece Margaret Monthermer, daughter and heir of Thomas Monthermer, was born at Thomas's manor of Stokenham in Devon on 18 October 1329. The proud father celebrated by hunting two does in his park there.[1] Margaret Monthermer and her cousin Isabella MacDuff, heir to the earldom of Fife, were the only two grandchildren of Joan of Acre and her second husband Ralph Monthermer. Margaret's mother, also Margaret, had been married before she wed Thomas Monthermer; her first husband was Sir Henry Tyes, executed as an adherent of Roger Damory in 1322. This perhaps suggests that Thomas Monthermer had sympathised with his half-sister Elizabeth Burgh and her third husband during the Contrariant rebellion of 1321/22. Thomas also supported the rebellion of Henry, Earl of Lancaster and Leicester, in late 1328 and early 1329, with his brother-in-law Hugh Audley.[2]

Elizabeth Burgh's eldest daughter Isabella Verdon, another grandchild of Joan of Acre, married Henry, Lord Ferrers of Groby sometime in the late 1320s or 1330. Ferrers acknowledged a debt of 500 marks to Elizabeth Burgh on 4 May 1328, which probably had something to do with the marriage, and visited her.[3] He was much his wife's senior, born in 1304 at the latest and perhaps in the 1290s, while she was born in March 1317. At an unknown date, Henry Ferrers presented a petition complaining that the royal favourite Roger Mortimer, Earl of March, had engineered an unfair division of the Verdon estate to the benefit of Isabella's older half-sisters Joan Furnival, Elizabeth Burghersh and Margery Blount.[4] These three young women were Mortimer's nieces, daughters of his late sister Maud, while Isabella herself was not. Isabella Ferrers née Verdon gave birth for the first time in February 1331 before she was even 14 years old, and Elizabeth Burgh sent a book costing £36 as a gift for her daughter's purification in March 1331.[5] Not surprisingly given Isabella's extreme youth, the child did not survive, and it is unclear whether it was a boy or a girl. Henry Ferrers had claimed his marital rights very early, and he and Isabella were lucky that she was not damaged by this experience of pregnancy and childbirth at such a young age and went on to bear other, healthy children.

Edward II's half-brother Edmund of Woodstock, Earl of Kent, had attended the former king's funeral in Gloucester in December 1327. Probably in 1328, the young man became convinced that Edward was still alive and being held somewhere in captivity, probably at Corfe Castle in Dorset. Kent spent much of 1329 and early 1330 looking for allies to help him free his brother and perhaps restore him to the throne, and was joined by numerous important men such as the archbishop of York, the bishop, mayor and sheriff of London, the Earl of Mar (in Scotland), various lords and sheriffs, and numerous others including former members of Edward II's household. Edward II's old friend Sir William Aune was another man who came to believe that he was alive, and on 24 May 1329 Aune had been appointed constable of Eleanor Despenser's castle of Caerphilly.[6]

Eleanor's son Huchon, in prison at Bristol Castle, offered his great-uncle the Earl of Kent his support, and so did the Clare sisters' half-brother Edward Monthermer (b. 1304) and Eleanor's son-in-law Richard Fitzalan (b. c. 1313), son of the Earl of Arundel executed in 1326. One surprising member of the Earl of Kent's faction was Eleanor's new husband William Zouche. There is no doubt that Zouche had been one of Queen Isabella's staunchest allies during the revolution of 1326/27, but apparently his marriage to Eleanor caused him to switch sides, and probably he was, like so many of the queen's former allies such as Hugh Audley, Thomas Wake and Henry Beaumont, dismayed by the grasping and self-interested regime of the late 1320s. The Earl of Kent, with numerous others, attended the belated coronation of the pregnant Queen Philippa at Westminster Abbey on 18 February 1330. Kent was dramatically arrested in Winchester on 13 March, and three days later made a long confession naming some of his important adherents in the matter of Edward of Caernarfon's ongoing captivity. He stated that he had met some of them while staying at Kensington at the time of the queen's coronation.

The Earl of Kent's confession shows that Sir Ingelram Berenger, a former sheriff of Buckinghamshire who served in the retinue of Eleanor Despenser's father-in-law Hugh Despenser the Elder for decades, vouched for the trustworthiness of William Zouche to him. Berenger and Zouche jointly acknowledged a debt to a rich merchant of London called John Pulteney on 15 March 1329, just days after Zouche and Eleanor Despenser had besieged her castle of Caerphilly. This might give some indication as to when the two men met and discussed the matter of Edward II's potential survival.[7] Kent and Zouche rode together the six miles between Woking and Guildford in Surrey on an unknown date as they discussed the issue, and Zouche told Kent to 'avoid the town of Guildford by reason of his niece [Eleanor] Despenser who was in the same town of Guildford'.[8] This is rather puzzling, as if Edward II were truly still alive, Eleanor would certainly have been one of the people most supportive of any efforts to help the uncle she had been so close to, and her eldest son, son-in-law, half-brother and husband were involved in the plot. Edward III was also at Guildford in Surrey from 23 to 28 February 1330, after his wife Philippa's belated coronation.[9] Eleanor Despenser's lands were confiscated on 12 February and she was pardoned on the 22nd, so it makes sense that she would have been in the king's company at this time. Her proximity to the king and his mother the dowager queen Isabella was presumably the reason why Kent was warned to avoid talking to her, and perhaps Zouche also wished to keep his wife out of further trouble given that she had enough problems already. The men secretly trying to aid Edward of Caernarfon and free him from captivity, perhaps even restore him to his lost throne, were risking a great deal—arrest or exile, forfeiture of all lands and goods, even execution—and they knew it.

An order was issued for the arrest of William Zouche and two other adherents of the Earl of Kent on 10 March 1330, three days before Kent himself was even arrested. The order was repeated on 18 March.[10] Zouche's lands and goods were seized, but restored to him on 10 April.[11] The Earl of Kent himself, who was the son, brother and uncle of kings, was beheaded in Winchester on 19 March 1330 for the 'crime' of trying to free a dead man from captivity. Many of his allies, including his brother-in-law Thomas Wake, Ingelram Berenger, and Eleanor Despenser's son-in-law Richard Fitzalan, fled the country, and Eleanor's half-brother Edward Monthermer was imprisoned in Winchester.[12] The archbishop of

York was indicted before King's Bench, the Earl of Kent's heavily pregnant widow Margaret Wake and their young children were imprisoned, and some of the earl's supporters who had fled abroad plotted an invasion of England from the continent in the summer of 1330. Whether Edward of Caernarfon truly was still alive is a matter for speculation, but certainly a lot of important men in 1329/30 acted as though they believed he was. Eleanor Despenser's opinion on the matter cannot be determined, but to hear that her uncle might still be alive, after she had perhaps come to terms with his and her first husband's downfall and death, must have been unsettling one way or the other. She may well have been pregnant at the time, given that her youngest child William Zouche the younger was born *c*. 1330.

In Ireland, meanwhile, Elizabeth Burgh's 17-year-old son William, Earl of Ulster, was feuding with Thomas FitzMaurice, Earl of Desmond. Edward III, or someone in his name, ordered the two men to cease making assemblies of armed men and attacking each other's lands on 19 June 1330.[13] Four days earlier, Queen Philippa had given birth to her and the king's first child, a son called Edward of Woodstock who immediately became heir to the throne. Edward III granted a yearly income of 40 marks to his servant Thomas Prior for bringing him news of his son's birth.[14] The young king, still only 17 (he was two months younger than William Burgh), visited his cousin Elizabeth Burgh on 22 August 1330 at Caythorpe in Lincolnshire, a manor she had held jointly with Roger Damory and which later passed to her and Roger's daughter Elizabeth and her husband John Bardolf.[15] Edward III was chafing against his mother Isabella's rule and longing to rule in his own right. On 19 October 1330, he had Roger Mortimer dramatically arrested at Nottingham Castle: Edward and twenty or so young knights used a secret tunnel into the castle and rushed into the room where Queen Isabella was holding a meeting with Mortimer and their few remaining allies. Some of the young knights were, and for many years would continue to be, Edward III's closest allies and friends. They included William Montacute, son of Edward II's great favourite of the same name who died in Gascony in 1319, and Ralph Stafford, who in 1336 would become Hugh and Margaret Audley's son-in-law.

Roger Mortimer was hanged at Tyburn on 29 November 1330, four years almost to the day since he had had Hugh Despenser the Younger grotesquely executed in Hereford. The dowager queen Isabella was committed to comfortable house arrest for a while, though spent Christmas 1330 with her son and daughter-in-law Philippa, and was made to give up her absurdly large income and the lands belonging to other people she had granted herself. Edward III invited all the adherents of the Earl of Kent who had fled from the country to come home, and pardoned everyone who had taken part in Kent's plot earlier in the year, including William Zouche. Richard Fitzalan was one of them and was restored to his executed father Edmund's inheritance, and days after the coup, the king appointed Hugh Audley's brother-in-law Ralph Neville as the steward of his household. After the turbulent and dramatic decades of Edward II's reign and its aftermath, things were finally returning to normal.

Chapter 22

A Belated Funeral

Edward III gave permission on 15 December 1330 for the 'friends of Hugh' to collect Hugh Despenser the Younger's remains from London Bridge, Bristol, Dover, York and Carlisle and to bury them honourably.[1] Even though she was married to her second husband and bore a child this year, Eleanor Despenser must have taken charge of her late husband's burial. Hugh was interred at Tewkesbury Abbey which stood on her own lands and where her brother, father, grandfather and other Clare ancestors were buried. In 2004, several bones of a medieval man who appeared to have suffered the traitor's death, excavated on land where Hulton Abbey in Staffordshire had once stood, were examined. The Audley family had been patrons of Hulton, and it was speculated that Hugh and Margaret Audley buried their brother-in-law Hugh Despenser the Younger there.[2] This is basically impossible; Despenser was the last person in the country to whom Hugh Audley would have given Christian burial on his own land, and he is far more likely to have had Despenser's bones flung into the nearest river. It also seems to have been Hugh Audley's brother James and nephew the younger James who were patrons of Hulton, not Hugh himself.[3] There is no reason to doubt that Eleanor Despenser buried her husband at Tewkesbury Abbey, and his tomb in the ambulatory behind the high altar, much vandalised centuries later at the Dissolution, can still be seen there. In 1349, his and Eleanor's eldest son Huchon was buried in the same position on the other side of the altar.

In January 1331, Edward III restored Glamorgan, Tewkesbury and Hanley to Eleanor Despenser and William Zouche on condition that they pay him £10,000, of which he almost immediately respited half.[4] By 5 April 1332 they had paid £1,333 of it, and were meant to pay instalments of 250 marks twice yearly, though in January 1333 this was reduced to 100 marks twice yearly.[5] The king stated that he was making this grant of her lands to his cousin to 'ease his conscience' which suggests he realised how badly his mother and Roger Mortimer had treated Eleanor.[6] (Eleanor's first husband and uncle had of course treated plenty of people equally badly, including her two sisters, but the revolution of 1326/27 was meant to have ushered in a more just era.) Much of the money was still unpaid when Eleanor and Zouche died.[7]

Also in January 1331, William Zouche was appointed as one of the mainpernors of Roger Mortimer's son Geoffrey, arrested with Roger at Nottingham in October 1330 but soon released, and the mainpernors promised to ensure that he 'shall behave himself well in the king's realm'.[8] Despite his and Eleanor's wealth, William Zouche frequently borrowed large sums of money in the early 1330s, which indicates that he lived well beyond his means. John Hotham, bishop of Ely, lent him £2,000 in May 1333, and another debt of £1,000 acknowledged by Zouche in 1333 was to Benedict Fulsham, a rich and important merchant of London who had been involved in Eleanor Despenser's supposed theft of jewels from the Tower of London. In January 1331 Fulsham was alleged to have received the jewels from Eleanor, and was ordered not to leave London.[9] Zouche and six other men acknowledged a joint debt of £2,900 to John Pulteney, merchant and mayor of London, in February 1331. One of the six men was Elizabeth Burgh's close adherent Sir Robert Chedworth, who, with his brother Thomas, still served Elizabeth into the late 1330s.[10] As well as the joint debt acknowledged with Robert Chedworth, Zouche appointed Robert as one of his attorneys in April 1332 when he went overseas on the king's service.[11] This connection suggests that there may have been rather more contact between Eleanor Despenser and her sister Elizabeth Burgh than is visible in extant records. Elizabeth sent Eleanor cloth in 1330/31, though apart from this, the payments Elizabeth made to her eldest sister for the lordship of Usk and the association of Zouche and Chedworth, there is little or no evidence of any real closeness.[12] Given the way Eleanor had encouraged and supported her husband Hugh's schemes in the 1320s, including against Elizabeth, this is hardly surprising.

Hugh Audley, high in the young king's favour and pardoned for his role in the Earl of Lancaster's 1328/29 rebellion, was named as a knight banneret of Edward's household in 1330, and appointed as one of the men sent to treat with Philip VI, king of France (r. 1328–50), in January 1331. The envoys were to 'treat of the mutual debts of the two kings' and to 'treat of all matters in dispute'.[13] The Earl of Lancaster, the king's great-uncle and also forgiven for his rebellion, was another of the envoys who travelled with Audley, and Margaret may have travelled with her husband.[14] A treaty with Philip VI's envoys was signed on 9 March 1331, and the following month the two kings met in person at Pont-Sainte-Maxence after Edward III left England secretly and disguised as a merchant. Shortly before Hugh Audley's departure, he and Margaret asked for Edward II's grants of various manors to them in July 1319 to be exemplified and confirmed, as their original documents 'had been stolen from them with other muniments in the quarrel of Thomas, Earl of Lancaster' (i.e. during and after the Contrariant rebellion of 1321/22).[15]

Elizabeth Burgh was at her manor of Clare in Suffolk in January 1331 when her brother-in-law Audley travelled overseas, and received a visit from her kinswoman and friend of many years, Marie de St Pol, Dowager Countess of Pembroke (*c.* 1303–77). Marie, like the Clare sisters, was a great-granddaughter of Henry III and hence their second cousin, and was the widow of Aymer Valence, Earl of Pembroke, himself a nephew of Henry III and decades Marie's senior. Marie had also been a victim of Hugh Despenser the Younger after her husband's death in June 1324, when Despenser tried to keep some of her dower lands for himself.[16] Elizabeth became a grandmother for the first time in February 1331 when her daughter Isabella Ferrers née Verdon, not yet 14, bore a child who did not survive. Elizabeth herself was 35.

Eleanor Despenser's eldest son and heir Hugh 'Huchon' Despenser was finally released from prison at Bristol Castle on 5 July 1331 after almost five years of imprisonment since his father left him at Caerphilly at the end of October 1326, when a dozen knights mainperned to produce him before his cousin the king at the parliament to be held at the end of September 1331. One of the knights was Hugh Audley's brother-in-law Sir Ralph Neville, steward of Edward III's household, which perhaps indicates that there was some measure of sympathy in the Audley family for their Despenser nephew, however much they had loathed his father. Two others were Sir Eble Lestrange (d. 1335) and Sir Richard Talbot, both married to women—Alice Lacy and Elizabeth Comyn respectively— who had been victims of Hugh Despenser the Younger's extortion in 1322 and 1324/25. A fourth was Sir John Ros, perhaps the man of this name who was beaten up by Huchon's father at the Lincoln parliament of early 1316. This all suggests a pleasing lack of vindictiveness on the men's part, and a willingness to allow a young nobleman to prove himself and not to visit the sins of his father upon his head.[17] Huchon petitioned the king pointing out that he had been pardoned of the forfeiture of life and limb for holding Caerphilly Castle against Queen Isabella, and enclosed a copy of the pardon with his petition.[18] There was perhaps a measure of defiance in Huchon naming himself 'Hugh son of Hugh Despenser' in the petition, and the young man must have wondered why he alone had not been released or pardoned when Edward III set matters straight after the downfall of Isabella and Roger Mortimer and did his best to heal the wounds of the previous few years. (His mother Eleanor chose to retain the name of her first husband throughout her second marriage.) Huchon appeared before parliament as requested, and was officially pardoned on 30 September 1331.[19] He was now 22 or 23 years old, and for all his high birth and close family relationship to the king of England—whom he had known well years before when they were boys—he had an awful lot of work to do to restore his and his family's reputation. He bore the name Hugh Despenser, the most reviled name in England in the late 1320s and 1330s.

Eleanor Despenser and William Zouche went overseas in May 1332 as part of the retinue of Edward III's sister Eleanor of Woodstock, elder of the two daughters of Edward II and Isabella of France, and Eleanor Despenser's first cousin.[20] Eleanor of Woodstock was not quite 14 years old, and was marrying Count Reynald II of Guelders, in the modern-day Netherlands close to the German border, a man who was decades her senior and had four daughters from his first marriage. The party left London on 1 May, sailed from Dover on 5 May and returned to London on 11 June after attending the wedding in Nijmegen. The twins Edward and William Bohun, nephews of Edward II and thus first cousins of both Eleanors, also went, and so did, interestingly, Hugh Audley and his brother-in-law Ralph Neville, and John Grey, presumably the man of this name who was still claiming Eleanor Despenser as his wife.[21] Eleanor's son Huchon also accompanied them. Apparently the young man had not yet been knighted, as his name was not followed by the word 'knight' in the list unlike those of several other men accompanying William Zouche.[22] Earlier that year, however, Edward III had promised to give Huchon 200 marks of lands and rents a year. This was a small income for such a high-ranking nobleman, but it was at least a first step on Despenser's long journey to prove himself and to restore his reputation, as was Edward's courteously acknowledging him as 'the king's kinsman'. To provide him with the promised income, the king granted Despenser three manors, Freeby in Lincolnshire and Mapledurwell and Ashley in Hampshire, all of which had once belonged to his grandfather Hugh Despenser the Elder.[23] Despenser was said in late April 1332 to be going on pilgrimage to Santiago de Compostela in northern Spain, a journey he presumably undertook after the visit to Nijmegen.[24] He had certainly been knighted when he participated in a jousting tournament in Dunstable sometime in Edward III's seventh regnal year, probably in January 1334, when he appears as *Monsire* [Sir] *Hugh le Despenser* in the list of participants, carrying the Despenser coat of arms. Another knight at Dunstable was Sir John Grey of Rotherfield, who a few months previously had finally given up his claim to be married to Huchon's mother.[25]

As Hugh Audley went on the journey to Nijmegen, doubtless his wife Margaret did too. One wonders what Eleanor Despenser found to say to her sister and brother-in-law, and what her husband Zouche and her putative husband Grey found to say to each other. Grey had not yet given up his claim that Eleanor was rightfully his wife (even though she had borne Zouche a child by then), and the journey to Nijmegen took place mere weeks after Grey came close to stabbing Zouche, so the situation must have been very awkward. This journey is one of the very few pieces of evidence we have of contact between Eleanor Despenser and Margaret Audley after Hugh Despenser the Younger forced the Audleys to sign over their lordship of Gwynllŵg to him in 1318. Perhaps the Clare sisters were willing to let bygones be bygones, or perhaps events of the late 1310s and 1320s had left a legacy of bitterness which they could not overcome. Margaret must have been aware that her older sister had stayed at her castle of Tonbridge several times while she herself had been incarcerated in a convent, and that Eleanor had been incredibly close to the man who ordered her incarceration, perhaps even his lover. Relations were somewhat better between the Audleys and Elizabeth Burgh, though not especially friendly: Hugh Audley sent his sister-in-law occasional letters and visited her in June 1339, while she seems to have visited him eight years later. There is little, however, to demonstrate any closeness between Margaret and Elizabeth other than a few letters exchanged between 1338 and 1342.[26]

Edward II's sister Mary, the reluctant and rather secular nun of Amesbury Priory and aunt of the three Clare sisters, died at the age of 53 on 29 May 1332, just days after her niece Eleanor of Woodstock married her much older husband hundreds of miles away. Mary may, or may not, have been the last surviving child of Edward I and Leonor of Castile; it is unclear when her older sister Margaret, Duchess of Brabant died, and although her younger brother Edward II had officially been dead since September 1327, there is evidence that he lived for years past that date. The only child of Edward I who certainly outlived Mary was her much younger half-brother Thomas of Brotherton, Earl of Norfolk, elder of the two sons of Edward I and Marguerite of France, who lived until 1338. Mary and Thomas's nephew King Edward III planned a visit to Ireland in the summer of 1332, though in the end the Battle of Dupplin Moor in Scotland, where an English army won a surprise victory that August, overtook his plans and he did not depart. Among the men the king ordered to accompany him to Ireland were William Zouche and Hugh Audley, Elizabeth Burgh's son-in-law Henry Ferrers and all three husbands of her Verdon stepdaughters, and Hugh Despenser the Younger's nephew Amaury St Amand.[27] The division of the late Theobald Verdon's inheritance into four parts for his four daughters continued to cause problems which were made worse after Elizabeth Burgh's daughter Isabella Verdon came of age (14, because she was already married) in March 1331, and perhaps the king thought it wise to have all four Verdon husbands under his eye.[28]

Chapter 23

Death of an Earl

Elizabeth Burgh, still only 36 years old, became a grandmother for the second time on 6 July 1332, when William Burgh and Maud of Lancaster's daughter was born in Ireland and named Elizabeth in her honour. Exactly eleven months later, on 6 June 1333, 20-year-old William was murdered near Belfast. The assassination was carried out by some of his own vassals on the orders of Gylle, widow of William's cousin Walter Burgh, whom he had starved to death in captivity. William's widow Maud fled back to England with her baby daughter, and may have given birth to twins later in 1333: there are references on the Patent Roll in 1338 and 1340 to two other daughters of William Burgh. In July 1338, mention is made of 'Isabella, daughter and heir of William, late Earl of Ulster', and in June 1340 Edward III gave the marriage of 'Margaret, daughter and heir of William Burgh, Earl of Ulster' to his brother-in-law Reynald of Guelders, for the use of Reynald and Eleanor of Woodstock's second son Eduard (b. 1336).[1] Assuming the girls existed and are not clerical errors, they cannot have lived long past 1340, as young Elizabeth Burgh was the sole heir of her father and of her grandmother the elder Elizabeth. Elizabeth Burgh the elder became a grandmother again in February 1333 when William Ferrers, eldest surviving child of her daughter Isabella Verdon, was born. Isabella was still not 16 years old, and had already given birth twice. She had a daughter Elizabeth Ferrers born around the mid-1330s, who later became Countess of Atholl, at least nominally; the earldom lay in Scotland, but her husband's family lived in England and did not hold the lands they claimed to own. Another daughter, Philippa Ferrers, would have become Countess of Warwick, but her husband Guy Beauchamp died in his father's lifetime.

Hugh Audley, in the 1330s, enjoyed a friendship with Isabella of Lancaster, second of the six daughters of Henry, Earl of Lancaster and sister-in-law of Elizabeth Burgh's late son William. Isabella—who had gone on pilgrimage with Elizabeth Burgh and her aunt Mary as a child in 1317—became a nun at the ever-popular Amesbury Priory in Wiltshire in 1327, but often left the priory to visit her father and siblings at Earl Henry's castles of Kenilworth and Tutbury. Isabella of Lancaster's accounts happen to survive for a few months in the early 1330s, and reveal that she and Audley frequently sent each other letters, and even exchanged greyhounds for hunting. Audley sent Isabella a gift of expensive lampreys on two occasions, while she gave gifts to the marshal of his hall and wrote to his steward of Heytesbury in Wiltshire.[2] As Isabella of Lancaster was veiled as a nun and later became prioress of Amesbury, this was clearly not a romantic affair, but appears to have been a genuine and perhaps rather unexpected friendship. Isabella of Lancaster also left Amesbury on one occasion to visit her aunt Isabella, Lady Hastings (d. 1334), a woman on good terms with Elizabeth Burgh.

On 29 September 1333, Hugh Audley was said to be going overseas on pilgrimage.[3] There is no mention of his wife Margaret accompanying him (though as married women rarely appear in records relating to their husbands, she may well have done) or where he went; perhaps to Santiago de Compostela in northern Spain, an enormously popular pilgrim destination. One of the two men Hugh appointed to act as his attorneys in his absence was his elder brother James Audley, and he intended to be overseas until two weeks after Easter 1334. Hugh Audley's desire to go on pilgrimage and leave the country for a while might have been a result of a feud he was involved in with his brother-in-law William Zouche. Apparently as prone to quarrelling as Eleanor Despenser's first husband had been, Zouche was 'making gatherings and meetings of armed men' in both Wales and England 'by reason of the dissensions between him and Hugh Daudele [Audley]'. Edward III ordered both men to cease threatening each other on 19 August 1333.[4] Somewhat ironically, William Zouche had been appointed to 'keep the king's peace in the land of Wales' on 26 June that year.[5]

On the same day as the record on the Patent Roll relating to his pilgrimage, Audley was pardoned a debt of £12,000 which he had acknowledged to Hugh Despenser father and son fifteen years before and which had fallen to the king by the Despensers' forfeiture. Elizabeth Burgh must have noted this with some interest, as she also asked shortly afterwards for her late husband Roger Damory's own debt of £12,000 to the Despensers to be pardoned. In June 1334, it was. Hugh Despenser father and son, Hugh Audley, Roger Damory and William Montacute had all acknowledged debts to each other of £6,000 in 1318, which perhaps represented a mutual alliance against Thomas, Earl of Lancaster, Edward II's powerful cousin. Audley and Elizabeth were pardoned the £12,000 which Audley and Damory owed to the two Hugh Despensers because, so they claimed, the 'recognisances were made under compulsion' and were obtained 'by force against his [Audley's] will'.[6] The two did not explain how their brother-in-law and his father were able to coerce Audley and Damory into making the recognisances to them before Despenser the Younger became a powerful royal favourite; claiming that they had was simply a convenient way to absolve themselves of the enormous debt.

Edward III spent much time on campaign against Scotland in the 1330s; its king, David II (b. 1324, r. 1329–71), was in fact his brother-in-law, but Edward had had no say in the marriage of his youngest sibling Joan of the Tower to the young David in 1328 and strenuously objected to it. One English nobleman who played little part in his cousin the king's wars in Scotland and France was John Bohun, Earl of Hereford, eldest son of Edward II's sister Elizabeth. Elizabeth Burgh was named after Hereford's mother, her aunt, and the earl visited her at Clare for a couple of days in May 1334 and again later in the year. She had a gold ring made for him in 1333.[7] The third Bohun brother William later became Earl of Northampton, and the second, Humphrey, succeeded the childless John as Earl of Hereford in 1336. Humphrey, like his older brother, seems to have suffered from some long-term illness or disability, and like John played no part in Edward III's wars. Their brother Northampton was, however, one of the king's chief commanders and an early member of the king's chivalric order the Knights of the Garter at the end of the 1340s. He visited his cousin Elizabeth Burgh often, and the two frequently exchanged letters and gifts. In 1339/40, Elizabeth paid over £7 for a palfrey horse for Northampton, called Grisel Pomeld, and was clearly extremely fond of her Bohun cousins including their sister Margaret Courtenay, Countess of Devon.[8]

The intensely masculine and intensely militaristic nature of Edward III's regime created numerous exciting opportunities for noblemen to fight, both in wars in Scotland and France and also on the jousting field. Edward II had often banned tournaments and himself never participated in a jousting contest (that we know of), but his son, who both as a man and a king was far more conventional than his father by the standards of the fourteenth century, adored jousting and both held and personally took part in many tournaments. As women, the Clare sisters could not of course participate in such events and their husbands were rather too old to do so, especially William Zouche. Life in Edward III's reign was vastly easier for the sisters than it had been in his father's and during the regime of his mother Isabella from 1327 to 1330, but they were also much less caught up in political events and the life of the court.

Chapter 24

A Third Abduction and a Death

Sometime not long before 28 February 1336, Margaret and Hugh Audley's only child and heir Margaret Audley the younger was abducted from their manor of Thaxted in Essex. The abduction was recorded on the Patent Roll on 28 February, when Edward III ordered two men to investigate what had happened.[1] It seems highly likely that at this point, neither Hugh and Margaret nor the king had any idea where their daughter was, or who was responsible for breaking into their manor and abducting her as well as stealing some of their goods. By 6 July 1336, Audley had learned what had happened: his daughter had been taken by, and forcibly married to, Sir Ralph Stafford (1301–72). Stafford had gone to Thaxted with eighteen named men and unnamed others, some of them his relatives, snatched Margaret Audley from her home, and married her without the consent of her father (or of herself, one assumes, though this was not recorded).[2] Edward III, then on campaign in Scotland, gave a commission to four men to 'hear and determine' what had happened, but the problem for the Audleys was that Sir Ralph Stafford was a close ally and friend of the king; he had been one of the knights who helped Edward III arrest Roger Mortimer at Nottingham in October 1330, and was very high in his favour. It was going to be difficult for them to obtain justice for their daughter's traumatic experience.

And so it proved: Stafford did not suffer so much as a slap on the wrist for his abduction of a noblewoman, the king's close kinswoman. Margaret Stafford née Audley's aunts Elizabeth Burgh and Eleanor Despenser had both been abducted and forcibly married for their wealth in 1316 and 1329, and now the nightmare scenario had befallen her too. It must have been obvious to Ralph Stafford by 1336 that the Audleys would never have more children—the older Margaret was now over 40—and that the younger Margaret would be their sole heir, and her third of the earldom of Gloucester would fall to him and his heirs if he married her.

Edward II's Nieces: The Clare Sisters

Yet again, the Clare inheritance had proved a poisoned chalice, and yet again, a man had forced himself into a share of it by abducting a woman. Margaret Stafford was probably only 13 or 14 when Ralph abducted her; she was possibly as old as 16, but it seems odd by the standards of her era and her class that she was not yet married if she was as old as 16. In fact, it even seems a little odd that she was not yet married at 14, given that she was one of the greatest heiresses in the country, and marrying her off very young—as horrible as this seems to modern sensibilities—would have protected her from abduction, forced marriage and what amounted to rape. Hugh Audley evidently overestimated his ability to keep his daughter safe, and perhaps he had not expected Ralph Stafford of all men to kidnap her: Stafford was given letters of protection to accompany Audley overseas in April 1332, so the two men had known each other well for a while. This most probably related to the journey to Nijmegen, when Edward III's sister Eleanor of Woodstock married the Count of Guelders.[3]

Margaret Stafford was not the only abducted noblewoman in England in the mid-1330s. It also happened to the Clare sisters' kinswoman Alice Lacy, Countess of Lincoln in her own right and widow of Thomas, Earl of Lancaster and Eble Lestrange. Within months of her second husband's death in September 1335 and at almost exactly the same time as the young Margaret's ordeal, an obscure knight called Sir Hugh Frene captured Alice at her own home of Bolingbroke Castle in Lincolnshire, took her to Somerton Castle thirty miles away, and married her against her will. Frene subsequently took Alice to the Tower of London, and she remained there 'in such confinement that none of her friends or well-wishers could go near her or talk to her'. She was in her mid-50s—her new husband Frene must have been at least a couple of decades younger—and a vow of chastity she had taken after her second husband Lestrange's death did not protect her.[4] A large inheritance and wealth could be, and frequently was, dangerous for medieval women.

Hugh Audley and Ralph Stafford jointly acknowledged a debt of 600 marks on 9 February 1339, so perhaps Hugh had come to terms with Stafford's shocking act by then.[5] He, his wife Margaret and their daughter had little other choice. Whether they wanted to or not, both Margaret Stafford and Alice Lacy had no choice but to remain married to Stafford and Frene. There was no way to undo the marriages, as divorce as such did not exist, only annulment which required a pre-existing impediment.

Kidnap, rape and lack of consent to her marriage on the woman's part did not count as impediments. Ralph Stafford was a widower who was a good twenty years his wife's senior, and had two daughters from his first marriage. He and Margaret were to have two sons and four daughters, and had numerous descendants including the Stafford dukes of Buckingham in the fifteenth and sixteenth centuries, all the kings of France from Louis XIII (r. 1610–43) onwards, kings of Spain, Hungary, Bohemia and Poland, Holy Roman Emperors, and Marie Antoinette. Their first son Ralph died as a child in or before 1347, and their heir was their second son Hugh, named after his grandfather Hugh Audley and born sometime between 1342 and 1346.[6]

The three Clare sisters collaborated for once, probably for the first time in many years, in or shortly before May 1336. They presented a joint petition to the king regarding the debts owed by their father Gilbert 'the Red' Clare to their grandfather Edward I which they claimed had been paid in full. Eleanor and Margaret's husbands William Zouche and Hugh Audley added their names to the petition. Hugh and Margaret Audley were at their favourite castle of Tonbridge on 5 October 1336, when they granted two acres of land in Caerwent, Monmouthshire to the archdeacon of Llandaff.[7] On 16 March 1337, Edward III made Hugh Audley Earl of Gloucester, the title formerly held by his wife's brother Gilbert Clare and dormant since Gilbert's death at the Battle of Bannockburn in 1314. Other supporters of the king were rewarded: the king's and the Clare sisters' cousin William Bohun became Earl of Northampton, Robert Ufford became Earl of Suffolk, William Clinton Earl of Huntingdon, and another royal kinsman, Henry of Grosmont, Earl of Derby (he was in line to inherit the earldoms of Lancaster, Leicester and Lincoln as well). Margaret Audley, who had been Countess of Cornwall since her marriage to Piers Gaveston thirty years previously, was now a countess twice over. She must have been delighted that she and her husband held the earldom which had once belonged to her brother, father and grandfather.

Eleanor Despenser was surely considerably less thrilled at her sister and brother-in-law's promotion, and may have considered that the earldom of Gloucester belonged by right to her son Huchon as the eldest nephew of the last earl. She died on 30 June 1337 at the age of 44, having lived for only four months after the death of her second husband William Zouche on 28 February 1337 (he left his teenage son Alan Zouche from his first marriage to Alice Toeni, the half-brother of the Earl of Warwick, as his heir).[8] On 21 May 1337, just weeks before her death, her cousin Edward III sent the sheriff of Gloucestershire to obtain £328 from her which she owed him as an instalment of the debt of £5,000 she had acknowledged in 1331, but Eleanor died without paying the sum.[9] There is unfortunately no way of knowing the cause of her death at the early age of 44. Eleanor had two grandchildren when she died: Edmund Fitzalan who was already 10 or 11 in 1337, and her second son Edward's eldest son Edward, future lord of Glamorgan, born in March 1336. Her youngest child William Zouche the younger, future monk of Glastonbury, was at most 7 years old when he lost his mother. Not long before her own death, Eleanor had also buried William Zouche at Tewkesbury Abbey, and he had appointed her one of the executors of his will. This suggests that even if he had abducted and married her without her consent eight years earlier, and even if she objected to marrying a man who captured her first husband and her uncle and besieged her eldest son at Caerphilly with a view to handing him over to Queen Isabella for execution, they made something of a success of their marriage.

Eleanor Despenser née Clare was buried at Tewkesbury Abbey in Gloucestershire, where her first husband, brother, father, grandfather and other members of her family were buried, and where her eldest son, grandson and many other descendants would also be buried in later decades. Tewkesbury Abbey lies just ten miles from St Peter's Abbey (later Gloucester Cathedral), where Eleanor's beloved uncle Edward II had supposedly been buried in December 1327. Around the time of Eleanor's death, however, an Italian papal notary and future bishop of Vercelli called Manuele Fieschi sent a letter to Edward III explaining in detail how Edward II had escaped from Berkeley Castle and made his way to Ireland, Avignon, Cologne and ultimately to a hermitage south of Milan. This story has never been proved, but there was something decidedly odd about Edward II's sudden death in September 1327 and the circumstances around it, and it is not absolutely certain that he died at that time and was buried at Gloucester.

The church of Tewkesbury Abbey survived the Dissolution of the Monasteries in the sixteenth century and still exists, though the location of Eleanor's grave there is not known, and nothing is known about her funeral or who attended. It is possible that she was buried in the Lady

Chapel which was pulled down in the sixteenth century; according to the chronicle of Tewkesbury Abbey, she had William Zouche buried in that chapel.[10] A small stained-glass image inside the abbey church of a kneeling naked woman, representing humility, may be a contemporary depiction of Eleanor, placed there either in her own lifetime or her son's. Her heir to her vast landholdings, including Glamorgan, was Huchon, who was 28 or 29 years old in July 1337 when Eleanor's Inquisition Post Mortem was held. Edward III ordered his officials on 21 July to give all Eleanor's lands to Huchon even before her IPM officially returned him as Eleanor's heir.[11] Eleanor was lucky enough not to have outlived most of her children, though her fourth daughter Margaret Despenser died the same year she did at Watton Priory in Yorkshire, at only 13 or 14 years old. Margaret's aunt Elizabeth Burgh, who often showed kindness to her Despenser nephews and nieces, sent wax images and a painting of the four evangelists for her sepulchre.[12]

Chapter 25

The Young Generation

Eleanor did not live long enough to see the marriage of her fifth and youngest daughter Elizabeth Despenser to Maurice Berkeley, son and heir of Thomas, Lord Berkeley, a great nobleman and landowner in Gloucestershire and Somerset, in August 1338. The marriage was arranged partly to resolve the conflict and hostility between the Despenser and Berkeley families during and after the Contrariant rebellion of 1321/22, and also as a means to ensure that the Despensers would not attempt to claim Berkeley lands in the future, as Hugh Despenser the Younger had held them in the 1320s when they were forfeit to the Crown. For Elizabeth Despenser, it was perhaps quite a surreal experience to go to live at the castle where her great-uncle Edward II had allegedly been murdered, and to have a father-in-law who had attended her father's execution. Her young husband Maurice Berkeley, born *c*. 1330 and some years her junior, was a grandson of none other than Roger Mortimer, lord of Wigmore and first Earl of March, via Mortimer's eldest daughter Margaret; one can imagine Despenser and Mortimer turning in their graves to see their daughter and grandson united in matrimony. Elizabeth and Maurice's eldest son Thomas, Lord Berkeley the younger was born in January 1353 when Elizabeth was probably 27 and Maurice about 22 or 23, and they had three younger sons and apparently three daughters.[1]

Despite their father Hugh Despenser the Younger's actions against her in the 1320s and her understandable hatred of him, after her sister Eleanor's death Elizabeth Burgh reached out to her Despenser nieces and nephews. Gilbert, the third Despenser son, joined her household for a while in the late 1340s, and went hunting on her estates at Trelleck and Caerleon which had, ironically, been taken from Elizabeth in 1322 by Gilbert's father. The fifth Despenser daughter Elizabeth also joined her aunt's household for a while before she went to live with her young husband Maurice Berkeley and his family in Gloucestershire. Elizabeth

Burgh sent items for the funeral of her fourth Despenser niece Margaret in 1337, received a gift from her eldest niece Isabella Fitzalan née Despenser, Countess of Arundel, and was visited by her eldest nephew Huchon Despenser and his wife. In November 1339 Elizabeth sent her falconer to Huchon, and in February and August 1340 sent letters to him in London.[2] Elizabeth Burgh may have been involved in the marriage of Eleanor's second son Edward Despenser: Edward wed Anne Ferrers, the much younger sister of Elizabeth's son-in-law Henry, Lord Ferrers, on 20 April 1335 at Ferrers' chief manor of Groby in Leicestershire.[3] The eldest of Edward and Anne's four sons was Edward the younger, born eleven months after his parents' wedding on 24 March 1336, who joined his great-aunt Elizabeth's household for a while in 1346 when he was 10 years old. In January 1347, this Edward attended the funeral of Elizabeth's councillor Sir John Wauton, who fought at the Battle of Crécy in 1346 and died during Edward III's siege of Calais. The Despenser brothers Huchon and Gilbert and their youngest sister Elizabeth Berkeley all spent time together at their aunt's homes in Wales in the summer of 1348, as did Eleanor Zouche, widow of their stepbrother Alan Zouche (her second husband was Elizabeth Burgh's long-term retainer Sir Nichol Damory), and Margaret, Lady Monthermer, widow of their half-uncle Thomas Monthermer.[4] Elizabeth Burgh also rented out the Oxfordshire manor of Bletchingdon to her nephew William Zouche, Eleanor Despenser's youngest child who later became a monk of Glastonbury, so must have kept in touch with him as well.[5] The lady's kindness and generosity to her Despenser kin speaks well of her. With the exception of Huchon, lord of Glamorgan, who spent most of the 1330s and 1340s doing his utmost to restore his family's name, there was little if anything the Despenser siblings could do for their aunt in return for her support of them, and Elizabeth did not help them in expectation of receiving anything in exchange for her efforts. She was not a woman to visit the sins of the father onto his children, and her support of Hugh Despenser the Younger's children speaks volumes about her character.

Another insight into Elizabeth Burgh's character is revealed by her generous endowment in 1338 of a hall founded at Cambridge University a dozen years before. University Hall was founded in 1326 by the university chancellor, but twelve years later it was struggling financially, so Elizabeth stepped in, saved the hall and renamed it after her birth family and one of her favourite residences, Clare in Suffolk. It was known as 'Clare Hall,' and began to be called Clare College 500 years later in the middle of the nineteenth century. Twenty-one years after her endowment, in 1359, Elizabeth issued statutes of the college which stated in part:

> We, therefore, desiring to assist true religion and to further the public good by promoting learning so far as God has put it in our power to do so, have turned our attention to the University of Cambridge in the diocese of Ely, where there is a body of students. Our purpose is that through their study and teaching at the university they should discover and acquire the precious pearl of learning, so that it does not stay hidden under a bushel but is displayed abroad to enlighten those who walk in the dark paths of ignorance.[6]

By July 1353 the hall Elizabeth had founded and endowed was already 'grievously wasted and dilapidated', and her cousin Edward III sent five men to investigate how this had happened and to ascertain whether any of the scholars needed to be 'chastised ... and if necessary to be removed from the hall' for allowing it to fall into such a state.[7] Elizabeth wrote her will in September 1355, and bequeathed 'my hall called Clarehall in Cambridge' numerous items including nine books, all her chapel furnishings, high-quality vestments and ample silverware.[8] Elizabeth's kinswoman and good friend Marie de St Pol, Dowager Countess of Pembroke and widow of Aymer Valence, followed her lead, and in 1347 founded a college at Cambridge which she called the Hall of Valence Marie, and which later became known as Pembroke College. Elizabeth's uncle Edward II had founded Oriel College at Oxford in 1326 and, on the tenth anniversary of his accession to the throne in July 1317, the King's Hall at Cambridge. King's Hall was incorporated into the new foundation of Trinity College in 1546, and Clare College, Pembroke College and Oriel College all still exist in the twenty-first century.

Elizabeth Burgh was a lover of books. In 1324, during the period of Despenser tyranny, she paid a scribe 8 shillings to make her a copy of the *Vitae Patrum*, 'Lives of the Fathers'. In February 1327, the month of Edward III's coronation, she borrowed seven books from the royal collection: four romances and, rather oddly, three books about surgery.

When Elizabeth visited London in 1350/51, she sent seven horses home with her book purchases, and bought and commissioned other books nearer to home, paying to have them covered with silver or decorative covers.[9] Her grandmother Queen Leonor had owned a fine book collection which she probably bequeathed to her daughters on her death in 1290, including the Clare sisters' mother Joan of Acre. The sisters' great-grandmother Isabella Clare née Marshal, Countess of Gloucester and Cornwall (d. 1240), left a large number of items including books to Tewkesbury Abbey which Eleanor Despenser, as the abbey's patron, must have known. It is possible that all three Clare sisters owned books which had belonged to their mother, grandmother and great-grandmother.[10] We have no direct evidence that any of the sisters could write, but their contemporary Margaret Wake, who was born in the mid- or late 1290s and who married their half-uncle the Earl of Kent in late 1325, was certainly able to write.[11] If a woman from a fairly minor baronial house in the north of England was literate, surely the great Earl of Gloucester's daughters and Edward I's granddaughters were as well.

Elizabeth wrote to Margaret Audley, Countess of Gloucester, at Tonbridge on 8 June 1339. This is one of the very few indications that the sisters kept in touch, and is another indication that Tonbridge was the residence which Margaret enjoyed the most. She spent most of her time there, and she and Hugh Audley would both be buried in the priory there. Elizabeth also sent letters at this time to her daughter Elizabeth Bardolf at Wormegay in Norfolk, John Bardolf's main seat, and to her cousin William Bohun, Earl of Northampton, at Rochford in Essex.[12] Elizabeth Burgh had strong family feelings: in December 1339 she buried her half-brother Sir Edward Monthermer, Joan of Acre's eighth and youngest child, at the Augustinian friary in Clare, Suffolk, with their mother. Her sense of duty towards Edward and her burying him with their mother, and her support of her Despenser and Audley kin, reveal a great deal about her affection for and feelings of obligation towards her close family. She sent servants to Bury St Edmunds to purchase meat, fish, poultry and dairy for the attendees of Monthermer's funeral, and gave 69 shillings-worth of bread and herring to paupers in exchange for their prayers for his soul. Her grandson William Ferrers, son and heir of Isabella Verdon, attended his great-uncle's funeral; he was 6 years old at the time.[13] Edward Monthermer, curiously for a medieval nobleman, never married, and died at the age of only 35, a few weeks after taking part in military action in October 1339. His two destriers or war-horses were listed among Elizabeth's horses in 1339/40, and one was called Bay Monthermer. Of Elizabeth's other destriers, one was called Bay Bardolf, as it had been a gift from her son-in-law John Bardolf in exchange for one called Grey Hundon.[14]

Elizabeth's half-sister Joan Monthermer, probably born in 1299, joined their aunt Mary in becoming a nun at Amesbury Priory in Wiltshire, but nothing is known of Joan's life, not even the year when she died. Mary MacDuff, Countess of Fife, Elizabeth's other Monthermer half-sister, went to live in Scotland in 1320 and it is unclear whether the two women had any contact. Mary MacDuff was the only child of Joan of Acre who outlived Elizabeth Burgh: she lived until *c.* 1371 when she was in her 70s, and her only child Isabella MacDuff, Countess of Fife in her own right, married four times but had no children. The remaining Monthermer sibling was Thomas (b. 1301), who survived his brother Edward by only a few months and died shortly after the naval Battle of Sluys in the summer of 1340, leaving his daughter Margaret as his heir. There was also Elizabeth Burgh's much older half-sister Isabella Clare, eldest child of Gilbert 'the Red', who was thirty-three years Elizabeth's senior. Isabella was widowed in 1326 when her husband Maurice, Lord Berkeley died imprisoned as a Contrariant. She lived into the 1330s, but was probably already dead when her step-grandson, the younger Maurice Berkeley, married her niece Elizabeth Despenser in 1338. Joan MacDuff, Countess of Fife, Gilbert the Red's other daughter from his first marriage to Alice Lusignan and Mary MacDuff's mother-in-law, vanishes from the record after 1322 and presumably died in Scotland.

The Clare sisters' cousin Edward III had claimed the throne of France in 1337 as the only surviving grandson of King Philip IV of France, Queen Isabella's father (Edward's younger brother John of Eltham, Earl of Cornwall—under the care of Eleanor Despenser when he was a child—died at the age of 20 in September 1336). The Clares' Monthermer half-brothers took part in the king's French wars, as did their cousin the Earl of Northampton, Margaret Audley's son-in-law Ralph Stafford (later the first Earl of Stafford), and Eleanor Despenser's son-in-law Richard Fitzalan, Earl of Arundel. Edward III stayed outside England for much of the period 1338 to 1340, seeking allies against his mother's cousin

Philip VI, who had taken the French throne in 1328 as the first Valois king. Queen Philippa accompanied him overseas, and gave birth to two of their sons, Lionel of Antwerp and John of Gaunt (i.e. Ghent), in November 1338 and March 1340. The king returned to England for a while, and on 22 June 1340 embarked for the continent again from the River Orwell in Suffolk. He stayed with his cousin Elizabeth Burgh at Clare for three days on his way to the port, from 27 to 29 May 1340. Elizabeth's servants had to provide hay for 180 horses, and the king's retinue consumed 170 gallons of ale, 200 eggs, 120 mackerel and 700 herring on the first day of the visit alone.[15]

At least in public, Edward III and Elizabeth appear to have enjoyed a reasonably cordial relationship, and certainly one much better and easier than Elizabeth's tense relationship with Edward's father. Edward III always courteously referred to Elizabeth as 'the king's kinswoman', yet the two do not seem to have been close on a personal level, and Elizabeth's biographer considers that the lady felt a 'muted dislike' for her cousin and deliberately provoked him on several occasions with her demands.[16] Elizabeth got on much better with Edward III and Queen Philippa's three eldest sons Edward of Woodstock, Lionel of Antwerp (who became Elizabeth's grandson-in-law when he was a young child in 1342) and John of Gaunt. Edward of Woodstock, made Prince of Wales in 1343 and heir to the throne since his birth in June 1330, developed a remarkably close friendship with his kinswoman Elizabeth, despite an age difference between them of three-and-a-half decades. He visited her no fewer than twenty-three times in twenty months in the 1350s.[17]

Elizabeth's four Despenser nephews Huchon, Edward, Gilbert and John also played enthusiastic roles in their cousin the king's French wars. Gilbert Despenser became a household knight of the king, and later also served in the retinue of Edward III's young grandson Richard II. Sometime in early 1338, Huchon sent a letter to Edward III jointly with his uncle Hugh Audley, Earl of Gloucester, and his brother-in-law Richard Fitzalan, Earl of Arundel, who was unhappily married to the eldest Despenser sister Isabella.[18] Huchon made an excellent marriage sometime before 27 April 1341, to Elizabeth Montacute, daughter of William, Earl of Salisbury. She was the granddaughter of the William Montacute who, alongside Roger Damory and Hugh Audley, had been powerful at Edward II's court in the 1310s and who died in Gascony in 1319.[19] Elizabeth Montacute's sister Sybil married Huchon's nephew Edmund Fitzalan, his sister Isabella Despenser's son. Another Montacute sister, Philippa, married Roger Mortimer of Wigmore's grandson and heir Roger Mortimer the younger (1328–60), who was made second Earl of March in 1354. This must have led to some interesting conversations around the Montacute family dinner table. Elizabeth Montacute was many years Huchon's junior; her date of birth is not known, but her brother William, their father's heir, was born in June 1328, and their parents probably married in 1327 or shortly before.[20] Elizabeth is likely to have been the eldest Montacute daughter as she was named after her paternal grandmother Elizabeth Montfort, and Sybil was probably the second eldest as she was named after their maternal grandmother Sybil Tregoz. William Montacute, Earl of Salisbury, was Edward III's closest friend, and it is likely that the king had a hand in promoting the marriage of Salisbury's daughter and his kinsman Huchon. Despite her youth, Elizabeth Despenser née Montacute was already the widow of Bartholomew Badlesmere's son and heir Giles (1314–38), who was Huchon's second cousin, and thus the couple had to ask for a dispensation from the pope before they could marry.[21] Huchon settled eight of his manors on himself and Elizabeth Montacute jointly.[22] She was old enough to consummate their marriage by the mid-1340s or earlier, but they were to have no children. Elizabeth did have children with her third husband, so probably Huchon was infertile.

Huchon's aunt Margaret Audley, Countess of Cornwall and Gloucester, died in early April 1342, aged 47 or 48. The date of her death is usually given as 9 or 13 April, though her Inquisition Post Mortem says she died on 'Tuesday the morrow of the Close of Easter last', and Easter Sunday fell on 31 March in 1342, which would seem to give a correct date of 2 April for Margaret's death. The order to take her lands into the king's hand, as always happened when a tenant in chief died, was issued on 15 April, and the writ to hold her IPM on 24 April.[23] Margaret's heir was her only surviving child Margaret Stafford, and had her elder daughter Joan Gaveston still been alive, the two half-sisters would have inherited equally. By the custom called the 'courtesy of England' her widower Hugh Audley was entitled to hold all her lands for the rest of his life, and Hugh thus managed to keep his wife's share of the Clare inheritance out of his son-in-law Ralph Stafford's grasp for another few years. Margaret and Hugh had been married for almost exactly a quarter of a century, since

28 April 1317; the marriage, arranged by her uncle Edward II for no better reason than he was currently infatuated with Audley, had endured and seemingly thrived. Margaret was buried at Tonbridge Priory, and her husband would be buried there with her a few years later. Margaret was the quietest of the three Clare sisters and her private life is the most difficult of all of them to illuminate in a biography, but her life was as eventful as those of her sisters: she survived years of incarceration in a convent, marriage to two of her uncle's favourites and perhaps lovers, and the abduction of her pubescent daughter. Although she had only one child who lived into adulthood and had children of her own, the modern-day descendants of Margaret Gaveston Audley née Clare number in the millions.

Chapter 26

The Last Sister

And so only Elizabeth Burgh was left of the three Clare sisters. She had prayers said for Margaret's soul in the years 1351 to 1353, and presumably in other years as well, on the anniversary of her sister's death.[1] In the years after Margaret Audley died, Elizabeth invited her niece Margaret Stafford and her husband Ralph Stafford to stay with her; with her strong sense of family, she reached out to all her nieces and nephews after her sisters' deaths.[2] A few months after she lost her sister, in mid-August 1342, Elizabeth witnessed the wedding of her namesake granddaughter and heir Elizabeth Burgh to Edward III's second son Lionel of Antwerp; the pair had been betrothed since May 1341. The younger Elizabeth was 10 when she married, and Lionel, born in late November 1338, was 3 years and 8-and-a-half months. The tiny couple subsequently lived in the care of Lionel's mother Queen Philippa with Lionel's older sisters Isabella and Joan and younger brothers John of Gaunt and Edmund of Langley.

The elder Elizabeth Burgh's nephew Edward Despenser, second son of her late sister Eleanor, was killed at the Battle of Morlaix in Brittany on 30 September 1342. Edward was killed fighting under his elder brother Huchon's banner and under the overall command of his cousin the Earl of Northampton, and the battle took place during the War of the Breton Succession when Edward III of England supported the claims of John Montfort to the duchy of Brittany against Montfort's niece Jeanne de Penthièvre. Edward Despenser left his widow Anne née Ferrers, sister-in-law of Elizabeth Burgh's daughter Isabella Verdon, and their four sons. Edward Despenser the eldest son (b. March 1336) was heir to his childless uncle Huchon Despenser and to his grandmother Eleanor Despenser's share of the Clare inheritance, the middle two sons were Hugh and Thomas, and Henry the youngest was born in 1341 or early 1342 and became bishop of Norwich in 1370.[3]

Elizabeth Burgh's youngest child Elizabeth Bardolf née Damory seems to have spent most of her life in Norfolk where her husband's estates were mostly concentrated, and often visited her mother in Cambridgeshire and Essex. Elizabeth Burgh, being much wealthier than her daughter, paid the travel costs. Elizabeth Bardolf usually spent time with her mother every Christmas and again in the summer, and she had her own chambers at Elizabeth's manors; her chamber at Anglesey in Cambridgeshire had its own fireplace and chimney. The two Elizabeths, mother and daughter, seem to have been genuinely close and to have thoroughly enjoyed each other's company, one happy result of the third marriage to Roger Damory which Elizabeth had undertaken, perhaps reluctantly, at her uncle Edward II's behest in 1317. Margaret Damory, Roger and Elizabeth's elder daughter, must have died sometime in the 1330s. The younger Elizabeth and her husband John Bardolf accompanied Elizabeth Burgh to Walsingham, where there had long been a great shrine to Our Lady and where Elizabeth Burgh founded a Franciscan friary in 1347, to the indignation of the Walsingham canons. Edward III sent a letter on 1 February 1347 stating that Elizabeth had been 'inflamed by the fervour of charity and devotion' to establish a Franciscan house in Walsingham.[4]

Isabella Ferrers née Verdon's daughter Elizabeth Ferrers—a confusingly large number of Elizabeth Burgh's female descendants were named after her—married David Strathbogie, heir to the titular earldom of Atholl, sometime after 1 August 1342.[5] David was born in the early 1330s, and lost his father David the elder in 1335. The Strathbogies lived permanently in England and adhered to the English kings, so their title was purely nominal and honorary; the real earldom of Atholl in Scotland and its lands were given to William Douglas and then to Robert Stewart in the 1340s. Elizabeth Strathbogie née Ferrers lived in her grandmother's household after her father Henry Ferrers died in 1343, and was referred to as 'Lady Elizabeth Atholl' in her grandmother's accounts. David Strathbogie himself, Elizabeth Burgh's grandson-in-law, had become a squire of the lady's household by 1343, as had his brother-in-law William Ferrers, Elizabeth's grandson (William was 10 years old in 1343 and David probably a little older). Elizabeth had bought William a pony in 1339/40 when he was 6 or 7. The English nobility of the fourteenth century very often married in childhood: William Ferrers wed the Earl of Suffolk's daughter Margaret Ufford in 1344 when he was 10 or 11 and she about the same age or younger.[6] Elizabeth Strathbogie and William Ferrers' sister Philippa, another granddaughter of Elizabeth Burgh, married Guy Beauchamp, heir to his father Thomas's earldom of Warwick, in or before 1351. After their father Henry Ferrers' death in September 1343, Elizabeth Burgh sent some of her household servants to Groby in Leicestershire to bring her widowed daughter Isabella née Verdon the 125 miles to her in Bardfield, Essex, and her granddaughters spent time with her after their father's death as well. Elizabeth was deeply attached to both her daughters and their children.[7]

Elizabeth Burgh's brother-in-law Hugh Audley went to the duchy of Brittany on Edward III's behalf sometime between January 1343 and January 1344, though was in England on 10 August 1343 and on 20 June 1344.[8] Duke John III of Brittany, a great-grandson of King Henry III of England and thus a cousin of the Clare sisters, had died childless in 1341, and his half-brother John Montfort and his late full brother's daughter Jeanne de Penthièvre battled for control of the duchy. The kings of both England and France took a keen interest in the War of the Breton Succession and both sent armies there, and ultimately Duke John III's half-brother John Montfort, the candidate backed by England, and his son emerged victorious. According to the chronicler Geoffrey le Baker, Audley's nephew Sir Hugh 'Huchon' Despenser was also one of the men sent to Brittany to aid John Montfort.[9] His younger brother Edward Despenser was killed fighting in Brittany in 1342.

Hugh Audley was now about 50 or 52. His and Margaret Audley's grandson and heir Ralph Stafford the younger, who cannot have been more than 8 years old and was probably younger, married the 4-year-old Maud of Lancaster, elder daughter and co-heir of Henry of Grosmont, Earl of Derby, in the town of Leicester on 30 November 1344. Grosmont held a jousting tournament in the town to mark the occasion. Hugh Audley, and Maud of Lancaster's elderly grandfather Henry, Earl of Lancaster and Leicester, were surely present.[10] It had been arranged in London on 10 October 1344 between Henry of Grosmont on one side, and Hugh Audley, his daughter Margaret Stafford and son-in-law the elder Ralph Stafford on the other, that Grosmont 'will have the custody and upbringing' of both his daughter Maud and young Ralph. Five manors were settled jointly on the young couple.[11]

The marriage of the two children did not last long. Young Ralph Stafford was already dead when his maternal grandfather Hugh Audley died in November 1347, and his parents' heir was his younger brother Hugh Stafford, who succeeded their father in 1372 as Earl of Stafford and inherited his grandmother Margaret Audley née Clare's third of the earldom of Gloucester.[12] The little widow Maud of Lancaster married her second husband Wilhelm of Bavaria in early 1352 when she was still not yet 12, and died childless in April 1362, leaving the entire vast Lancastrian inheritance to her younger sister Blanche of Lancaster, who married Edward III's third son John of Gaunt and was the mother of King Henry IV. The marriage, had young Ralph lived longer, would ultimately have given him one half of the Lancastrian patrimony (which included the earldoms of Lancaster, Leicester, Derby and Lincoln), and arranging such a splendid match had been a great triumph for the Audley/Staffords, but it was not to be. Arranging an excellent marriage for his eldest daughter Isabella Despenser to the heir to the earldoms of Arundel and Surrey had also been a triumph for Hugh Despenser the Younger in 1321, but in December 1344 Richard Fitzalan had his marriage to Isabella annulled, and thereby made their son Edmund illegitimate. Richard married Eleanor of Lancaster, fifth of the six daughters of Henry, Earl of Lancaster and Leicester (and Henry of Grosmont's sister), instead in early 1345. He gave Isabella Despenser six manors in Essex for her sustenance, and she lived in obscurity; almost nothing is known about Eleanor Despenser née Clare's eldest daughter after the annulment of her marriage except that she was still alive in 1356 and seems to have been dead by 1369.[13] Her son Edmund did not inherit his father's huge wealth and earldoms, but as his much younger half-brother Richard, their father's heir, ended up being beheaded by Edward III's grandson and successor Richard II, perhaps he had reason to be glad of it.

Henry, Earl of Lancaster and Leicester himself, the last surviving grandchild of King Henry III, died on 22 September 1345 a few months after his granddaughter Maud's wedding to young Ralph Stafford. The funeral of the greatest of English noblemen in Leicester in January 1346 was attended by his niece Queen Isabella, great-nephew Edward III, Queen Philippa, and much of the English nobility. Assuming he was well enough to travel there, Hugh Audley would certainly have been one of them, as would his sister-in-law Elizabeth Burgh, who had known Earl Henry well. Elizabeth Burgh the younger, Countess of Ulster and now Edward III's daughter-in-law, was their mutual granddaughter. Henry's heir was his only son Henry of Grosmont, now in his mid-30s or so, who at the time of his father's death was leading a gloriously successful campaign in Gascony against the French. Edward III upgraded one of Grosmont's titles in 1351 and made him the first Duke of Lancaster, and Grosmont showed great affection for his second cousin Elizabeth Burgh, who was a good fifteen years his senior: he visited her in January and May 1347, May 1350 and on another two occasions later that year, and wrote to her and sent her a gift of venison while he was crusading in Poland and Lithuania in 1351/52.[14] She left him items in her will.

Elizabeth Burgh began to show a greater interest in the religious life in the 1340s. In 1343 or before, sometime during her almost four decades of widowhood, she took a vow of chastity, and might in fact have taken the vow much earlier to avoid being forced into yet another marriage by her uncle Edward II or cousin Edward III. Her vow of chastity probably required her to wear a nun's habit and a ring, at least sometimes.[15] Elizabeth demonstrated a fascination with the order of Minoresses or Franciscan nuns. The pope gave her permission to enter enclosed Minoress spaces with three female attendants in 1343, and she was later also permitted to stay the night in a Minoress house with two female attendants.[16] Her close friend and kinswoman Marie de St Pol, Dowager Countess of Pembroke, founded a house of Minoresses at Denny in Cambridgeshire in 1342. Elizabeth herself would request burial at the Minoress house without Aldgate in London (also often called the 'Minories'), where in 1352 she built and occupied a large house in the outer courtyard which was later lived in by the Dowager Countess of Kent, Queen Philippa's niece Elisabeth of Jülich (d. 1411), and other noble ladies.[17] In 1347, Elizabeth Burgh founded a house of Franciscan friars in Walsingham, Norfolk out of 'charity and devotion'. Her daughter-in-law Maud of Lancaster, Dowager Countess of Ulster and William Burgh's widow (and one of Henry of Grosmont's six sisters), entered the religious life permanently in 1347 or 1348 after she was widowed from her second husband, and spent the remaining three decades of her life as a canoness at Campsea Ashe and Bruisyard priories in Suffolk. Elizabeth herself, however, though obviously finding the Minoresses' lifestyle highly appealing, was too attached to her life as a great lady dispensing patronage and hospitality and enjoying her estates and wealth to wish to give it all up completely. In 1340 she went on a three-week pilgrimage from East Anglia to Canterbury taking a large retinue of servants and seventy horses, a prime example of both her devotion to religion and to her secular lifestyle.

King Edward III left England for the continent in July 1346 with a large force including his 16-year-old eldest son Edward of Woodstock, now Prince of Wales, and his and the Clare sisters' cousin the Earl of Northampton. The king and his son inflicted a massive defeat on the forces of Philip VI of France at the Battle of Crécy on 26 August. On 8 July 1346, days before he departed from his kingdom, Edward III gave his kinsman Huchon Despenser permission that 'as soon as he dies the executors of his will shall have full and free administration of his goods and chattels', Huchon was pardoned on 30 October that year, in consideration of his good service in the wars against France, of 'all homicides, felonies, robberies and trespasses in England'.[18] Eleanor Despenser's eldest son, now in his late 30s, played a vital role in the Crécy campaign just days before the battle by leading a small force of men across a ford of the River Somme. A large French force shot at them from the other side with crossbows and longbows, and it took Huchon and his men forty-five minutes to wade through a mile and a half of waist-deep water, under fire the whole time. This remarkably brave action freed a way through the French lines for the English army and prevented them becoming trapped and destroyed between the Seine and Somme rivers.[19] Huchon Despenser had done his utmost to restore his and his family's name over the previous fifteen years, and his deeds in France earned him accolades. He was not, however, chosen as a Knight of the Garter when the order was instituted in 1348 though perhaps would have been had he not died in February 1349, and his nephew and heir Edward Despenser became a member of the order a few years later. Huchon's cousin Margaret Stafford née Audley's husband Ralph Stafford was the fifth Knight of the Garter, his abduction of a young noblewoman not being deemed a serious enough reason to keep him out of the highly prestigious order. Another founder member of the Garter was Hugh Audley's nephew James Audley, who also fought at Crécy.

For many years, Huchon's aunt Elizabeth Burgh kept in touch with her cousin Jeanne de Bar, Countess of Surrey, another granddaughter of Edward I. Jeanne had married John Warenne, Earl of Surrey, in May 1306 just before her cousin Eleanor Clare married Hugh Despenser the Younger, but the marriage proved a childless disaster. Surrey had tried to annul it in the 1310s and make his illegitimate sons with his mistress Maud Nerford his heirs, but this failed. By the mid-1340s Surrey had another mistress, Isabella Holland, and tried again to have his marriage to Jeanne annulled so that he could marry her. He claimed, most implausibly, to have had an affair before he married Jeanne with her aunt Mary, nun of Amesbury, a transparent ploy which he hoped would persuade the pope to annul the marriage on the grounds of incest. This also failed, and when Surrey died the day before his sixty-first birthday at the end of June 1347, Jeanne de Bar was still his wife. He left her nothing at all in his will and failed even to mention her, and referred to his mistress Isabella Holland as his *compaigne*, companion or consort, a word otherwise only used for wives. Elizabeth Burgh did, however, leave Jeanne something in her will: a 'gold image of St John the Baptist in the desert'.[20] Jeanne, who by birth was French—her father Henri was Count of Bar in eastern France—often travelled abroad which Elizabeth did not.[21] Elizabeth is not known to have travelled beyond England, Wales and Ireland at any time during her long life, unless she accompanied Roger Damory to France in the company of Edward II when Elizabeth's uncle paid homage to Philip V for his French lands in June 1320.

Margaret Audley's widower Hugh Audley, Earl of Gloucester, died on 10 November 1347, a few months after the Earl of Surrey, aged about 54 or 56.[22] Elizabeth Burgh appears to have visited her brother-in-law some months before his death, taking her daughter Isabella Ferrers with her: on 4 June 1347 the two women were at Desning near Bury St Edmunds in Suffolk, a manor which belonged to Hugh, and her younger daughter Elizabeth Bardolf probably also accompanied them.[23] Hugh was buried at Tonbridge Priory in Kent next to his wife. His nephews Peter and James Audley, sons of his obscure older brother James, were famous warriors in the Hundred Years' War, and his only daughter Margaret Stafford outlived him by less than two years. By the custom known as the 'courtesy of England' her widower Ralph Stafford kept her substantial inheritance in his own hands until his death in 1372 at the age of 71, when it passed to their only surviving son Hugh Stafford.

Hugh Audley had risen high in and after 1315 as a result of Edward II's infatuation with him, and he had done well to survive Edward's reign after switching sides and rebelling against the king, and after taking part in another rebellion against Edward III's mother and her chief counsellor in the late 1320s.

Chapter 27

The Final Years

The terrible years of 1348/49 saw the first mass outbreak of the Black Death in Europe which killed a huge percentage of the population, perhaps as many as half. Eleanor Despenser's eldest child Hugh 'Huchon' Despenser, lord of Glamorgan, died on 8 February 1349 at the age of 40, perhaps of the Black Death. Huchon, who had visited his aunt Elizabeth Burgh in Wales with his brother Gilbert and youngest sister Elizabeth Berkeley a few months before his death, was buried at Tewkesbury Abbey. His and his wife Elizabeth née Montacute's magnificent effigies can still be seen there. Elizabeth was buried next to Huchon ten years later, though had been married to and had children with her third husband Sir Guy Bryan (Bryan lived until 1390 and was also buried in Tewkesbury Abbey). As Huchon and Elizabeth had no children, his heir to Glamorgan and his other lands was his brother Edward's eldest son Edward Despenser, who was not quite 13 in February 1349.

Huchon's aunt Elizabeth Burgh lost her daughter Isabella Ferrers née Verdon on 25 July 1349, when Isabella was only 32 years old. Elizabeth made offerings on the anniversary of Isabella's death every year, and Isabella's teenaged daughters Elizabeth and Philippa stayed with their grandmother in the winter of 1349/50 after their mother's death.[1] Isabella's heir, also the heir of her late husband Henry Ferrers of Groby, was her 16-year-old son William, who passed into royal wardship and who was granted an annual income of £50 for his sustenance by the king in October 1349.[2] And Margaret Audley's only child to live into adulthood, Margaret Stafford, died sometime before 7 September 1349 leaving her son Hugh Stafford and her daughters Elizabeth, Joan, Beatrice and Katherine. She was only about 27. Her much older abductor and widower Ralph Stafford survived her by twenty-three years.

Elizabeth Burgh's youngest child Elizabeth Bardolf née Damory gave birth to her only son William Bardolf at Wormegay in Norfolk on

Monday, 21 October 1349. William was baptised in the parish church of Wormegay on the same day as his birth. The boy's father John Bardolf had a chamberlain named Richard Rysyng, who rode so hurriedly to fetch William's godfather for the baptism that his horse stumbled into a pit and he fell and broke his leg. A violent altercation of some kind took place in the church of Wormegay on the day of William's baptism which led to the shedding of blood, and after his baptism the church was therefore 'suspended from the celebration of all divine offices'.[3] Elizabeth Bardolf had been pregnant with her son when she lost her half-sister Isabella Ferrers, and while the Black Death was raging in England and elsewhere; it can hardly have been a happy pregnancy. As well as their son William, Elizabeth and John Bardolf had two daughters, Agnes and Isabella Bardolf, presumably named after John's mother Agnes Beauchamp and Elizabeth's half-sister Isabella Ferrers respectively. Both girls or young women were left bequests in their grandmother Elizabeth Burgh's will of 1355, but do not appear on any other known record, and do not seem to have married and had children. It is likely, therefore, that they died young.

Elizabeth Burgh, who was now 54 years old, spent the festive season of 1349/50 at her Welsh castle of Usk.[4] As well as her Ferrers granddaughters, she was visited there on 5 December 1349 by Marie de St Pol, Dowager Countess of Pembroke, and in early January by her recently widowed nephew-in-law Ralph, Lord Stafford, and niece-in-law Elizabeth Despenser née Montacute, widow of Huchon Despenser (who married her third husband Guy Bryan in 1350). Elizabeth Burgh spent a few days in mid-April 1350 at Tewkesbury in Gloucestershire where her sister Eleanor, brother Gilbert Clare, father Gilbert 'the Red', brother-in-law Hugh Despenser the Younger and nephew Huchon were buried in the abbey church. The manor of Tewkesbury passed from Huchon to his nephew Edward Despenser, though as Edward was still underage, it was currently in the king's hands. Elizabeth passed through Bletchingdon in Oxfordshire on 21 April, which she held herself and rented out to her nephew William Zouche (Eleanor Despenser's youngest child) some years later, though by right it should probably have belonged to her third husband Roger Damory's nephew Richard Damory.[5] She spent the period from early May to early June 1350 at her manor of Clare. Her guests here included her son-in-law John Bardolf, Edward III's eldest daughter Isabella of Woodstock and the king's first and third sons Edward of

Woodstock and John of Gaunt (aged 20 and 10 respectively), Elizabeth's cousin the Earl of Northampton and his wife Elizabeth Badlesmere, her kinsman Henry of Grosmont, and her granddaughter and heir the young Elizabeth Burgh, Countess of Ulster, who came for two weeks. Now in her mid-50s, Elizabeth entertained as often and as lavishly as she always had.

Countess Elizabeth of Ulster was now almost 18, though still had a few years to wait for her young husband Lionel of Antwerp, the king's second son, to mature enough to be her partner in more than name only: he was still only 11 in the summer of 1350, though they had now been married for eight years. Countess Elizabeth's mother Maud of Lancaster appears to have been on good terms with her mother-in-law Elizabeth Burgh the elder, and on one occasion before Maud entered a religious house in 1347/48, Elizabeth returned Maud's 'two lost spaniels' to her, implying that Maud had visited her and brought her dogs with her.[6] Until his death in September 1345, Elizabeth had also often kept in touch with the wealthy and influential Henry, Earl of Lancaster and Leicester, father of Henry of Grosmont and Maud of Lancaster. Henry hunted on Elizabeth's lands before he went blind probably sometime in the early or mid-1330s.[7]

Elizabeth's daughter Elizabeth Bardolf and granddaughter Elizabeth Strathbogie née Ferrers, titular Countess of Atholl, spent the festive season of 1351/52 with her. All three women made offerings on the feasts of St Stephen, or 26 December, and St Thomas Becket, or 29 December. Elizabeth's granddaughter the Countess of Ulster was not present, but her grandmother wrote to her on 30 December.[8] Elizabeth Burgh the elder became a great-grandmother probably in 1353 when she was in her late 50s, when her daughter Isabella Ferrers' daughter Philippa Beauchamp gave birth to the elder of her two daughters, Katherine Beauchamp (Katherine's sister, Philippa Beauchamp's younger daughter, was yet another Elizabeth). Philippa's husband Guy Beauchamp, heir to the earldom of Warwick, died in 1360 in his father's lifetime, and their two little daughters became nuns at Shouldham Priory; this disinherited them so that their uncle Thomas Beauchamp could succeed his father as Earl of Warwick.

Philippa of Ulster, daughter and ultimately the heir of the younger Elizabeth Burgh and her husband Lionel of Antwerp, Earl and Countess of Ulster, another great-granddaughter of the elder Elizabeth Burgh, was born at the royal palace of Eltham in Kent on 16 August 1355. She was named after her paternal grandmother Philippa of Hainault, queen of England, who was also her godmother. Little Philippa was born thirty-seven weeks after her father's sixteenth birthday, and perhaps he and his wife Elizabeth, who was 23 when her daughter was born, had finally consummated their marriage because he had turned 16. On 5 March 1356, when she was a few months old, Edward III sent his granddaughter Philippa to live at the priory of Campsea Ashe in Suffolk with her maternal grandmother Maud of Lancaster, William Burgh's widow.[9] Philippa married Edmund Mortimer, heir to the earldom of March, in or before December 1358 when she was 3 and he 6; Edmund was the great-grandson of the Roger Mortimer whom Edward III had had executed in 1330.[10] Elizabeth Burgh had, remarkably, lived long enough to see the marriage of one of her great-grandchildren. Another great-grandchild born in her lifetime was Henry Ferrers in February 1356, son of William Ferrers and grandson of Isabella Verdon, and Henry's sisters Margaret and Elizabeth Ferrers were probably born before Elizabeth died in November 1360 as well.

Elizabeth Burgh wrote her very long will on 25 September 1355, a few weeks after the birth of her great-granddaughter Philippa of Ulster. (If her sisters Eleanor Despenser and Margaret Audley also made wills, they no longer exist.) She was now 60 years old, and although she lived for another five years, making her will suggests she was ill at the time; in the fourteenth century, people generally only made their wills when they thought they might be dying. Elizabeth asked to be buried at the house of the Minoresses outside Aldgate in London, which had been founded in 1293 by Edward I's younger brother Edmund of Lancaster and his wife Blanche of Artois, Elizabeth's great-uncle and great-aunt. Perhaps it is revealing that she did not wish to be buried beside any of her three husbands, though she did leave £140 for prayers to be said for their souls in perpetuity, and for her own soul and for those of everyone who had died in her service. She also left 100 marks for five men-at-arms to go on crusade to the Holy Land, and to pray there for the souls of her three husbands and her own. Elizabeth was indeed buried some years later, as she had requested, at the house of the Minoresses outside Aldgate. It was once believed that she was buried in Ware, Hertfordshire next to Roger Damory, and an epitaph in Latin to that effect was seen and preserved by an eighteenth-century writer.[11] In May 1372, however, John Hastings, Earl of Pembroke, wrote in his will that he wished his tomb to be 'made as like as possible to the tomb of Elizabeth de Burgh who lies in the Minories, London, without Aldgate'.[12] As that was less than a dozen years after Elizabeth's death, and as Pembroke was a nobleman who must have known Elizabeth well, this is direct evidence of her correct burial site. As well as requesting burial at the Minories, Elizabeth gave them £20 and numerous items including five cloths of gold, a bed 'of black tartarin' (a kind of silk), and 'twelve green hangings with the border powdered with owls'. Her great-granddaughter Elizabeth Ferrers, one of the three children of her grandson William, Lord Ferrers of Groby (1333–71), became a nun at the Minoresses without Aldgate sometime before June 1368.[13]

The very first person mentioned in Elizabeth's will was her long-term official, adviser, attorney and perhaps friend Sir Nichol Damory, who may have been her third husband's illegitimate son, and Elizabeth left him several bequests. She also appointed Nichol as one of her fifteen executors, and he was named first among them. Elizabeth left items to her only surviving child Elizabeth Bardolf, perhaps Nichol Damory's half-sister, including her 'great coach' with all equipment and cushions. This was a generous gift as such coaches, in which wealthy noble ladies travelled, were hugely expensive. Elizabeth Bardolf's daughters Agnes and Isabella Bardolf received rich bequests 'to help [them] to marry', including a goblet of gold, a bed of sendal (expensive silk) with a coverlet lined with miniver (expensive white fur), an indigo bed with a blue coverlet, a silver cross, candlesticks and salt-cellars. Both Bardolf girls disappear from the record after this, and evidently did not marry and probably died young, unless they joined religious houses. Several of Elizabeth's other grandchildren received bequests: William, Lord Ferrers was left all the items in her Leicestershire manor of Lutterworth, including carthorses, oxen, wheat and rye, and William's sister Elizabeth Strathbogie, Countess of Atholl, was bequeathed two 'beds of tawny'. Elizabeth Burgh's granddaughter, namesake and primary heir Elizabeth Burgh, Countess of Ulster, was only bequeathed 'all the debt which my son, her father, owed me on the day he died'. Elizabeth probably intended this statement to be less sarcastic than it sounds, and the countess was heir to her grandmother's large landholdings. As the younger Elizabeth was a wealthy heiress and the king's daughter-in-law, Elizabeth Burgh did not feel the need to leave her items similar to those she left her other grandchildren, who had greater need of them.

Elizabeth also left generous sums of money and gifts to numerous religious houses, including £10 to the Augustinians of Clare where her mother Joan of Acre was buried, £5 and two cloths of gold to Croxden Abbey in Staffordshire where her second husband Theobald Verdon was buried in 1316, £2 to the Franciscans of Ware in Hertfordshire where her third husband Roger Damory may have been buried, and two reliquaries, and a cross and two cloths of gold to Tewkesbury Abbey in Gloucestershire, the mausoleum of her natal family the Clares. She also left £10 and two cloths of gold to Amesbury Priory in Wiltshire where her aunt Mary and half-sister Joan Monthermer had been nuns, and where she herself had lived in 1308/09 and 1316/17 (her daughter Isabella Verdon was born there). She bequeathed to her cousin the Countess of Surrey an image of John the Baptist, to her friend the Countess of Pembroke a 'little gold cross with a sapphire in the centre' and a gold diamond ring, to her kinsman the Prince of Wales a 'gold tabernacle with the image of Our Lady', two 'little angels' of shaped gold and other items, and to her kinsman Henry of Grosmont, Duke of Lancaster, her 'little psalter' and a square cross with a piece of the True Cross inside. Elizabeth also bequeathed items or gifts of money to numerous servants, including robes and the matching garments to her damsels: Suzanne Neketon received Elizabeth's best robe, Elizabeth Torel her second best, Margaret Banchon her third best, Isabel Morley her fourth best, Agnes Southern the fifth best and Alison Wodeham the sixth best. Near the end of her will Elizabeth commented on 'the peril which comes to wrongful occupiers of the goods of the dead and disturbers of their last wills' as a dire warning to anyone who might try to deprive anyone of their rightful bequests, and her opinion of the tumultuous century she lived in is apparent from her statement that 'diverse hindrances are often made through malice, and man's subtlety is greater than was usual before this time'.[14]

In the last years of her life, Elizabeth ceased to visit her Welsh properties, presumably finding the journey there too long and difficult. She divided her time between London, Clare and Bardfield (in Essex), and was in London from 9 July to 16 October 1355 when she wrote her will, with a short trip to Greenwich on 28 and 29 August. Elizabeth's guests in London at this time included Henry of Grosmont, Duke of Lancaster, and her much younger first cousin Joan, Countess of Kent (1326/27–85), daughter of Edward I's youngest son Edmund of Woodstock, Earl of Kent. Joan became her father's heir when her younger brother John, Earl of Kent died in late 1352, and in 1361 would marry Edward III's eldest son and heir the Prince of Wales and become the mother of Richard II. Elizabeth stayed in the capital again from 12 May to 10 September 1358, and her guests included her cousins the Earl of Northampton and the Countess of Surrey, her nephew-in-law Ralph, Earl of Stafford, the bishop of London, and the 'bishops of Armenia'. Her grandson-in-law Lionel of Antwerp also visited her three times in July and again on 21 August 1358.[15]

Elizabeth's aunt-in-law and Lionel's grandmother the Dowager Queen Isabella of France, who was almost exactly Elizabeth's own age, died at Hertford Castle on 22 August 1358. She was buried at the Greyfriars church in London on 27 November. Isabella's youngest child Joan of the Tower, queen of Scotland, who spent much time with Isabella— her marriage to David II was unhappy and childless and Joan lived in England for the last few years of her life—would be buried in the same church in 1362. Elizabeth did not stay in London long enough in 1358 to attend Isabella's funeral, and the two women do not appear to have visited each other, though did keep in occasional touch via letter. Elizabeth also lost the cousin she had long been close to, William Bohun, Earl of Northampton, on 16 September 1360.

Elizabeth Burgh died on 4 November 1360 at the age of 65, a few weeks after her cousin Northampton, probably at one of her East Anglian properties.[16] She was buried as she had requested at the Minoresses without Aldgate in London, though nothing is known about her funeral. Her landholdings passed to her granddaughter Elizabeth Burgh the younger and Elizabeth's husband Lionel of Antwerp, who were made Duke and Duchess of Clarence in November 1362 when Lionel's father the king celebrated his fiftieth birthday. Duchess Elizabeth died in Dublin on 10 December 1363, aged only 31, leaving her 8-year-old daughter Philippa Mortimer as her heir. Lionel of Antwerp married his second wife Violante Visconti of Milan in May 1368, but died less than five months after his wedding, a few weeks before his thirtieth birthday. His daughter Philippa gave birth to her first child and the elder Elizabeth

Burgh's eldest great-great-grandchild, Elizabeth Mortimer, later Percy, in February 1371 when she was 15.

Elizabeth Bardolf née Damory did not survive her mother very long; the date of her death is unknown, but she had already passed away when her husband John Bardolf died on or around 3 August 1363 in Assisi, Italy.[17] There is no record of Elizabeth Bardolf receiving dower after John's death so she must have predeceased him, and perhaps died in 1361 or 1362. Sir Nichol Damory, Elizabeth Burgh's adviser and retainer for decades, died at Depden, Suffolk in 1381 when he must have been well into his 70s. After he lost his first wife Eleanor, widow of Eleanor Despenser's stepson Alan Zouche (d. 1346), he married a woman named Joan Cotesford in or before 1363; her brother John, a Master of Arts, was a canon of Lincoln.[18] In early 1359, Damory had been appointed steward of the household of Edward III's eldest daughter Isabella of Woodstock, and performed so well in the role that seven months later Edward III granted him £40 a year in gratitude for his 'good service' to her.[19]

Elizabeth Burgh's cousin and friend Jeanne de Bar, Countess of Surrey, another granddaughter of Edward I, died on 29 August 1361 in her mid-60s.[20] Henry of Grosmont, Duke of Lancaster, Elizabeth's second cousin and a man with whom she had enjoyed a very close friendship, did not have long to enjoy the psalter and cross she had bequeathed him, as he died in Leicester on 23 March 1361 only a few months after Elizabeth. Marie de St Pol, arguably Elizabeth's closest friend and about eight years Elizabeth's junior, lived until May 1377 when she was over 70—neither she nor Jeanne de Bar left any children—and Elizabeth's first cousin King Edward III died the month after Marie, on 21 June 1377 at the age of 64. His eldest son Edward of Woodstock, Prince of Wales, had died the year before, and so Edward was succeeded as king by his 10-year-old grandson Richard II.

Sadly, it is impossible to visit any of the Clare sisters' graves today. Tonbridge Priory in Kent, where Margaret and Hugh Audley were buried in 1342 and 1347, was dissolved as early as 1525, and the few remaining ruins were knocked down in 1842 when a railway line was built across the site. Margaret's first husband Piers Gaveston was buried at the Dominican priory in Kings Langley, Hertfordshire, and his tomb was also lost at the Dissolution, though the tomb of Edward III's fourth son Edmund, first Duke of York (d. 1402) at Langley was saved and still exists. Elizabeth

Burgh's burial place of the Minoresses outside Aldgate in London was closed down in 1539 and nothing survives—a few ruins were destroyed by fire at the end of the 1700s—though the street where it once stood near the Tower of London still bears the name 'Minories'. Eleanor Despenser was luckier than her sisters: the church of Tewkesbury Abbey in Gloucestershire survived the Dissolution because the townspeople bought it from Henry VIII's commissioners in 1539 to use as their parish church, and thus the mausoleum of the Clares and the Despensers still exists, as do the tombs of Eleanor's first husband Hugh Despenser and their eldest son Huchon. The exact location of Eleanor's final resting place in the church is, however, not known.

All three of Elizabeth Burgh's children had offspring of their own, and their lines of descent continued in the late fourteenth century and into the fifteenth, and far beyond. King Edward IV (r. 1461–83) and his younger brother Richard III (r. 1483–85) were Elizabeth's descendants, via her son William Burgh, Earl of Ulster, his granddaughter Philippa Mortimer, Countess of March (1355–80), and Philippa's great-grandson Richard, Duke of York (1411–60), the kings' father. Elizabeth's elder daughter Isabella Ferrers née Verdon was the great-grandmother of Richard Beauchamp, Earl of Warwick (1382–1439), and Isabella had numerous other descendants including Henry Beaufort, Duke of Somerset (1436–64) and Henry Stafford, Duke of Buckingham (1455–83). The grandson of Elizabeth's second daughter Elizabeth Bardolf née Damory, Thomas, Lord Bardolf (b. 1369), died in rebellion against King Henry IV (r. 1399–1413) in 1408. Elizabeth Bardolf was also an ancestor of Richard III's great friend Francis Lovell (d. 1487) and of Henry Norris, executed in 1536 supposedly for being one of the lovers of Queen Anne Boleyn. Margaret Audley née Clare had only one child who lived into adulthood, but her five Stafford grandchildren had many children, and via her descendant Margaret de Foix née Kerdeston (d. 1486), Margaret Audley became the ancestor of numerous kings and queens of France, Spain, Poland, Bohemia and Hungary and Holy Roman Emperors. Margaret's Stafford descendants included Henry Stafford, Duke of Buckingham (also a descendant of her sister Elizabeth), executed by Richard III in 1483, and Henry's son Edward, Duke of Buckingham, executed by Henry VIII in 1521. Only three of Eleanor Despenser's ten children, Edward, Isabella and Elizabeth Despenser, had children of their own who outlived them. Her third son Gilbert (d. 1382) had a son John who died at age 14, her fourth son John Despenser (d. 1366) is oddly obscure and it is not clear whether he married and had children or not, and her middle three Despenser daughters and her youngest son William Zouche entered the religious life. Her eldest son Huchon was married but left no children. Eleanor's great-grandson Thomas Despenser (1373–1400), grandson of her second son Edward Despenser (*c*. 1310–42), was made Earl of Gloucester in 1397, and Thomas's posthumous daughter and heir Isabelle (1400–39) was Countess of Worcester and Warwick by her two marriages and the grandmother of Richard III's queen, Anne Neville (1456-85). Eleanor's youngest daughter Elizabeth Berkeley née Despenser was the mother of Thomas, Lord Berkeley (1353–1417) and was an ancestor of Henry Beaufort, Duke of Somerset (1436–64) and Eleanor Butler née Talbot (d. 1468), alleged to have married Edward IV before he married his queen Elizabeth Woodville. Elizabeth Despenser's second son James Berkeley (*c*. 1354/5–1405) is the ancestor of the later Berkeley family who own Berkeley Castle in Gloucestershire to this day. The Clare sisters all have millions of modern-day descendants; their fascinating, turbulent stories are part of our own history.

Appendix 1: Brief Biographical Details of the Clare Sisters

For ease of reference, the key dates in the sisters' lives:

Eleanor, born *c*. 14 October 1292 at Caerphilly Castle, South Wales; married 1) Hugh Despenser the Younger 26 May 1306, widowed 24 November 1326; married 2) William Zouche before 26 January 1329, widowed 28 February 1337; died 30 June 1337 aged 44, buried at Tewkesbury Abbey in Gloucestershire

Margaret, born sometime between the autumn of 1293 and the autumn of 1294, possibly in Ireland; married 1) Piers Gaveston, Earl of Cornwall, 1 November 1307, widowed 19 June 1312; married 2) Hugh Audley (later Earl of Gloucester, d. 10 November 1347), 28 April 1317; died 2 April 1342 aged 47 or 48, buried at Tonbridge Priory in Kent

Elizabeth, born 16 September 1295 in Tewkesbury, Gloucestershire; married 1) John Burgh 29 September 1308, widowed 18 June 1313; married 2) Theobald Verdon 4 February 1316, widowed 27 July 1316; married 3) Roger Damory *c*. 30 April/3 May 1317, widowed 12 or 13 March 1322; died 4 November 1360 aged 65, buried at the Minoresses outside Aldgate, London

Appendix 2: The Sisters' Children

Eleanor:

1. Hugh 'Huchon' Despenser, lord of Glamorgan, 1308/09 – 8 February 1349; m. Elizabeth Montacute
2. Edward Despenser, *c*. 1310 – 30 September 1342; m. Anne Ferrers
3. Isabella Despenser, *c*. 1312 – after 1356 and before 1369; m. Richard Fitzalan, Earl of Arundel
4. Joan Despenser, *c*. mid-1310s – 15 November 1384; a nun
5. Gilbert Despenser, *c*. mid- or late 1310s – 22 April 1382; m. Ela Calveley
6. Eleanor Despenser, *c*. late 1310s or early 1320s – shortly before 15 February 1351?; a nun
7. John Despenser, *c*. late 1310s or early 1320s – shortly before 10 June 1366; m. ?
8. Unnamed Despenser son, b. and d. shortly before 13 January 1321
9. Margaret Despenser, *c*. 2 August 1323 – 1337; a nun
10. Elizabeth Despenser, *c*. 2/14 December 1325 – 13 July 1389; m. 1) Maurice, Lord Berkeley and 2) Sir Maurice Wyth
11. William Zouche, *c*. 1330 – after 6 December 1390; a monk

(The birth order and birthdates of the Despenser children as shown here may not be completely accurate. Huchon and Edward were certainly the two eldest Despenser boys, and Gilbert was older than John and was the third eldest Despenser son to survive into adulthood. Isabella was certainly the eldest girl, and Margaret and Elizabeth were the fourth and fifth daughters respectively. It is highly likely that Joan was the second daughter, as she was betrothed in 1323, and Eleanor the third, as she was betrothed in 1325. Whether Gilbert and John were older or younger than their sisters Joan and Eleanor, and how the unnamed boy who died in infancy at the beginning of 1321 fits into the birth order, is uncertain.)

Edward II's Nieces: The Clare Sisters

Margaret:

1. Joan Gaveston, *c.* 12 January 1312 – 13 January 1325; betrothed to John Multon, son and heir of Thomas, Lord Multon of Egremont
2. Margaret Audley, *c.* 1321/22 – *c.* 7 September 1349; m. Ralph Stafford, later Earl of Stafford

Elizabeth:

1. William Burgh, Earl of Ulster, 17 September 1312 – 6 June 1333; m. Maud of Lancaster
2. Isabella Verdon, 21 March 1317 – 25 July 1349; m. Henry, Lord Ferrers of Groby
3. Damory child, probably Margaret, *c.* 23 May 1318 – between 1329 and 1337; apparently unmarried
4. Elizabeth Damory, *c.* 1321/2? – *c.* 1361/62?; m. John, Lord Bardolf

Appendix 3: The Descent of the Sisters' Inheritances

The schedules of the November 1317 division of the Clare inheritance are now in the National Archives in Kew: C 47/9/23 (Audley), 24 (Despenser) and 25 (Burgh/Damory). The Earl of Gloucester's Inquisition Post Mortem of July/August 1314 listing his lands in twenty English counties, Wales and Ireland is in *Calendar of Inquisitions Post Mortem 1307–17*, no. 538, pp. 325–54. The dower granted to his widow Maud on 5 December 1314 which was shared out among her three sisters-in-law and their husbands after her death in 1320 and amounted to well in excess of £2,000 annually can be seen in *Calendar of Close Rolls 1313–18*, pp. 131–9. Eleanor and Hugh Despenser the Younger received lands worth £1,415 a year in 1317, and a reversion of £945 from Countess Maud in 1320, to a total of £2,443; Hugh and Margaret Audley received lands worth £1,384 in 1317 and a reversion of £928, to a total of £2,314; and Elizabeth Burgh and Roger Damory received lands of £1,391 plus a reversion of £881, to a total of £2,274.[1]

Eleanor's heir on her death in 1337 was her eldest son Hugh 'Huchon' Despenser, then 28 or 29 years old. Huchon had no children from his marriage to the Earl of Salisbury's daughter Elizabeth Montacute, and his heir after he died in February 1349 was his nephew Edward (1336–75), eldest son of his brother, Eleanor Despenser's second son, Edward (*c.* 1310–42) and Anne Ferrers. The younger Edward married Elizabeth Burghersh, and their only surviving son was Thomas, who was 2 years old when Edward died in 1375. Thomas Despenser, lord of Glamorgan and briefly Earl of Gloucester from 1397 to 1399, married Edward III's granddaughter Constance of York in 1379 when they were both children. Thomas's heir was his daughter Isabelle Despenser, born posthumously on 27 July 1400 six-and-a-half months after his death. Isabelle had a son from her second marriage: Henry Beauchamp, Duke of Warwick, born 1425. After Henry and his little daughter Anne died in 1446 and 1449 respectively, Isabelle's heir was her daughter Anne Beauchamp, born 1426.

Anne married Richard Neville, Earl of Warwick, known to posterity as the 'Kingmaker'. Richard Neville and Anne née Beauchamp's daughters Isabel and Anne Neville, Eleanor Despenser's heirs, married Edward IV's brothers George, Duke of Clarence and Richard, Duke of Gloucester, later Richard III.

Margaret's heir on her death in 1342 was her only surviving child Margaret Stafford née Audley, though the older Margaret's widower Hugh Audley kept all her lands in his hands until his death in 1347, by the custom called the 'courtesy of England'. Margaret Stafford enjoyed her inheritance for less than two years: she died in 1349 in her late 20s. After her widower Ralph Stafford died in 1372, their heir was their second but only surviving son Hugh Stafford, Earl of Stafford. Hugh Stafford and his wife Philippa Beauchamp had five sons; Ralph, the eldest, was murdered by Richard II's half-brother John Holland in 1385 in Hugh's lifetime, and the earldom of Stafford and the Clare/Audley inheritance passed next in succession to Hugh's three sons Thomas, William and Edmund. Thomas Stafford died in 1392 and William in 1395, both childless. Edmund Stafford, the fourth son and Earl of Stafford, was killed at the Battle of Shrewsbury in July 1403, and left a son Humphrey, not yet a year old, from his marriage to Edward III's granddaughter Anne of Gloucester. Humphrey Stafford, Earl of Stafford, was made first Duke of Buckingham in 1444, and outlived his eldest son, also Humphrey. His heir on his death in 1460 was thus his grandson Henry Stafford, Duke of Buckingham and heir to the Clare/Audley lands. Henry Stafford was executed by Richard III in 1483, and his son and heir Edward, Duke of Buckingham, by Henry VIII in 1521.

Elizabeth's heir on her death in 1360 was her granddaughter Elizabeth Burgh, only child of Elizabeth's late son William, Earl of Ulster, then 28 years old. Elizabeth Burgh the younger had married Edward III's second son Lionel of Antwerp in August 1342 when she was 10 and he not yet 4. Lionel and Elizabeth were made Duke and Duchess of Clarence in 1362 the year before Elizabeth died, and their only child and heir Philippa was born at the royal palace of Eltham in Kent on 16 August 1355. Philippa of Clarence married Edmund Mortimer, great-grandson of the Roger Mortimer executed in 1330 and heir to his father's earldom of March, in or before December 1358 when she was 3 and he 6. Philippa and Edmund's second child and first son Roger Mortimer was born on

Appendix 3: The Descent of the Sisters' Inheritances

11 April 1374. When he came of age he inherited the earldoms of March and Ulster and Elizabeth Burgh's share of the Clare inheritance. Roger's son and heir Edmund was born in November 1391, and after he died childless in Ireland in January 1425 left his wealth, lands and titles to his sister Anne Mortimer's son Richard, third Duke of York (1411–60), the father of Edward IV and Richard III, and the heir of Elizabeth Burgh.

Abbreviations

C	Chancery (National Archives)
CCR	Calendar of Close Rolls
CChR	Calendar of Charter Rolls
CCW	Calendar of Chancery Warrants 1244–1326
CFR	Calendar of Fine Rolls
CIM	Calendar of Inquisitions Miscellaneous
CIPM	Calendar of Inquisitions Post Mortem
CMR	Calendar of Memoranda Rolls Michaelmas 1326–Michaelmas 1327
CP	The Complete Peerage of England, Scotland, Ireland, Great Britain and the United Kingdom, ed. V. Gibbs
CPL	Calendar of Entries in the Papal Registers: Letters
CPR	Calendar of Patent Rolls
DL	Duchy of Lancaster (National Archives)
E	Exchequer (National Archives)
EHR	English Historical Review
FCE	Fourteenth Century England
IPM	Inquisition Post Mortem
ODNB	Oxford Dictionary of National Biography
PROME	Parliament Rolls of Medieval England
SAL MS	Society of Antiquaries of London, manuscript
SC	Special Collections (National Archives)
Underhill	F. Underhill, For Her Good Estate: The Life of Elizabeth de Burgh
Vita	*Vita Edwardi Secundi*, ed. N. Denholm-Young

Endnotes

Chapter 1: The Clare Sisters

1. The National Archives E 101/333/15; M. Morris, *A Great and Terrible King: Edward I and the Forging of Britain* (2008), 100; M. Prestwich, *Edward I* (1988), 78; S. Cockerill, *Eleanor of Castile: The Shadow Queen* (2014), 177–8.
2. Oxford Dictionary of National Biography.
3. Cited in ODNB.
4. *Calendar of Close Rolls 1288–96*, 138, 151–2, *Calendar of Patent Rolls 1281–92*, 359–60, and *Calendar of Charter Rolls*, vol. 2, 1257–1300, 350–1, for Gilbert's surrender of his lands and the re-grant. See *Calendar of Inquisitions Post Mortem*, vol. 25, 1437–42 (2010), no. 319, for an example of the confirmation of the 1290 re-grant and the identities and birth order of Gilbert's heirs 150 years later in 1440.
5. For Maud's personality, feud with Gilbert and favouritism, see L. E. Mitchell, *Portraits of Medieval Women: Family, Marriage, and Politics in England 1225–1350* (2003), 37–9, 42. Maud died before 10 March 1289: *CCR 1288–96*, 6.
6. M. A. E. Green, *Lives of the Princesses of England*, vol. 2 (1867), 331.
7. Cockerill, *Eleanor of Castile*, 338.
8. Cockerill, *Eleanor of Castile*, 337.
9. ODNB; L. F. Salzman, *Edward I* (1968), 92–3.
10. Green, *Lives of the Princesses*, vol. 2, 334–5; *CCR 1288–96*, 89.
11. Cockerill, *Eleanor of Castile*, 341–2; Green, *Lives of the Princesses*, 335–6.
12. Cited in Morris, *Great and Terrible King*, 231.
13. *CIPM 1291–1300*, no. 371, and *CIPM 1300–7*, no. 435, are the IPMs of Joan and Gilbert 'the Red', and give the younger Gilbert's approximate date of birth. Eleanor of Provence, widow of Henry III and mother of Edward I, and Joan of Acre's last surviving grandparent, died a few weeks after the birth of her latest great-grandchild, at Amesbury Priory in Wiltshire on 24 June 1291.

14. *CCR 1288–96*, 169–70.
15. *CPR 1292–1301*, 592, 606.
16. L. Benz St John, *Three Medieval Queens: Queenship and the Crown in Fourteenth-Century England* (2012), 119.
17. F. Underhill, *For Her Good Estate: The Life of Elizabeth de Burgh* (1999), 7.
18. ODNB; Morris, *Great and Terrible King*, 256.
19. *CPR 1292–1301*, 183.
20. The date of birth is based on a comment by a priory annalist that Joan of Acre was purified on the feast of St Clement, i.e. 23 November, in 1292. The ceremony of purification or churching normally took place forty days after childbirth, which would place Eleanor's date of birth on or around 14 October. If Joan's purification took place only thirty days after birth, as was sometimes the case with female children in this era, Eleanor was born on or about 24 October 1292. *Annales Monastici*, vol. 4, ed. H. R. Luard (1869), 511; also *Annales de Wigornia*, 511, cited in *The Complete Peerage of England, Scotland, Ireland, Great Britain and the United Kingdom*, ed. V. Gibbs, vol. 4 (1916), 271 note e. I owe the *Annales Monastici* reference to Brad Verity.
21. SC 1/22/156; Prestwich, *Edward I*, 233–4.
22. *CPR 1292–1301*, 9–13, 19, 20, 22, etc.
23. Elizabeth's exact date and place of birth are given in *CP*, vol. 4, on the 'Addenda & Corrigenda' page near the front of the volume. Unfortunately, no source is cited for the statement.
24. *CPR 1292–1301*, 243.
25. *Annales Londonienses 1195–1330*, in ed. W. Stubbs, *Chronicles of the Reigns of Edward I and Edward II*, vol. 1 (1882), 133.
26. Underhill, 6.
27. E 101/369/11, fo. 96r (minstrels, gifts from the king, date of the wedding); C. Bullock-Davies, *Menestrellorum Multitudo: Minstrels at a Royal Feast* (1978), xxv (cloth). See also *The Chronicle of Pierre Langtoft*, ed. T. Wright, vol. 2 (1868), 368–9, a rhyming chronicle in French which says that at the time of mass knighting in May 1306 'Sir Hugh son of Hugh, called Despenser/Took there the maiden of noble kindred/ Whom Gilbert de Clare had begotten/On Joan the countess, surnamed of Acre' (*Sir Huge le fiz Hug, Despenser appellez/I prist la pucelle de gentil parentz/Quele Gilbert de Clare avoit engendrez/Sur Jone la countesse de Acres surnomez*).

28. *CCR 1307–13*, 5; *CPR 1301–7*, 443, 526–7, 536.
29. Béarn lay within the part of France then ruled by the English kings, so it is not entirely correct to call him 'French.'
30. *CCR 1302–7*, 533.
31. *Cartulary of the Augustinian Friars of Clare*, ed. C. Harper-Bill (1991), 12.

Chapter 2: The New King

1. *CPR 1301–7*, 460. Edward II duly granted Norfolk to his half-brother Thomas in late 1312.
2. *CIPM 1291–1300*, no. 604. Edmund was the only surviving legitimate son of Henry III's younger brother Richard, Earl of Cornwall (1209 -72) and married Margaret, sister of Gilbert `the Red' Clare, Earl of Gloucester, in 1272.
3. The National Archives E 41/460; *CChR 1300–26*, 108.
4. *CFR 1307–19*, 18.
5. Edward I gave Gaveston custody of the lands of the late Edmund Mortimer in July 1304 and he must have been at least 21 then. Gaveston's parents were already married by 30 June 1272 and he was their second child, with three younger siblings. *CPR 1301–7*, 244; J. S. Hamilton, *Piers Gaveston, Earl of Cornwall 1307–1312: Politics and Patronage in the Reign of Edward II* (1988), 21.
6. F. Devon, *Issues of the Exchequer* (1837), 119–20; C. Bullock-Davies, *A Register of Royal and Baronial Minstrels 1272–1327* (1986), 119.
7. Devon, *Issues*, 120.
8. N. Fryde, *The Tyranny and Fall of Edward II 1321–1326* (1979), 34.
9. *Scalacronica: The Reigns of Edward I, Edward II and Edward III, as Recorded by Sir Thomas Gray*, ed. H. Maxwell (1907), 50.
10. *Vita Edwardi Secundi Monachi Cuiusdam Malmesberiensis*, ed. N. Denholm-Young (1957), 16.
11. *Chronicon Galfridi de Baker de Swynebroke*, ed. E. M. Thompson (1889), 4.
12. Cited in Hamilton, *Piers Gaveston*, 110.
13. *Vita Edwardi Secundi*, 14–15, for the quotation.
14. *Chronique Métrique de Godefroy de Paris*, ed. J. A. Buchon (1827), 182, 196, 244.
15. *Scalacronica*, ed. Maxwell, 45; *Scalacronica: By Sir Thomas Gray of Heton, Knight*, ed. J. Stevenson (1836), 136: *de soun corps vn dez plus*

fortz hom de soun realme. Eleanor's seal can be seen in W. de Gray Birch, *A History of Margam Abbey* (1897), opposite p. 301.
16. *CPR 1307–13*, 1, 21, 50.
17. *CFR 1307–19*, 18, dated 16 March 1308.
18. *CPR 1307–13*, 74, 78–9.
19. R. M. Haines, *Edward II: His Life, His Reign, and Its Aftermath, 1284–1330* (2003), 61–2.
20. *The Chronicle of Lanercost 1272–1346*, ed. H. Maxwell (1913), 187.
21. P. Chaplais, *Piers Gaveston: Edward II's Adoptive Brother* (1994), 45; *Calendar of Chancery Warrants*, vol. 1: 1244–1326 (1927), 275; E. Hallam, *The Itinerary of Edward II and his Household 1307–1327* (1984), 32.
22. See Hamilton, *Piers Gaveston*, for a discussion of Gaveston's competent leadership in Ireland.
23. Underhill, 10, 157 note 26.
24. *The Anonimalle Chronicle 1307 to 1334*, ed. W. R. Childs and J. Taylor (1991), 132.
25. *CPR 1301–7*, 443.

Chapter 3: Journeys to Ireland

1. J. C. Davies, *The Baronial Opposition to Edward II: Its Character and Policy* (1917), 91 note 3.
2. Davies, *Baronial Opposition*, 91 note 3.
3. Davies, *Baronial Opposition*, 91 note 7.
4. *Collectanea Topographica et Genealogica*, vol. 4, eds. F. Madden, B. Bandinel and J. G. Nichols (1837), 64.
5. *Vita*, 7–8.
6. G. L. Haskins, 'A Chronicle of the Civil Wars of Edward II', *Speculum*, 14 (1939), 76 (wicked and impious); *Vita*, 1–3, for the other details.
7. *Recueil de Lettres Anglo-Françaises 1265–1399*, ed. F. J. Tanqueray (1916), 96.
8. Underhill, 10.
9. *Vita*, 8.
10. C 53/96, no. 24: Despenser witnessed a royal charter on 24 December 1309.
11. *CCR 1307–13*, 237; *CCW*, 308; *CFR 1307–19*, 54; *CCR 1307–13*, 198; *Calendar of Inquisitions Miscellaneous (Chancery)*, vol. 2, 1308–48 (1916), 20.

Endnotes   213

12. Devon, *Issues of the Exchequer*, 124.
13. See for example the case of Henry, Lord Beaumont, born in the duchy of Brabant in late 1339, who was not returned as his grandmother's heir in 1349 as he should have been, and Edward III had to change the law: *CIPM 1347–52*, no. 415; *CPR 1340–3*, 72–3; *CPR 1350–4*, 63.
14. *CCW*, 357.
15. *The Household Book of Queen Isabella of England for the Fifth Regnal Year of Edward II, 8th July 1311 to 7th July 1312*, eds. F. D. Blackley and G. Hermansen (1971), 19, 157.
16. *CCR 1307–13*, 351; *Household Book*, xiv; *CIPM 1272–1300*, 227, for Barnwell.
17. E 101/380/4, fos. 16r and 22r, and *CCW*, 263 (Emma and Joan); SC 8/147/7323 (Maud); J. Ward, *Elizabeth de Burgh, Lady of Clare (1295–1360)* (2014), 69, 77, 141, and Underhill, 115 (Suzanne and Anne); *Petitions to the Pope 1342–1419*, ed. W. H. Bliss (1896), 74 (Petronilla and Agnes). Pernel or Petronilla Pagham later served Maud of Lancaster's daughter Elizabeth Burgh (1332–63), namesake granddaughter and heir of Elizabeth Burgh née Clare: *CPR 1350–4*, 307.
18. *Household Book of Queen Isabella*, xiv, xv, xxvi, 31, 157, 203; E 101/380/4, fo. 22r, for 1324/25.
19. An attendant of Queen Isabella called Cecily, wife of John Chaucomb, is mentioned in 1324/25 and 1327; possibly this was Cecily Leygrave's married name. E 101/380/4, fo. 22r; *CPR 1327–30*, 27.
20. *Annales Londonienses*, 200.
21. *CPR 1307–13*, 397.
22. *Vita*, 20–21.
23. *CPR 1307–13*, 405.
24. J. R. S. Phillips, *Aymer de Valence, Earl of Pembroke 1307–1324: Baronial Politics in the Reign of Edward II* (1972), 131.
25. *Household Book*, 31, 37, 139, 20; *CFR 1307–19*, 117–8 (Wallingford and Gaveston's other lands).
26. *Gesta Edwardi de Carnarvon Auctore Canonico Bridlingtoniensi*, in ed. W. Stubbs, *Chronicles of the Reigns of Edward I and Edward II*, vol. 2 (1883), 42, records the birth of the Gavestons' infant, but does not name her; Chaplais, *Piers Gaveston*, 78–9; Hamilton, *Piers Gaveston*, 93–4.
27. Hamilton, *Piers Gaveston*, 94.
28. Chaplais, *Piers Gaveston*, 77.

29. *CCR 1307–13*, 448–9; *Foedera, Conventiones, Literae*, vol. 2.1, 1307–27, ed. T. Rymer (1818), 153.

Chapter 4: Two Young Widows

1. Bullock-Davies, *Register of Minstrels*, 143; R. Rastall, 'Secular Musicians in Late Medieval England', Univ. of Manchester PhD thesis, (1968), 62.
2. *Flores Historiarum*, ed. H. R. Luard, vol. 3 (1890), 335.
3. *Monasticon Anglicanum*, ed. W. Dugdale, vol. 2 (new edition, 1819), 61. I owe this reference to Brad Verity.
4. J. R. Maddicott, *Thomas of Lancaster 1307–1322: A Study in the Reign of Edward II* (1970), 127.
5. *Vita Edwardi Secundi*, 25.
6. *Flores Historiarum*, vol. 3, 152–3.
7. *Annales Londonienses*, 206–7.
8. *Vita*, 25.
9. *Annales Paulini 1307–1340*, in ed. W. Stubbs, *Chronicles of the Reigns of Edward I and Edward II*, vol. 1 (1882), 271; *Anonimalle Chronicle*, 86.
10. *Vita*, 26.
11. *Johannis de Trokelowe et Henrici de Blaneforde Chronica et Annales*, ed. H. T. Riley (1866), 77.
12. *Vita*, 26.
13. *Vita*, 26–8.
14. *Vita*, 26–7.
15. *Vita*, 27, and for Gaveston's execution, see also: *Annales Londonienses*, 207; *Annales Paulini*, 271; *Anonimalle*, 86; *Chronicon Galfridi de Baker*, 5; *Gesta Edwardi de Carnarvon*, 44; *Flores Historiarum*, vol. 3, 152; *Lanercost*, 198; *Adae Murimuth Continuatio Chronicarum*, ed. E. M. Thompson (1889), 17–18; *Johannis de Trokelowe*, 77.
16. *Foedera 1307–27*, 203–5.
17. *CFR 1307–19*, 136–7; *CCR 1307–13*, 427–8; *CPR 1307–13*, 465.
18. *Anonimalle*, 86; *The Brut or the Chronicles of England*, part 1, ed. F. W. D. Brie (1906), 207; *Vita*, 30; *Johannis de Trokelowe*, 77.
19. *Vita*, 29.
20. *Lanercost*, 203; Davies, *Baronial Opposition*, 85.
21. *CPR 1324–7*, 281.
22. Hamilton, *Piers Gaveston*, 99.

23. *CChR 1300–26*, 111, 131; *CPR 1307–13*, 497, 502; *CCR 1307–13*, 225–6, 538; *CPR 1313–17,* 576–8. The older Margaret, Countess of Cornwall, died shortly before 16 September 1312: *CFR 1307–19*, 146.
24. SC 8/192/9551; *CCW*, 433. The petition begins *Mon tresch[er] e treshon [ur]able seign[eur] a v[ost]re hautesce monstre Margarete de Gavastoun contesse de Cornewaille.*
25. *CCW*, 394; *CPR 1313–17,* 87. Her brother the Earl of Gloucester was also in Canterbury at this time: C 53/100, no. 16.
26. Davies, *Baronial Opposition*, 91 note 7.

Chapter 5: The Earl of Gloucester's Heirs

1. T. Stapleton, 'A Brief Summary of the Wardrobe Accounts of the Tenth, Eleventh and Fourteenth Years of King Edward the Second', *Archaeologia*, 26 (1836), 341.
2. Thomas Clare (*c*. 1245–87), younger brother of Gilbert 'the Red', left sons Gilbert and Richard, but they died in 1307 and 1318, and when Richard's infant son Thomas died in 1321, the male Clare line ended completely. The heirs of Thomas Clare (d. 1287) were his daughters Margaret Badlesmere and Maud Clifford: *CIPM 1317–27*, no. 275.
3. *CFR 1307–19*, 201; *CIPM 1307–17*, 325; *1313–18*, 131–9 (lists Maud's dower); T. B. Pugh, 'The Marcher Lords of Glamorgan and Morgannwg, 1317–1485', in ed. T. B. Pugh, *Glamorgan County History, III: The Middle Ages* (1971), 167. The earl's IPM: *CIPM 1307–17*, no. 538, pp. 325–54.
4. *CFR 1307–19*, 202.
5. *CIPM 1307–17*, 352–3.
6. *CFR 1307–19*, 224–5. Damory was with the king on 3 February 1315: *CPR 1313–17,* 248. He is presumably the 'Roger Amory' who was involved, with a large group of other men, in an assault on the sheriff of Cornwall in or before July 1309: *CPR 1307–13*, 236–7.
7. *CPR 1313–17*, 622, 666; Davies, *Baronial Opposition*, 221.
8. *CFR 1307–19*, 353, 355, 363.
9. *CIPM 1327–36*, no. 275.
10. *Vita*, 123; SC 8/42/2053, *CIM 1308–48*, no. 509 and *CCR 1318–23*, 596, for Bletchingdon; M. Altschul, *A Baronial Family in Medieval England: The Clares, 1217–1314* (1965), 305, for Easton; also see

216   Edward II's Nieces: The Clare Sisters

http://www.british-history.ac.uk/vch/bucks/vol4/pp237-242 (accessed 25 May 2018). Evidently the Damory brothers were on good terms: Roger appointed Richard as his attorney in June 1320 when he went overseas. *CPR 1317–21*, 455.
11. *CFR 1307–19*, 228, 230, 234, 237; *CCR 1313–18*, 307.
12. *CCR 1313–18*, 139.
13. *Foedera 1307–27*, 259 (Oxford); TNA E/101/375/15; E/101/376/2; E/101/375/16 (Gaveston's funeral arrangements); C. F. R. Palmer, 'The Friar-Preachers of Kings Langley', *The Reliquary*, 23 (1882–3), 156 (£15); Hamilton, *Piers Gaveston*, 166 note 84 (£144).
14. Hamilton, *Gaveston*, 100, 166–7.

Chapter 6: The First Abduction

1. Fryde, *Tyranny and Fall of Edward II*, 33, claims that Despenser took the castle from Maud directly with his 'characteristic brutality'. There is no evidence whatsoever that Maud was at Tonbridge at the time, or that anyone was hurt during the episode.
2. *CPR 1313–17*, 306–7; *CFR 1307–19*, 248; *CIPM 1307–17*, 351–2.
3. *CIPM 1307–17*, 352; *CCR 1313–18*, 301.
4. *CIPM 1307–17*, 353.
5. *The Parliament Rolls of Medieval England*, ed. Brand, Curry et al (2005), January/February 1316 Parliament, 352–3.
6. C. Moor, *Knights of Edward I*, vol. 5 (1932), 105; *The Parliamentary Writs and Writs of Military Summons*, ed. F. Palgrave, vol. 1 (1827), 295.
7. *CPR 1307–13*, 568. He was replaced on 4 January 1315, just after Gaveston's funeral: *CPR 1313–17*, 207.
8. *PROME*, January/February 1316 parliament, 352–3.
9. *CPR 1327–30*, 481; *CCR 1330–3*, 53.
10. Margaret Badlesmere née Clare was one of the two daughters and ultimately the two co-heirs of Thomas Clare (*c.* 1245–87), lord of Thomond in Ireland and younger brother of Gilbert 'the Red'. Thomas's elder son Gilbert (1281–1307) was briefly married to Hugh Despenser the Younger's sister Isabella.
11. Cited in *The Political Songs of England*, ed. T. Wright (1839), 264.

12. J. R. Maddicott's biography of Badlesmere in the ODNB calls him an 'able man' and states that Edward II's inability to retain his loyalty speaks volumes about the king's failings.
13. *CPR 1317–21*, 467–8, 473.
14. *CPR 1313–17*, 384, 432–3.
15. M. Vale, *The Princely Court: Medieval Courts and Culture in North-West Europe* (2001), 109.

Chapter 7: Widowed Again

1. His IPM is in *CIPM 1317–27*, no. 54. The Staffordshire jurors stated on 8 October 1316 that Elizabeth Burgh was 'pregnant with a living child'. The Shropshire and Oxfordshire jurors also knew she was pregnant, but Wiltshire, Herefordshire, Warwickshire and Leicestershire appear not to have heard.
2. *CFR 1307–19*, 294, 116–17.
3. He was buried at Croxden Abbey in Staffordshire, just a couple of miles from his main seat at Alton; Elizabeth left a bequest of money to the abbey in her will thirty-nine years later.
4. SC 1/63/150; the transcription and translation are mine. A bachelor was a knight in another knight's or lord's retinue.
5. Damory witnessed a grant to Bartholomew Badlesmere on 24 October 1308 with other members of Gloucester's retinue such as Richard Clare, Roger Tyrell and Fulk Peyferer: *CCR 1307–13*, 246. *Collectanea Topographica et Genealogica*, vol. 4, 64, for Dunstable.
6. Stapleton, 'Brief Summary of the Wardrobe Accounts', 320.
7. *CCR 1313–18*, 430.
8. *Johannis de Trokelowe*, 95; Stapleton, 'Brief Summary', 320.
9. Maddicott, *Thomas of Lancaster*, 187.
10. *CPR 1313–17*, 576–8; *CCW*, 433, 459, 463.
11. Davies, *Baronial Opposition*, 433.
12. *CPR 1313–17*, 162; *Calendar of Documents Relating to Scotland*, vol. 3, 1307–1357, ed. J. Bain (1887), nos. 383, 583.
13. *CFR 1319–27*, 51–2; *CPR 1327–30*, 30; *CCR 1327–30*, 27.
14. C 53/103, nos. 38, 43.
15. Stapleton, 'Brief Summary', 343.

Chapter 8: Two Favourites, Two Weddings

1. *CFR 1307–19*, 316–17; *CPR 1317–21*, 125.
2. *CPR 1313–17*, 535.
3. Stapleton, 'Brief Summary', 339. Joan Montacute née Verdon married her second husband Thomas Furnival in February 1318, still only 14-and-a-half-years old.
4. *Vita Edwardi Secundi*, 87; *Flores Historiarum*, 178; Phillips, *Aymer de Valence*, 119.
5. *Vita*, 80.
6. *Vita*, 87.
7. Stapleton, 'Brief Summary', 338; *CIPM 1327–36*, no. 395.
8. *CIPM 1327–36*, nos. 83, 389.
9. *CIPM 1327–36*, no. 395 (visit); *CPR 1313–17*, 641 (Scales). The favour to Scales was recorded at Clarendon, and Elizabeth might have travelled there to meet her uncle and returned to Amesbury with him and Damory, bearing in mind that subjects were supposed to travel to their king and not vice versa.
10. Elizabeth's brother-in-law Hugh Despenser the Younger witnessed three of Edward's charters in Andover on 11 April (C 53/203, nos. 16, 18, 32), though Roger Damory himself did not.
11. *CPR 1313–17*, 644.
12. *CPR 1313–17*, 662–3; *CPR 1317–21*, 26.
13. Underhill, 18, 135; E 101/377/2.
14. *Petitions to the Pope 1342–1419*, 22 (vow); Ward, *Lady of Clare*, 143 (will). See also S. S. Morrison's *Women Pilgrims in Late Medieval England* (2002) for Elizabeth's love of pilgrimage.
15. *CPR 1317–21*, 42.
16. *CPR 1313–17*, 664.
17. Underhill, 19. She is much more indulgent towards Verdon and his abduction of Elizabeth from Bristol Castle, speculating that Elizabeth consented to and desired the match: 15–16.
18. Moor, *Knights of Edward I*, vol. 1, 10–11. The Damory brothers' mother, or stepmother, was called Juliana, and they had a sister Katherine, who married Sir Walter Poer or Poure of Oxfordshire. *Inquisitions and Assessments Relating to Feudal Aids 1284–1431*, vol. 1, ed. A. S. Maskelyne (1899), 81.

19. Stapleton, 'Brief Summary', 337–8.
20. Underhill, 135.
21. *CCW*, 468; *CPR 1313–17*, 664. She surrendered them to the king sometime before her wedding, and she and Audley received them back jointly.
22. *CP*, vol. 1, 347. Hugh Audley's mother Isolde, wife of Walter Balun (d. 1287) and secondly of Hugh Audley the Elder, was long believed to have been a member of the Mortimer family, though genealogist Douglas Richardson has discovered evidence that she was the daughter of Sir Roger le Rous (d. 1294) of Gloucestershire. See his post on www.soc.genealogy.medieval, 'C. P. Addition: Isolde le Rous, wife of Walter de Balun and Hugh de Audley, Lord Audley', dated 17 December 2017 (accessed 13 February 2018). Alice Audley married Ralph Greystoke, who was born in 1299, so she was probably a few years younger than her brothers James and Hugh and born *c.* late 1290s or 1300.
23. T. F. Tout, *The Place of the Reign of Edward II in English History* (second edition, 1936), 315.
24. *CPR 1313–17*, 578.
25. *CCW*, 470; *CPR 1313–7*, 660–1, 666.
26. *Johannis de Trokelowe*, 98–9.

Chapter 9: A Rich Inheritance

1. *CCR 1313–18*, 404–5, 469, 560, 576.
2. The division is C 47/9/23, 24 and 25.
3. Pugh, 'Marcher Lords', 167, 603 note 1.
4. Alice Lacy's grandfather Edmund Lacy was the brother of the Clare sisters' grandmother Maud Clare née Lacy, Countess of Gloucester. Like the Clare sisters, Alice was a great-granddaughter of Margaret Quincy, Countess of Lincoln.
5. *CPR 1317–21*, 5–6, 10; E 40/1432; SC 8/18/868A to H.
6. *CPR 1317–21*, 415, 587.
7. *CPR 1317–21*, 46; *CCR 1313–18*, 575; *Foedera*, 345–6; Stapleton, 'Brief Summary', 329, for the surrender of Knaresborough to Edward; *CIM*, no, 392.
8. *CFR 1307–19*, 225, 316.
9. *CPR 1317–21*, 34, 46, 58.

220   Edward II's Nieces: The Clare Sisters

10. *CPR 1317–21*, 2, 23, 39, 44, 79, 81, 99, and many more.
11. M. Saaler, *Edward II* (1997), 97.
12. See Appendix 2 of my Hugh biography, *Downfall of a King's Favourite*.
13. *CPR 1317–21*, 133, 292; *CCR 1313–18*, 542; *CCR 1318–23*, 71; SC 8/83/4018A. C 53/104, 105 and 106 are the charters issued by Edward II in the eleventh, twelfth and thirteenth years of his reign; Hugh Audley witnessed five charters in the eleventh regnal year which ran from 8 July 1317 to 7 July 1318, but none at all in the twelfth or thirteenth, July 1318 to July 1320. All five charters are dated August 1317, and an unspecified 'Hugh Audley' witnessed another on 7 December 1317. It is not always possible to determine in the records of Edward II's reign whether Audley or his father of the same name was meant.
14. Phillips, *Aymer de Valence*, 139–47, 317–19,
15. *CPR 1317–21*, 60, 103, 120–1; *CCR 1313–18*, 531–2.
16. *CPR 1317–21*, 208, 257, 456.
17. *PROME*, August 1321 parliament; *CCR 1318–23*, 494.
18. *Flores Historiarum*, vol. 3, 342.
19. *Lanercost*, 230; *Vita*, 115.
20. M. Prestwich, 'The Court of Edward II', *The Reign of Edward II: New Perspectives*, ed. G. Dodd and A. Musson (2006), 66–7.
21. *CPR 1317–21*, 66–7.
22. Stapleton, 'Brief Summary', 337.

Chapter 10: The New Favourite

1. *CPR 1317–21*, 125; Elizabeth Verdon is wrongly called 'Isabella'.
2. Stapleton, 'Brief Summary', 338; *CPR 1317–21*, 146, 181. For Roger Damory and Elizabeth Burgh's children, see also Chapter 13.
3. M. Prestwich, *The Three Edwards: War and State in England 1272–1377* (1980), 161.
4. C. M. Woolgar, *The Great Household in Late Medieval England* (1999), 27.
5. *Vita*, 87.
6. Maddicott, *Thomas of Lancaster*, 224; *Aymer de Valence*, 131.
7. *Foedera 1307–27*, 370; *CCR 1318–23*, 112–4.
8. *Foedera 1307–27*, 377; Tout, *Place of the Reign*, 315, 350.
9. *CCR 1313–18*, 109–10.

10. His third son Edward Montacute, who later married Edward II's niece Alice of Norfolk, accompanied him to Gascony, and there is a reference in one of Edward II's accounts to his boat there, *La Peronele*. The younger William Montacute also appears in the king's accounts some years later. E 101/380/4, fo. 7v.
11. E 101/506/23, mems. 1, 2; C 53/105, nos. 26, 31; *CPR 1317–21*, 292; *CCR 1318–23*, 10, 31.
12. *CCR 1318–23*, 143; *CPR 1317–21*, 251; *CFR 1307–19*, 374.
13. *CPR 1317–21*, 583.
14. *CCR 1318–23*, 81.
15. *CPR 1317–21*, 342, 362; *CCR 1318–23*, 71, 138; C 53/104.
16. *CP*, vol. 6, 190 note d.
17. E 101/506/23, mem. 1; C 53/105, nos. 26, 31; C 53/106, no. 34; *CCR 1318–23*, 138. He had, however, become enormously wealthy as a result of the king's infatuation with him: in July 1319 seven men acknowledged that they owed him almost £2,500, and he had a few debtors in Ireland as well. *CCR 1318–23*, 154, 202.
18. J. S. Hamilton, 'Charter Witness Lists for the Reign of Edward II', *Fourteenth Century England I*, ed. Nigel Saul (2000), 5–6, 17; C 53/112 and 113.
19. *Cartae et Alia Munimenta quae ad Domimium de Glamorgancia Pertinent*, vol. 3 (1910), 1063–5.
20. *Anonimalle Chronicle*, 92–3; *Chronicon Galfridi de Baker de Swynebroke*, 10; *Lanercost*, 208, 229; *Scalacronica*, ed. Maxwell, 70.
21. Cited in S. Phillips, *Edward II* (2010), 98.
22. *True Chronicles of Jean le Bel, 1290–1360*, trans. and ed. Nigel Bryant (2011), 31.
23. See Chapter 17 below.
24. SC 8/56/2760, 61 and 62; SC 8/162/8098; *CPR 1317–21*, 440–1, 510.
25. *CPR 1317–21*, 468, 472.
26. J. S. Hamilton, 'Some Notes on 'Royal' Medicine', *Fourteenth Century England II*, ed. C. Given-Wilson (2002), 37; Phillips, *Edward II*, 363 note 222; Prestwich, 'Court of Edward II', *Reign of Edward II*, ed. Dodd and Musson, 71.
27. *Recueil de Lettres Anglo-Françaises 1265–1399*, ed. F. J. Tanqueray, 313–14, Lassam or Lysan d'Avene was a keeper of the peace in Glamorgan. Eleanor sent Inge another letter dated at Westminster on 29 January,

probably either in 1318 or 1321, in which she referred to a debt she owed to her father-in-law's long-term adherent Sir Ingelram Berenger: *Calendar of Ancient Correspondence Concerning Wales*, ed. J. Goronwy Edwards (1935), 219.
28. SC 1/36/88; E 199/31/8.
29. Woolgar, *Great Household*, 12, 46, 190.
30. *CPR 1317–21*, 418, 421, 426, 449, 452, 455.
31. E 40/386 *Cartulary of the Augustinian Friars of Clare*, 32–3; C53/107, nos. 24, 27–32.
32. *Flores Historiarum*, 342.
33. *CCR 1318–23*, 494.
34. *CFR 1319–27*, 2–3.
35. *CCR 1318–23*, 268.
36. *Vita*, 109.
37. *CPR 1317–21*, 531–2. Eleanor and Hugh Despenser the Younger's son and heir Huchon asked for the same grant to be inspected and confirmed in November 1343, as it had been 'lost by accident'. *CPR 1343–5*, 132.

Chapter 11: The Despenser War

1. Stapleton, 'Brief Summary', 340.
2. Stapleton, 'Brief Summary', 338.
3. *Ancient Correspondence Concerning Wales*, 180–1.
4. *CPR 1317–21*, 572–3, 578; *CFR 1319–27*, 51–2; *CCR 1318–23*, 365.
5. W. H. Stevenson, 'A Letter of the Younger Despenser on the Eve of the Barons' Rebellion, 21 March 1321', *EHR*, 12 (1897), 759 (in French; my translation).
6. *CFR 1319–27*, 51–3, 55, 57, 58 etc; *CCR 1327–30*, 27.
7. *CPR 1317–21*, 587; *CFR 1319–27*, 57.
8. *CPR 1321–4*, 65; SC 8/57/2829.
9. SC 8/99/4925. The man was Matthew Crauthorne; his appointment is in *CFR 1319–27*, 59.
10. Stevenson, 'Letter', 760–1.
11. *CFR 1319–27*, 51, 55.
12. SC 8/123/6145.
13. *CCR 1318–23*, 368, 371.

14. *The Brut or the Chronicles of England*, 213; *Johannis de Trokelowe*, 109; *Annales Paulini*, 303.
15. *CCR 1318–23*, 541–3.
16. *CCR 1318–23*, 541–2; *CPR 1321–4*, 294; J. C. Davies, 'The Despenser War in Glamorgan', *Transactions of the Royal Historical Society*, 9 (1915), 55–6.
17. *CCR 1318–23*, 541–2; *Vita*, 110–11.
18. *CPR 1321–4*, 164–5, 169, 319.
19. *CPR 1321–4*, 15–18.
20. *CCR 1318–23*, 402, 408; *CFR 1319–27*, 70.
21. *CFR 1319–27*, 80; *CPR 1321–4*, 37.
22. *Calendar of Ancient Petitions Relating to Wales*, ed. W. Rees (1975), 139–40.

Chapter 12: Contrariants

1. *CCR 1318–23*, 516; S. Waugh, 'The Profits of Violence: The Minor Gentry in the Rebellion of 1322 in Gloucestershire and Herefordshire', *Speculum*, 52 (1977), 850.
2. Maddicott, *Thomas of Lancaster*, 305; *CCR 1318–23*, 511–12.
3. *CCR 1318–23*, 526.
4. *CCR 1318–23*, 522.
5. *CCR 1318–23*, 522.
6. Palgrave, *Parliamentary Writs*, vol. 2, 261: *mes Roger pur ceo qe notre seignour le Roi vous ad en temps moult amez e fuistes de sa meygne e prives de lui e auez sa niece esposee, notre dit seignour le Roi de sa grace e sa realte met en respit execucioun de ce jugement a sa volunte.*
7. *The Brut or the Chronicles of England*, 216–17
8. Ward, *Lady of Clare*, 84.
9. J. Ward, *Women of the English Nobility and Gentry 1066–1500* (1995), 84, 184: Elizabeth paid 3 shillings to keep her father's anniversary on 7 December 1351. Ward, *Lady of Clare*, 76: she kept her brother's anniversary on 23 June in 1352 and paid 2 shillings and 3 pence, and John Burgh's on 18 June and Theobald Verdon's on 27 July (the exact dates of their deaths), giving 1 shilling and 4 pence and 2 shillings and 1 pence respectively. On 12 March 1351, the twenty-ninth anniversary of Damory's death, she provided enough wheat to bake 1,240 loaves for the poor, and 900 herring.

10. *Vita*, 123.
11. G. A. Holmes, 'A Protest Against the Despensers, 1326', *Speculum*, 30 (1955), 210: *feut pursui et oppres tant qil deuya*.
12. Underhill, 29.
13. *Calendar of Entries in the Papal Registers Relating to Great Britain and Ireland: Papal Letters*, vol. 3, 1342–62, ed. W. H. Bliss and C. Johnson (1897), 113.
14. *A Collection of All the Wills, Now Known to be Extant, of the Kings and Queens of England*, ed. J. Nichols (1780), 29; *CPR 1334–8*, 102.
15. Holmes, 'Protest', 210; *CCR 1318–23*, 428.
16. *CCR 1318–23*, 578, 651; *CCR 1323–7*, 65.
17. *Ancient Petitions Relating to Wales*, 139–40.
18. In her will of 1355, Elizabeth left a bequest to the Franciscan friary in Ware, which might suggest that Damory was buried there. The friary was not, however, founded until 1338 so Roger cannot have been buried there in 1322, but it may be that his body was moved there a few years later. In 1322 and 1338 the manor of Ware belonged to Thomas, Lord Wake (1298–1349), who is not known to have had any close connections to the Damorys (or to Elizabeth, for that matter).
19. *CCR 1318–23*, 421, 425, 428; *CFR 1319–1327*, 99; *CCR 1323–7*, 51; Tout, *Place of the Reign*, 315.
20. *CCR 1318–23*, 429.
21. SC 8/6/299.
22. V. Gibbs, 'The Battle of Boroughbridge and the Boroughbridge Roll', *The Genealogist*, new series, 21 (1905), 223.
23. Gibbs, 'Battle of Boroughbridge', 225; C. Moor, *Knights of Edward I*, vol. 2, 157–8; *CP*, vol. 6, 190.
24. *Calendar of Memoranda Rolls (Exchequer): Michaelmas 1326–Michaelmas 1327* (1968), no. 2160. Gwenllian was a great-granddaughter of King John, Margaret Audley's great-great-grandfather, and was the only child of Llywelyn ap Gruffudd. She was taken to Sempringham on the death of her father in December 1282 when she was only about 6 months old, and died there in 1337.
25. *Le Livere de Reis de Britanie e le Livere de Reis de Engletere*, ed. J. Glover (1865), 345.
26. *CCR 1318–23*, 440; Underhill, 33–4.
27. *CMR*, nos. 1593, 2160, 2198.
28. *CPR 1321–4*, 269.

Chapter 13: In the King's Favour

1. Cited in Phillips, *Edward*, 363–4 note 222, and Prestwich. 'Court of Edward II', *Reign of Edward II: New Perspectives*, 71.
2. E 101/380/4, fo. 31r; Society of Antiquaries of London Manuscript 122, 40.
3. E 101/380/4, fos. 19v, 22v; SAL MS 122, 7, 28, 29, 41, 46.
4. Phillips, *Edward*, 98 (husband); *True Chronicles of Jean le Bel, 1290–1360*, 31; *Galfridi de Baker*, 10; *Anonimalle*, 92–3.
5. *Flores*, vol. 3, 229: *concubitus illicitos peccatis*.
6. *Scalacronica*, ed. Maxwell, 70. Prestwich, 'Court of Edward II', 71, gives the rumours of an affair between Edward II and Eleanor Despenser some credence.
7. Paul Doherty, *Isabella and the Strange Death of Edward II* (2003), 101–2, talks of 'wife-swapping' and suggests that Edward allowed Despenser to have sex with Isabella or even sexually assault her, for which there is no evidence.
8. *La Alianore la Despensere* is mentioned in E 101/379/7, fo. 7, E 101/380/4, fo. 32v, and SAL MS 122, 4. *La Despenser* is mentioned in E 101/380/4, fo. 19r (which says that it was 'bought for the use of the king by Sir Hugh Despenser the son'), SAL MS 122, 7, 16, and *CPR 1324–7*, 172, 278, 325.
9. *CChR 1300–26*, 448–51; *CPR 1321–4*, 183, 327.
10. E 101/332/27, mem. 5; *CPR 1321–4*, 176, 183, 191; *CPR 1327–30*, 32; *CChR 1300–26*, 448–9; *Cartae ... de Glamorgancia Pertinent*, vol. 3, 1100–1.
11. *CChR 1300–26*, 442.
12. Holmes, 'Protest Against the Despensers', 210–11; *CCR 1318–23*, 624.
13. E 101/379/7, fo. 3.
14. *Cartae ... de Glamorgancia Pertinent*, vol. 3, 1101–4.
15. *Cartae ... de Glamorgancia Pertinent*, vol. 3, 1103.
16. Ward, *Lady of Clare*, xvii note 14, citing SC 6/927/31.
17. Stapleton, 'Brief Summary', 338, for 1318. I owe the 1329 reference to Roger Damory and Elizabeth Burgh's daughter Margaret to Douglas Richardson's post of 9 October 2018 in soc.genealogy.medieval, citing http://aalt.law.uh.edu/AALT4/JUST1/Just1no1403/aJUST1no1403 fronts/IMG_6495.htm (both accessed 10 October 2018).

18. Elizabeth Bardolf née Damory was called Roger's heir in 1337, 1338 and 1360/61, and thus, by contemporary inheritance laws in England, must have been his only surviving legitimate child then: *CChR 1327–41*, 426, *CIPM 1352–60*, no. 637 (pp. 507, 509), and *CPR 1334–8*, 491. If Damory had had a legitimate son, the boy would have been his sole heir, and Elizabeth Damory's sister Margaret mentioned in 1329 would have been their father's joint heir if she had lived. Margaret Damory seems therefore to have died between 1329 and 1337. The 1320 agreement with Ulster is E 40/386.
19. *CIPM 1336–46*, 253–5; *CIPM 1347–52*, no. 56. The Lincolnshire jurors thought she was 33 in November 1347, which would place her date of birth three years before her parents even married.
20. Ward, *Lady of Clare*, 129; Underhill, 100.
21. *CP*, vol. 4, 48 note c. The modern name Nicholas was spelled Nichol in the fourteenth century. Elizabeth's biographer F. Underhill (*For Her Good Estate*, 100) suggests that 'the kinship was so distant he [Nichol] can hardly be classified as [Roger Damory's] family'. She does not consider the possibility that Nichol was Roger's son or even his nephew, or that the young Roger Damory was. J. Ward, *English Noblewomen in the Later Middle Ages* (1992), 103, 140, also suggests that Nichol was Roger's nephew.
22. Ward, *Lady of Clare*, 2; *CP*, vol. 4, 48 note c; Ward, *English Noblewomen in the Later Middle Ages*, 140.
23. It is certain, however, that Elizabeth Bardolf née Damory, his daughter with Elizabeth Burgh, was his only legitimate child who survived into adulthood. If Nichol Damory had been Roger's son from a previous marriage he would have been Roger's heir, unless Roger's first marriage was annulled and Nichol thus made illegitimate.
24. *CPR 1338–40*, 477; *CPR 1358–61*, 300; *CPR 1361–4*, 377; *CPR 1364–7*, 34; *CIPM 1361–5*, no. 573. Holton was granted to Roger Damory in 1317: *CPR 1313–17*, 615, 677; *CPR 1317–21*, 248.
25. *CCR 1354–60*, 16.
26. *CPR 1358–61*, 166; Devon, *Issues of the Exchequer*, 183; W. M. Ormrod, *Edward III* (2011), 469.
27. K. L. Wood-Legh, 'The Knights' Attendance in the Parliaments of Edward III', *EHR*, 47 (1932), 412, describes Nichol Damory as a man 'of more than ordinary knowledge and ability'.

Chapter 14: Unequal Treatment

1. *CMR*, no. 2133.
2. SAL MS 122, 81.
3. SAL MS 122, 2.
4. SC 1/37/4 and 45.
5. E 101/379/7, fo. 8.
6. See K. Warner, *Edward II: The Unconventional King* (2014), 165–6, and Warner, *Isabella of France: The Rebel Queen* (2016), 155–7, for the Tynemouth affair.
7. Prestwich, 'Court of Edward II', 71.
8. I explore this possibility in Chapter 16.
9. *Chronicon Henrici Knighton, Monachi Leycestrensis*, vol. 1, ed. J. R. Lumby (1889), 434: *quae ut regina habebatur in regno dum regina in remotis agebat*.
10. *CPR 1327–30*, 439, for her gifts to Damory. She wrote to the receiver of Ponthieu regarding 'the affairs of the Earl of Cornwall' in late 1311, which probably relates to financial support of some kind.
11. *CPR 1321–4*, 227, 229.
12. *CPR 1324–7*, 277, 304.
13. *CChR 1300–26*, 444, 446, 448–51; *CPR 1321–4*, 183, 327.
14. *CPR 1321–4*, 349.
15. E 101/379/17, mem. 2: *son gesine*.
16. *CCR 1327–30*, 47–8.
17. Davies, *Baronial Opposition*, 97.
18. John Rylands MS Latin 132, fos. 7a and 10b, cited in F. Taylor, *A Descriptive Catalogue of the Latin Manuscripts in the John Rylands University Library of Manchester*, part 1 (reprinted 1980), 235. I am grateful to Dr Jo Edge for bringing this document to my attention.
19. SC 1/46/4: *n're tresch'e dame la Roine*.
20. *CChR 1300–26*, 466.
21. *CPR 1330–4*, 345.
22. See Chapter 11 of K. Warner, *Downfall of a King's Favourite: Edward II and Hugh Despenser the Younger* (2018), and K. Warner, "We Might be Prepared to Harm You': An Investigation into Some of the Extortions of Hugh Despenser the Younger', *Journal of the Mortimer History Society*, 2 (2018), 55–69, for more details, and for Despenser's threats.
23. SC 8/176/8753; SC 8/59/2947; *Cartae*, vol. 3, 1101–4.
24. *CCR 1323–7*, 65.

228   Edward II's Nieces: The Clare Sisters

25. SC 8/35/1723 (petition); *CPR 1321–4*, 431 (Sandal); *CChR 1300–26*, 442 (Kennington).
26. *CPR 1321–4*, 382.
27. Ward, *Lady of Clare*, 63–4. Margaret Courtenay was born in April 1311 so was only 13/14 years old in 1324/25, and was born the year before Elizabeth's son.
28. Ward, *Lady of Clare*, 64; Twigs Way, *Virgins, Weeders and Queens: A History of Women in the Garden* (2005).
29. E 101/380/4, fos. 11v, 16r, 24v.
30. Holmes, 'Protest Against the Despensers', 211. The park was back in Elizabeth's hands by early May 1327, in her cousin Edward III's reign: *CPR 1327–30*, 207.

Chapter 15: A Secret Lover

1. *CCR 1323–7*, 216.
2. E 101/380/4, fo. 19r: *des quex le Roy fist p'uement son deduyt a cele place encont' la Tour*. The dictionary at www.anglo-norman.net (accessed 25 January 2019) translates *faire son deduit* as 'to have one's pleasure (of a woman)', and *faire lur deduit* as 'to make love'.
3. E 101/380/4, fo. 20r. Many payments to men working on the houses, including carpenters and plasterers, can be found in the same document. The owner of La Rosere was Agnes Dunley, or *Anneys de Doneleye* as the account calls her.
4. C 53/111, no. 18; *CCR 1323–7*, 319, implies that he was at court on the 24th.
5. E 101/380/4, fo. 20v.
6. *Flores*, 229.
7. E 101/380/4, fo. 19v: *j robe de iiij garnamenz*.
8. Ward, *Lady of Clare*, 141–2; *Collection of All the Wills*, 24–5.
9. SAL MS 122, 41.
10. *CChR 1300–26*, 448–51; *CCR 1323–7*, 519.
11. *CCR 1323–7*, 335.
12. SC 8/43/2017; *CCR 1323–7*, 125.
13. Pugh, 'Marcher Lords', 174.
14. E 101/380/4, fo. 22r.
15. E 101/380/4, fos. 22r, 22v.

16. C 53/111, nos. 12, 14.
17. SAL MS 122, 8.
18. *Lanercost*, 249; *Flores*, 226.
19. E 101/380/4, fo. 22r; Saaler, *Edward II*, 97 (sturgeon).
20. *CPR 1327–30*, 27.
21. E 101/380/4, fos. 22v, 23r.
22. *The War of Saint-Sardos (1323–1325): Gascon Correspondence and Diplomatic Documents*, ed. P. Chaplais (1954), 199–200; *Historiae Anglicanae Scriptores Decem*, ed. Roger Twysden (1652), column 2767–8.
23. *CIM*, no. 1329.
24. E 101/380/4, fo. 23r: *qils eient lalme mons' Pieres de Gauerston counte de Cornewaille le plus en remembraunce.*
25. *CCR 1313–18*, 468; *CCR 1330–3*, 547.
26. E 101/380/4, fo. 16r.
27. *CPR 1324–7*, 95, 153; *CCR 1318–23*, 288, 395; *CIPM 1317–27*, 393.
28. E 101/380/4, fo. 10v: *l'res de secree seal a counte de Cestre et Huchoun le Despens'.*
29. SAL MS 122, 41–3, 73.
30. E 101/380/4, fo. 20v.
31. *CChR 1300–26*, 448–9.
32. E 101/380/4, fo. 29r.
33. E 101/380/4, fos. 24r, 27r. The unconventional king himself bought two types of fish called roach and dace from a fisherman near La Rosere at this time, as he often did; his chamber accounts are full of entries about fish 'bought by the king himself'.
34. E 101/380/4, fo. 29v. The Earl of Winchester was also at court on 14 February and 2 April, when he witnessed royal charters: C53/111, nos. 9, 10.
35. E 101/380/4, fos. 30v, 32r.
36. E 101/380/4, fo. 31r.
37. *CPR 1324–7*, 124.
38. SAL MS 122, 7, 8, 15.

Chapter 16: Intruder and Pharisee

1. *War of Saint Sardos*, ed. Chaplais, 199–200.
2. *Vita*, 140, 142; *Adae Murimuth*, 44.

3. SAL MS 122, 75.
4. SAL MS 122, 25, 27.
5. SAL MS 122, 28 (Caerphilly); *CCR 1323–7*, 510 (Sutton). See Chapter 11 of *Downfall of a King's Favourite* for more details. Edward II had granted the manor of Banstead to Queen Isabella in 1318, though it was currently in his own hands, as with the rest of her lands: *CPR 1317–21*, 115.
6. SAL MS 122, 28–9, 36; E. B. Fryde, 'The Deposits of Hugh Despenser the Younger with Italian Bankers', *Economic History Review*, 2nd series, 3 (1951), 361–2; SC 1/49/146 and 146A.
7. *CCR 1323–7*, 519, is the loan; *CPR 1313–18*, 459, identifies Madefrey; *CCR 1323–7*, 418, 423, and *CMR*, no. 2255 for Audley.
8. *Vita*, 142–3.
9. *Vita*, 144–5.
10. SAL MS 122, 38: *Jak Pyk counta au Roi qe le dit mons' Hugh fust tue*.
11. *Historiae Anglicanae Scriptores Decem*, ed. Roger Twysden, column 2767–8.
12. *CCR 1323–7*, 580–1; *Foedera 1307–27*, 615.
13. SAL MS 122, 28, 40–41.
14. SAL MS 122, 41; *A Descriptive Catalogue of Ancient Deeds*, ed. H. C. Maxwell, vol. 6 (1915), no. C.5924; SC 1/49/147 and 148; Fryde, 'Deposits of Hugh Despenser the Younger', 352 note 1; *CPR 1324–7*, 199.
15. SAL MS 122, 73, which refers to the young man as *Huchon le Despenser fuitz le fuitz*, 'Huchon Despenser son of the son'.
16. SAL MS 122, 43: *p' p'er a n're dame p' la dame la Despens' q' dieu la donast hastiue deliu'aunce de son enfaunt xxxs* ('to pay to Our Lady for the Lady Despenser that God granted her a prompt delivery of her child, 30 shillings').

Chapter 17: A Protest Against the Regime

1. SAL MS 122, 45, 46.
2. *CCR 1323–7*, 537–8.
3. *CPR 1321–4*, 15–16.
4. *CCR 1323–7*, 442.
5. *CCR 1323–7*, 543–4.
6. *CCR 1313–18*, 443; *CPR 1321–4*, 15, 179; *CFR 1319–27*, 167.
7. Ward, *Lady of Clare*, 1–3; Underhill, 39.

8. SAL MS 122, 51–2; *CFR 1319–27*, 375. Eleanor's town of Melton Mowbray lay within the hundred of Framland.
9. SAL MS 122, 53.
10. SAL MS 122, 92.
11. *CPR 1324–7*, 266.
12. SAL MS 122, 66 (journey from Sheen and carts); *CMR*, no. 2264 (John at Kenilworth); P. Dryburgh, 'Living in the Shadows: John of Eltham, Earl of Cornwall (1316–36)', *Fourteenth Century England IX*, ed. J. Bothwell and G. Dodd (2016), 28 (120 days).
13. Underhill, 37, 165–6 note 125, and see also below, Chapter 18. Elizabeth's document is printed in the original French in Holmes, 'Protest Against the Despensers', and in English translation in Ward, *Women of the English Nobility and Gentry*, 116–19.
14. *CFR 1319–27*, 389; *CCW*, 579.
15. SAL MS 122, 78. Joan Jermy was the sister of Alice Hales, wife of Edward II's half-brother Thomas, Earl of Norfolk (b. 1300).
16. *CPL 1342–62*, 164, 254.
17. *CPL 1342–62*, 164; *Petitions to the Pope 1342–1419*, 75, 81.
18. M. Burtscher, *The Fitzalans, Earls of Arundel and Surrey* (2008), 45.

Chapter 18: The End of Hugh Despenser

1. SAL MS 122, 65–7, 68–9; *CPR 1324–7*, 277; *CMR*, no. 267. Eleanor was called 'my lady, Lady Eleanor Despenser, consort of Sir Hugh' in Edward's chamber account at this time.
2. SAL MS 122, 69 (archers), 75 (meal). Will Balsham was called Queen Isabella's cook in July 1329: *CPR 1327–30*, 404.
3. *Annales Paulini*, 312–13; *Croniques de London*, ed. G. J. Aungier (1844), 50; SAL MS 122, 66.
4. For Isabella as *ma dame*, see for example the Household Ordinance of 6 December 1318, cited in Tout, *Place of the Reign of Edward II*, 276, and for Philippa, *Life-Records of Chaucer*, ed. M. M. Crow and C. C. Olson (1966), 164, 169; *CPR 1324–7*, 304 (Eleanor at Henley); SAL MS 122, 78–9 (all other details in this paragraph), 92 (Tristan and Isolde). Unfortunately, none of the letters from Edward to Hugh and Eleanor Despenser or vice versa survive, only records of payments to the messengers who carried them.

5. SC 8/42/2054; SC 8/50/2492.
6. *CPR 1321–4*, 175, 269; *CCR 1323–7*, 133–4.
7. Ward, *Lady of Clare*, 64.
8. Ward, *Lady of Clare*, 2–4.
9. Ward, *English Noblewomen in the Later Middle Ages*, 95; Underhill, 40–41.
10. SC 8/165/8222; *CPR 1327–30*, 31, 69.
11. *CPR 1324–7*, 201, and *CFR 1319–27*, 370; and for Hugh's move to Nottingham, *CCR 1323–7*, 418, 423, and *CMR*, no. 2255.
12. *CPR 1334–8*, 528.
13. *CIPM 1317–27*, no. 657; *CCR 1323–7*, 463.
14. Ward, *Lady of Clare*, 1–2, 4. Ward identifies 'Lady Maria' as Elizabeth's friend Marie de St Pol, Countess of Pembroke, but Marie would have been referred to by her title rather than her first name, as she was in Elizabeth's other accounts: see *Lady of Clare*, 42, 43, 77.
15. The last two chamber accounts of Edward II's reign are E 101/380/4 and SAL MS 122. Mary was born in March 1279, so was five years older than her brother.
16. Ward, *Lady of Clare*, 1–3.
17. *Records of the Borough of Leicester*, ed. M. Bateson, vol. 1 (1899), 353.
18. *Anonimalle*, 124–7.
19. *Anonimalle*, 124–7, 129–30.
20. *CPR 1330–4*, 172.
21. *CCR 1323–7*, 655.
22. J. Ward, *Women in England in the Middle Ages* (2006), 113–4; Ward, *Lady of Clare*, xvii.
23. Ward, *Lady of Clare*, xvii-xviii, note 20, citing E 101/91/22; Underhill, 37, 87, 165–6 note 125.
24. Ward, *Lady of Clare*, 3.
25. *CCR 1323–7*, 620; *CCR 1327–30*, 16.
26. One of the two men chiefly responsible for bringing Despenser to the queen was Sir Robert Stangrave, whom Audley appointed as his attorney four months later: *CPR 1327–30*, 36.

Chapter 19: Deposition

1. Ward, *Women in England in the Middle Ages*, 113–14.
2. *CMR*, no. 2160.

3. *CCR 1323–7*, 624; *CMR*, no. 437.
4. *CPR 1327–30*, 16, 27, 66; SC 1/41/124.
5. *CPR 1324–7*, 346.
6. *CPR 1327–30*, 30; *CCR 1327–30*, 27.
7. *CPR 1324–7*, 338.
8. *CCR 1327–30*, 79.
9. *CPR 1321–4*, 16.
10. *CPR 1327–30*, 32.
11. *CCR 1327–30*, 15–16.
12. *CPR 1327–30*, 39.
13. K. Fowler, *The King's Lieutenant: Henry of Grosmont, First Duke of Lancaster 1310–1361* (1969), 256 note 16; *CPR 1327–30*, 8.
14. *CPR 1327–30*, 271; *CFR 1327–37*, 3; *CCR 1327–30*, 196.
15. Fowler, *King's Lieutenant*, 28; *CP*, vol. 12B, 178; Underhill, 93.
16. *CPR 1327–30*, 198.
17. *CPR 1334–8*, 490.
18. *CIPM 1327–36*, no. 243; *CPR 1327–30*, 198; *CFR 1327–37*, 157.
19. *CPR 1330–4*, 476; *CPR 1334–8*, 384–5.
20. Underhill, 40–41.
21. *CPR 1327–30*, 243, 266; *CCR 1327–30*, 275–6.
22. *CIPM 1413–18*, no. 632.
23. John Haudlo, one of the most loyal of all Despenser adherents since before 1300, and his wife Maud (sister and heir of Hugh Despenser the Younger's late brother-in-law Edward Burnell), went overseas on pilgrimage in 1327, and although this is only speculation, it is not impossible that they took Edward Despenser with them. *CPR 1327–30*, 171, 175, 188.

Chapter 20: Rebellion and Abduction

1. *CIM 1308–48*, nos. 1039, 1111.
2. *CIM 1308–48*, no. 1111; *CFR 1327–37*, 116–7; *CPR 1327–30*, 357.
3. *CCR 1327–30*, 528, 530–1, 593–4; *CCR 1330–3*, 286–7; *CPR 1327–30*, 484; *CPR 1330–4*, 26, 35.
4. *CPR 1327–30*, 376, 381, 485.
5. *CCR 1327–30*, 501.
6. *CPR 1327–30*, 422.

234   Edward II's Nieces: The Clare Sisters

7. *CCR 1327–30*, 81, 121.
8. *CPR 1327–30*, 360, 374, 422.
9. *CP*, vol. 12B, 957.
10. Underhill, 63 (Bletchingdon); *CPR 1358–61*, 538 (a monk); *CFR 1377–83*, 46 (100 shillings); *CFR 1383–91*, 346 (alive in 1390); *Monasticon Anglicanum*, ed. W. Dugdale, vol. 2, 62, for Hugh Zouche, who was presumably named in honour of Hugh Mortimer (d. 1304), elder brother of William Zouche.
11. *CPR 1321–4*, 185, 190. His proof of age which gives his date of birth is in *CIPM 1317–27*, no. 336, and his IPM in *CIPM 1353–60*, no. 518; he died 1 September 1359.
12. ODNB; *CFR 1327–37*, 298; *CPR 1330–4*, 203, 292; *CCR 1333–7*, 110.
13. *CPL 1305–41*, 394; ODNB.
14. *CPR 1327–30*, 347; *CCR 1327–30*, 590; *CCR 1330–3*, 182.
15. *CPR 1327–30*, 500–1, 512, 541; *CFR 1327–37*, 161; *CCR 1330–3*, 5, 37. Isabella was at Tewkesbury on 26 June 1330: SC 1/38/195. Edward III was at Burford (Oxfordshire) on 21 June, Tewkesbury on the 27th and at Hanley at the 29th: Ormrod, *Edward III*, 613.
16. *CPR 1327–30*, 544; *CPR 1330–4*, 244.
17. *CMR*, no 2270; CCR 1323–7, 517, 645; *CPR 1327–30*, 552.
18. SC 8/157/7801; *CCR 1330–3*, 7; *Adae Murimuth*, 255.
19. *CFR 1327–37*, 118–9.
20. *CFR 1327–37*, 93.
21. *CPR 1327–30*, 492.

Chapter 21: The King Lives

1. *CIPM 1336–46*, no. 476.
2. *CCR 1327–30*, 530; *CPR 1327–30*, 547. Margaret Monthermer had no children with Henry Tyes, and his sister Alice Lisle was his heir: *CIPM 1327–36*, no. 48.
3. *CCR 1327–30*, 379; Underhill, 167 note 138, citing E 101/91/17.
4. *CIPM 1327–36*, no. 389.
5. Underhill, 95.
6. *CFR 1327–37*, 134–5.
7. *CCR 1327–30*, 526. The two acknowledged another joint debt on 3 July 1329: *CCR 1327–30*, 555.

8. *Adae Murimuth*, 255.
9. Ormrod, *Edward III*, 613.
10. *CPR 1327–30*, 557; *CFR 1327–37*, 168. The other two were Sir Fulk FitzWarin (who had pronounced the death sentence and reprieve on Roger Damory in March 1322) and George Percy.
11. *CCR 1330–3*, 17–18.
12. *CFR 1327–37*, 175, 181; *CCR 1330–3*, 14.
13. *CCR 1330–3*, 143.
14. *CPR 1330–4*, 74.
15. Underhill, 45; Ormrod, *Edward III*, 613; *CIPM 1361–5*, no. 573.

Chapter 22: A Belated Funeral

1. *CCR 1330–3*, 175.
2. See http://www.reading.ac.uk/archaeology/research/projects/arch-ml-hugh-despenser.aspx (accessed 2 March 2018).
3. See *CPR 1348–50*, 48.
4. *CCR 1330–3*, 179, 182; *CPR 1330–4*, 53.
5. *CFR 1327–37*, 308, 344; *CPR 1334–8*, 171, 230.
6. *CPR 1330–4*, 51; SC 8/157/7801.
7. *CCR 1333–7*, 199; *CCR 1337–9*, 302.
8. *CCR 1330–3*, 178.
9. C 241/130/185; C 241/105/256; *CCR 1330–3*, 182.
10. *CCR 1330–3*, 284; Ward, *Lady of Clare*, 27, 42, 48, and Underhill, 126–7, for Chedworth. For other large debts of Zouche, see *CCR 1330–3*, 531, 551, 554, 557.
11. *CPR 1330-4*, 278.
12. Underhill, 87, for the cloth.
13. *CMR*, no, 2271 (banneret); *CPR 1330–4*, 41–2, 48; *Foedera 1327–44*, 805–6.
14. E 101/310/24. Curiously, Lancaster's name does not appear on the list of envoys on the Patent Roll or Foedera (*CPR 1330–4*, 90–95, and *Foedera 1327–44*, 813) but certainly went, as this document, his and his household's list of expenses, makes apparent.
15. *CPR 1330–4*, 49.
16. Phillips, *Aymer de Valence*, 234–5. Among the food the two ladies consumed during Marie's visit to Clare were a swan, two curlews, sturgeon and whale-meat. Ward, *Lady of Clare*, 86.

17. *CCR 1330–3*, 325–6; *CPR 1330–4*, 246. Talbot became a household knight of Hugh Despenser the Younger in 1322, and married Despenser's victim Elizabeth Comyn in or before July 1326 to Despenser's evident amusement, as he lent Talbot 10 marks soon after hearing the news. Eble Lestrange was the second husband of Alice Lacy, Countess of Lincoln and the widow of Thomas of Lancaster, whom Despenser and Edward II persecuted in 1322.
18. SC 8/42/2091 and 2092.
19. *PROME*, September 1331.
20. *CFR 1327–37*, 308.
21. Vale, *Princely Court*, 238, 311–3. The Bohun twins were the third and fourth sons of Edward II's sister Elizabeth, Countess of Hereford (1282–1316), and were born around 1309 or 1312/13.
22. *CPR 1330–4*, 278.
23. *CPR 1330–4*, 267, 342, 377, 462.
24. *CPR 1330–4*, 273, 277.
25. *Collectanea et Topographica*, vol. 4, 390, 394; for the tournament, see J. Munby, R. Barber and R. Brown, *Edward III's Round Table at Windsor* (2007), 35.
26. Underhill, 88, 182 note 14.
27. *CCR 1330–3*, 586; the three husbands were Thomas Furnival, Bartholomew Burghersh and William Blount.
28. *CIPM 1327–36*, nos. 389, 395.

Chapter 23: Death of an Earl

1. *CPR 1338–40*, 115, 445.
2. R. B. Pugh, 'A Fragment of an Account of Isabel of Lancaster, Nun of Amesbury, 1333–4', *Festschrift zur Feier des zweihundertjährigen Bestandes des Haus-, Hof- und Staatsarchivs*, vol. 1, ed. L. Santifaller (1949), 489, 491, 498.
3. *CPR 1330–4*, 467.
4. *CCR 1333–7*, 131.
5. *CPR 1330–4*, 495.
6. *CPR 1330–4*, 470, 551.
7. Ward, *Lady of Clare*, 75, 87; Underhill, 113.
8. Underhill, 113–4; Ward, *Lady of Clare*, 25.

Chapter 24: A Third Abduction and a Death

1. *CPR 1334–8*, 283.
2. *CPR 1334–8*, 298.
3. *CPR 1330–4*, 276. Stafford was not, however, named among the knights given gifts by Eleanor of Woodstock on this occasion: Vale, *Princely Court*, 312–13.
4. *CPL 1305–41*, 544, for the vow; SC 8/64/3163 is Alice's petition.
5. C 131/177/11.
6. *CIPM 1370–3*, no. 210: he was said to be between 26 and 30 years old when his father died in 1372.
7. SC 8/179/8915; *CCR 1333–7*, 580–1; *CPR 1334–8*, 394 (Caerwent).
8. *CIPM 1336–46*, no. 112.
9. *CCR 1337–9*, 302.
10. Cited in *CP*, vol. 4, 271 note d.
11. *CIPM 1336–46*, no. 132; *CFR 1337–47*, 25.
12. Underhill, 90.

Chapter 25: The Young Generation

1. John Smyth of Nibley's *The Berkeley Manuscripts: The Lives of the Berkeleys, Lords of the Honour, Castle and Manor of Berkeley*, vol. 1 (published in Gloucester in 1883; originally written before 1640), 374, 377 gives them three daughters, Katherine, Agnes and Elizabeth. Assuming they really existed, none of them ever married. Katherine the eldest was said to have become a nun at Whirwell.
2. Underhill, 88–90; Ward, *Lady of Clare*, 25, 44–5, 51.
3. *CIPM 1352–60*, no. 333.
4. Underhill, 52, 89; Ward, *Lady of Clare*, 85. The younger Edward Despenser (1336–75), Eleanor Despenser's grandson, married Elizabeth Burghersh, granddaughter of Elizabeth Burgh's stepdaughter Elizabeth Verdon, so perhaps the lady was involved with this marriage as well.
5. Underhill, 63.
6. See http://www.clare.cam.ac.uk/data/uploads/about/ClareCollege Statutes.pdf, accessed 28 February 2018.
7. *CPR 1350–4*, 510.
8. Ward, *Lady of Clare*, 144; *Collection of All the Wills*, 30 (*ma sale appelle Clarehall en Cantebrig*).

238   Edward II's Nieces: The Clare Sisters

9. F. A. Underhill, 'Elizabeth de Burgh: Connoisseur and Patron', in ed. J. H. McCash, *The Cultural Patronage of Medieval Women* (1996), 273.
10. A. R. Meyer, 'The Despensers and the "Gawain" Poet: A Gloucestershire Link to the Alliterative Master of the Northwest Midlands', *Chaucer Review*, 35 (2001), 417–18. Isabella was a daughter of William Marshal, Earl of Pembroke (d. 1219) and by her first marriage was the mother of Richard Clare, Earl of Gloucester (1222–62), father of Gilbert 'the Red.'
11. *Adae Murimuth*, 256–7.
12. Ward, *Lady of Clare*, 49.
13. J. Ward, 'Noble Consumption in the Fourteenth Century: Supplying the Household of Elizabeth de Burgh, Lady of Clare', *Proceedings of the Suffolk Institute of Archaeology and History*, 41 (2005/8), 454; Underhill, 96, 138.
14. Ward, *Lady of Clare*, 61–2. Elizabeth's other horses included palfreys called Bay Stanford and Sorrel Hobyn, and packhorses called Blauncherd of Walsingham and Grey Turnebole.
15. Ward, *Lady of Clare*, 87–8.
16. Underhill, 112–13.
17. Underhill, 110–12.
18. SC 1/54/28.
19. Her father, born probably in 1301, played dice with Edward II in Nottingham at Christmas 1324. His elder brother John, who died at age 18 in 1317, was briefly married to Elizabeth Burgh's eldest stepdaughter Joan Verdon.
20. The younger William Montacute was born in Donyatt, Somerset on Sunday, 19 June 1328 ('Sunday before the Nativity of St John the Baptist, 2 Edward III'): *CIPM 1347–52*, no. 244.
21. *CPL 1305–41*, 553. Giles Badlesmere's mother was Margaret Clare, first cousin of the Clare sisters, and rescued by Hugh Despenser the Younger in 1319 when she was besieged in a house by a gang of armed men.
22. *CPR 1343–5*, 268.
23. *CIPM 1336–46*, no. 382; *CFR 1337–47*, 289.

Chapter 26: The Last Sister

1. Underhill, 182 note 14, citing E 101/93/12.
2. Ward, *Women of the English Nobility and Gentry*, 182–3.

Endnotes   239

3. Henry Despenser was 19 in February 1361; see *Petitions to the Pope 1342–1419*, 364.
4. Ward, *Women of the English Nobility and Gentry*, 81; Ward, *Lady of Clare*, 45, 136–7; Underhill, 101–2, 139–40; *CPR 1345–8*, 255.
5. *CPR 1340–3*, 500–1.
6. Underhill, 97–8; Ward, *Lady of Clare*, 62, 69, 77, 85; Ward, *English Noblewomen in the Later Middle Ages*, 100. William Ferrers was born in Newbold, Leicestershire on 28 February 1333: *CIPM 1352–60*, no. 195.
7. Ward, *English Noblewomen of the Later Middle Ages*, 99.
8. E 101/23/36; *CCR 1343–6*, 174; *CPR 1343–5*, 307.
9. *The Chronicle of Geoffrey le Baker of Swinbrook*, trans. D. Preest (2012), 67.
10. *Knighton's Chronicle 1337–1396*, vol. 2, ed. G. H. Martin (1995), 30; *CPR 1343–5*, 366, 384; DL 25/2184. Grosmont was the brother of Elizabeth Burgh's daughter-in-law Maud of Lancaster, and uncle of her granddaughter the younger Elizabeth Burgh; another of his six sisters, Isabella the nun of Amesbury, was Hugh Audley's correspondent in the 1330s.
11. DL 27/36; DL 27/143 and 144; DL 25/733.
12. *CIPM 1347–52*, no. 56; *CCR 1346–9*, 344–5.
13. See Appendix 1 of K. Warner, *Edward II and Hugh Despenser the Younger: Downfall of a King's Favourite*.
14. Underhill, 110.
15. Underhill, 135–6; *CPL 1305–41*, 544, mentions the habit and ring as part of Alice de Lacy, Countess of Lincoln's own vow of chastity in and after 1335.
16. *Petitions to the Pope 1342–1419*, 102, 300; *CPL 1342–62*, 113, 190, 561, 586.
17. Ward, *Lady of Clare*, xviii.
18. *CPR 1345–8*, 158, 477.
19. M. Livingstone and M. Witzel, *The Road to Crécy: The English Invasion of France, 1346* (2005), 256–9.
20. Ward, *Lady of Clare*, 147.
21. *CPR 1327–30*, 42; *CPR 1348–50*, 514, for Jeanne.
22. *CIPM 1347–52*, nos. 56, 57.
23. Ward, *Lady of Clare*, 89, 93–5.

Chapter 27: The Final Years

1. Ward, *Lady of Clare*, 76; Underhill, 96.
2. *CPR 1348–50*, 411.
3. *CIPM 1361–5*, no. 573; *CIPM 1370–3*, no. 136.
4. Ward, *Women of the English Nobility and Gentry*, 182–3, for the details in this paragraph.
5. Bletchingdon was in Elizabeth's hands in September 1349: *CIPM 1347–52*, no. 205. The elder Richard Damory gave it to her husband Roger for life in 1312, and it reverted to him on Roger's death in 1322 and was in his possession when he died in 1330: *CIPM 1327–36*, no. 275. It is not entirely clear why Elizabeth held the manor, and later in the century it passed to the Poure family, descendants of Roger and Richard Damory's sister Katherine.
6. Underhill, 94; Ward, *Lady of Clare*, 46.
7. Underhill, 109.
8. Ward, *Women of the English Nobility*, 184.
9. *CPR 1354–8*, 352.
10. Devon, *Issues*, 172; W. M. Ormrod, 'Edward III and his Family', *Journal of British Studies*, 26 (1987), 410 note 46.
11. *Collection of All the Wills*, 22. The epitaph reads *Hic jacet Rogerus Damory, baro, tempore Edwardi Secundi, et Elizabetha, tertia filia Gilberti Clare, comitis Gloucestriae, et Johannae uxoris ejus*: 'Here lies Roger Damory, baron, of the era of Edward II, and Elizabeth, third daughter of Gilbert Clare, Earl of Gloucester, and his wife Joan'.
12. *Testamenta Vetusta: Being Illustrations from Wills*, ed. N. Harris Nicolas, vol. 1 (1826), 87.
13. *Testamenta Vetusta*, vol. 1, 76.
14. Elizabeth's will is printed in Ward, *Lady of Clare*, 141–9 (the entire will, in English translation); *Testamenta Vetusta*, vol. 1, 56–9 (an abridged version, in English); *Collection of All the Wills*, 22–42 (the entire will, in the French original). The translations used here are Ward's.
15. J. Ward, 'Elizabeth de Burgh, Lady of Clare (d. 1360), in C. Barron and A. Sutton, eds., *Medieval London Widows, 1300–1500* (1994), 40–45, for Elizabeth's visits to London and guests.
16. Underhill, 59.
17. *CIPM 1361–5*, no. 573.

18. *Petitions to the Pope 1342–1419*, 478. He wrote his will on 3 February 1381: *CP*, vol. 4, 48 note c.
19. *CPR 1358–61*, 166, 294.
20. *CIPM 1361–5*, no. 215 ('Sunday the feast of the Decollation of St John the Baptist last').

Appendix 3: The Descent of the Sisters' Inheritances

1. Figures from Pugh, 'Marcher Lords', 603 note 2.

Bibliography

Primary Sources

A Descriptive Catalogue of Ancient Deeds, ed. H. C. Maxwell, 6 vols. (1890–1915).
A Descriptive Catalogue of the Latin Manuscripts in the John Rylands University Library of Manchester, part 1, ed. F. Taylor (reprinted 1980).
Adae Murimuth Continuatio Chronicarum, ed. E. M. Thompson (1889).
Annales Londonienses 1195–1330, in W. Stubbs, ed., *Chronicles of the Reigns of Edward I and Edward II*, vol. 1 (1882).
Annales Monastici, vol. 4, ed. H. R. Luard (1869).
Annales Paulini 1307–1340, in Stubbs, *Chronicles of the Reigns*, vol. 1.
The Anonimalle Chronicle 1307 to 1334, ed. W. R. Childs and J. Taylor (1991).
The Brut or the Chronicles of England, part 1, ed. F. W. D. Brie (1906).
Calendar of Ancient Correspondence Concerning Wales, ed. J. Goronwy Edwards (1935).
Calendar of Ancient Petitions Relating to Wales, ed. W. Rees (1975).
Calendar of Chancery Warrants, vol. 1, 1244–1326 (1927).
Calendar of the Charter Rolls, 2 vols., 1300–41 (1908).
Calendar of the Close Rolls, 18 vols., 1288–1360 (1898–1906).
Calendar of Documents Relating to Scotland, vol. 3, 1307–1357, ed. J. Bain (1887).
Calendar of Entries in the Papal Registers Relating to Great Britain and Ireland: Papal Letters, 2 vols., 1305–62 (1897).
Calendar of Entries in the Papal Registers Relating to Great Britain and Ireland: Petitions to the Pope 1342–1419, ed. W. H. Bliss (1896).
Calendar of the Fine Rolls, 7 vols., 1272–1368 (1911–13).
Calendar of Inquisitions Miscellaneous (Chancery), vol. 2, 1308–48 (1916).
Calendar of Inquisitions Post Mortem, 11 vols., 1272–1369 (1906–38).
Calendar of the Patent Rolls, 19 vols., 1281–1361 (1891–1903).

Calendar of Memoranda Rolls (Exchequer): Michaelmas 1326–Michaelmas 1327 (1968).
Cartae et Alia Munimenta quae ad Domimium de Glamorgancia Pertinent, vol. 3 (1910).
Croniques de London, ed. G. J. Aungier (1844).
Haskins, G. L., 'A Chronicle of the Civil Wars of Edward II', *Speculum*, 14 (1939).
The Chronicle of Geoffrey le Baker of Swinbrook, trans. D. Preest (2012).
The Chronicle of Pierre de Langtoft, vol. 2, ed. T. Wright (1868).
Chronicon Galfridi de Baker de Swynebroke, ed. E. M. Thompson (1889).
Chronicon Henrici Knighton, Monachi Leycestrensis, vol. 1, ed. J. R. Lumby (1889).
Chronique Métrique de Godefroy de Paris, ed. J. A. Buchon (1827).
Collectanea Topographica et Genealogica, vol. 4, ed. F. Madden, B. Bandinel and J. G. Nichols (1837).
Flores Historiarum, vol. 3, ed. H. R. Luard (1890).
Foedera, Conventiones, Literae, 3 vols., 1307–1361, ed. T. Rymer (1818–25).
Gesta Edwardi de Carnarvon Auctore Canonico Bridlingtoniensi, in W. Stubbs, ed., *Chronicles of the Reigns of Edward I and Edward II*, vol. 2 (1883).
Historiae Anglicanae Scriptores Decem, ed. Roger Twysden (1652).
The Household Book of Queen Isabella of England for the Fifth Regnal Year of Edward II, 8th July 1311 to 7th July 1312, eds. F. D. Blackley and G. Hermansen (1971).
Inquisitions and Assessments Relating to Feudal Aids 1284–1431, 6 vols., eds. A. S. Maskelyne, C. Johnson, A. E. Stamp and J. V. Lyle (1899–1920).
Issues of the Exchequer, ed. Frederick Devon (1837).
Johannis de Trokelowe et Henrici de Blaneforde Chronica et Annales, ed. H. T. Riley (1866).
Knighton's Chronicle 1337–1396, vol. 2, ed. G. H. Martin (1995).
The Chronicle of Lanercost 1272–1346, ed. Herbert Maxwell (1913).
Le Livere de Reis de Britanie e le Livere de Reis de Engletere, ed. J. Glover (1865).
Monasticon Anglicanum, ed. W. Dugdale, vol. 2 (new edition, 1819).
National Archives records, mostly SC 1 (Ancient Correspondence, including SC 1/46/4, a letter from Eleanor in 1324), SC 8 (Ancient Petitions), C 53 (Charter Rolls), and E 101 (Accounts Various, including E 101/380/4, Edward II's chamber account of 1324/25).

The Parliament Rolls of Medieval England, eds. Brand, Curry, Given-Wilson, Horrox, Martin, Ormrod and Phillips (2005).
The Parliamentary Writs and Writs of Military Summons, ed. F. Palgrave, vol. 1 and 2 (1827–30).
The Political Songs of England, ed. T. Wright (1839).
Records of the Borough of Leicester, ed. M. Bateson, vol. 1 (1899).
Recueil de Lettres Anglo-Françaises 1265–1399, ed. F.J. Tanqueray (1916).
Royal Charter Witness Lists for the Reign of Edward II 1307–1326, ed. J. S. Hamilton (2001).
Scalacronica: The Reigns of Edward I, Edward II and Edward III, ed. H. Maxwell (1907).
Scalacronica: By Sir Thomas Gray of Heton, Knight, ed. J. Stevenson (1836).
Society of Antiquaries of London Manuscript 122 (Edward II's chamber account of 1325–6).
Statutes of the Realm, vol. 1: 1100–1377 (1810).
Testamenta Vetusta: Being Illustrations from Wills, ed. N. Harris Nicolas, vol. 1 (1826).
True Chronicles of Jean le Bel, 1290–1360, trans. and ed. Nigel Bryant (2011).
Vita Edwardi Secundi Monachi Cuiusdam Malmesberiensis, ed. N. Denholm-Young (1957).
The War of Saint-Sardos (1323–1325): Gascon Correspondence and Diplomatic Documents, ed. P. Chaplais (1954).

Secondary Sources

Altschul, M., *A Baronial Family in Medieval England: The Clares, 1217–1314* (1965).
Benz St John, L., *Three Medieval Queens: Queenship and the Crown in Fourteenth-Century England* (2012).
Bullock-Davies, C., *Menestrellorum Multitudo: Minstrels at a Royal Feast* (1978).
Bullock-Davies, C., *A Register of Royal and Baronial Minstrels 1272–1327* (1986).
Burtscher, M., *The Fitzalans, Earls of Arundel and Surrey* (2008).

Bibliography 245

Chaplais, P., *Piers Gaveston: Edward II's Adoptive Brother* (1994).
Cockerill, S., *Eleanor of Castile: The Shadow Queen* (2014).
Davies, J. C., *The Baronial Opposition to Edward II: Its Character and Policy* (1918).
Davies, J. C., 'The Despenser War in Glamorgan', *Transactions of the Royal Historical Society*, 9 (1915), 21–64.
Davies, J. C., 'The First Journal of Edward II's Chamber', *EHR*, 30 (1915), 662–80.
Dodd, G. and A. Musson, eds., *The Reign of Edward II: New Perspectives* (2006).
Dryburgh, P., 'Living in the Shadows: John of Eltham, Earl of Cornwall (1316–36)', *Fourteenth Century England IX*, ed. J. Bothwell and G. Dodd (2016), 23–47.
Fryde, E. B., 'The Deposits of Hugh Despenser the Younger with Italian Bankers', *Economic History Review*, 2nd series, 3 (1951), 344–62.
Fryde, N., *The Tyranny and Fall of Edward II 1321–1326* (1979).
Gibbs, V., and H. A Doubleday, *The Complete Peerage of England, Scotland, Ireland, Great Britain and the United Kingdom*, 14 vols. (1910–40).
Gibbs, V., 'The Battle of Boroughbridge and the Boroughbridge Roll', *The Genealogist*, new series, 21 (1905), 222–6.
Gray Birch, W. de, *A History of Margam Abbey* (1897).
Green, M. A. E., *Lives of the Princesses of England*, vol. 2 (1867).
Haines, R. M., *King Edward II: His Life, His Reign, and Its Aftermath, 1384–1330* (2003).
Hallam, E. M., *The Itinerary of Edward II and his Household, 1307–1327* (1984).
Hamilton, J. S., *Piers Gaveston, Earl of Cornwall 1307–1312: Politics and Patronage in the Reign of Edward II* (1988).
Hamilton, J. S., 'Charter Witness Lists for the Reign of Edward II', in ed. N. Saul, *FCE I* (2000), 1–20.
Hamilton, J. S., 'Some Notes on 'Royal' Medicine in the Reign of Edward II', in ed. C. Given-Wilson, *FCE II* (2002), 33–43.
Harper-Bill, C., ed., *Cartulary of the Augustinian Friars of Clare* (1991).
Holmes, G. A., 'The Judgement on the Younger Despenser, 1326', *EHR*, 70 (1955), 261–7.
Holmes, G. A., 'A Protest Against the Despensers, 1326', *Speculum*, 30 (1955), 207–12.

Livingstone, M. and Witzel, M., *The Road to Crécy: The English Invasion of France, 1346* (2005).
Maddicott, J. R., *Thomas of Lancaster 1307–1322: A Study in the Reign of Edward II* (1970).
Meyer, A. R., 'The Despensers and the "Gawain" Poet: A Gloucestershire Link to the Alliterative Master of the Northwest Midlands', *Chaucer Review*, 35 (2001), 413–29.
Mitchell, L. E., *Portraits of Medieval Women: Family, Marriage, and Politics in England 1225–1350* (2003).
Moor, C., *The Knights of Edward I*, 5 vols. (1929–32).
Morris, M., *A Great and Terrible King: Edward I and the Forging of Britain* (2008).
Morris, R., 'Tewkesbury Abbey: The Despenser Mausoleum', *Transactions of the Bristol and Gloucestershire Archaeological Society*, 93 (1974), 142–55.
Morrison, S. S., *Women Pilgrims in Late Medieval England* (2002).
Ormrod, W. M., *Edward III* (2011).
Oxford Dictionary of National Biography, online edition, available at http://www.oxforddnb.com/.
Palmer, C. F. R., 'The Friar-Preachers of Kings Langley', *The Reliquary*, 23 (1882–3).
Phillips, J. R. S., *Aymer de Valence, Earl of Pembroke 1307–1324: Baronial Politics in the Reign of Edward II* (1972).
Phillips, S., *Edward II* (2010).
Prestwich. M., 'The Court of Edward II', *The Reign of Edward II: New Perspectives*, in eds. G. Dodd and A. Musson (2006) 61–75.
Prestwich, M., *Edward I* (1988).
Prestwich, M., *The Three Edwards: War and State in England 1272–1377* (1980).
Pugh, R. B., 'A Fragment of an Account of Isabel of Lancaster, Nun of Amesbury, 1333–4', in ed. L. Santifaller, *Festschrift zur Feier des Zweihundertjährigen Bestandes des Haus-, Hof- und Staatsarchivs*, vol. 1 (1949), 487–98.
Pugh, T. B., 'The Marcher Lords of Glamorgan and Morgannwg, 1317–1485', in ed. T. B. Pugh, *Glamorgan County History, III: The Middle Ages* (1971), 167–86.
Rastall, R., 'Secular Musicians in Late Medieval England', Univ. of Manchester PhD thesis (1968).

Rees, W., *Caerphilly Castle: A History and Description* (1937).
Saaler, M., *Edward II* (1997).
Salzman, L. F., *Edward I* (1968).
Saul, N., 'The Despensers and the Downfall of Edward II', *EHR*, 99 (1984), 1–33.
Stapleton, T., 'A Brief Summary of the Wardrobe Accounts of the Tenth, Eleventh and Fourteenth Years of King Edward the Second', *Archaeologia*, 26 (1836), 318–45.
Stevenson, W. H., 'A Letter of the Younger Despenser on the Eve of the Barons' Rebellion, 21 March 1321', *EHR*, 12 (1897), 755–61.
Tomkinson, A., 'Retinues at the Tournament of Dunstable, 1309', *EHR*, 74 (1959), 70–87.
Toomey, J. P., *Records of Hanley Castle, Worcestershire, c. 1147–1547* (2001).
Tout, T. F., *The Place of the Reign of Edward II in English History* (2nd edn., 1936).
Underhill, F. A., 'Elizabeth de Burgh: Connoisseur and Patron', in ed. J. H. McCash, *The Cultural Patronage of Medieval Women* (1996), 266–87.
Underhill, F., *For Her Good Estate: The Life of Elizabeth de Burgh* (1999).
Vale, M., *The Princely Court: Medieval Courts and Culture in North-West Europe* (2001).
Ward, J., *Elizabeth de Burgh, Lady of Clare (1295–1360)* (2014).
Ward, J., 'Elizabeth de Burgh, Lady of Clare (d. 1360)',' in eds. C. Barron and A. F. Sutton, *Medieval London Widows, 1300–1500* (1994) 29–45.
Ward, J., *English Noblewomen in the Later Middle Ages* (1992).
Ward, J., 'The Estates of the Clare Family, 1066–1317', Univ. of London PhD thesis (1962).
Ward, J., 'Noble Consumption in the Fourteenth Century: Supplying the Household of Elizabeth de Burgh, Lady of Clare', *Proceedings of the Suffolk Institute of Archaeology and History*, 41 (2006) 447–60.
Ward, J., *Women in England in the Middle Ages* (2006).
Ward, J., *Women of the English Nobility and Gentry, 1066–1500* (1995).
Warner, K., 'The Adherents of Edmund of Woodstock, Earl of Kent, in March 1330', *EHR*, 126 (2011), 779–805.
Warner, K., *Blood Roses: The Houses of Lancaster and York Before the Wars of the Roses* (2018).

Warner, K., "Bought by the King Himself': Edward II, His Chamber, His Family and His Interests in 1325/26', *Fourteenth Century England X*, ed. Gwilym Dodd (2018), 1–23.

Warner, K., *Edward II: The Unconventional King* (2014).

Warner, K., *Edward II and Hugh Despenser the Younger: Downfall of a King's Favourite* (2018).

Warner, K., *Isabella of France: The Rebel Queen* (2016).

Warner, K., '"We Might be Prepared to Harm You": An Investigation into Some of the Extortions of Hugh Despenser the Younger', *Journal of the Mortimer History Society*, 2 (2018), 55–69.

Waugh, S., 'For King, Country and Patron: The Despensers and Local Administration 1321–1322', *Journal of British Studies*, 22 (1983), 23–58.

Waugh, S., 'The Profits of Violence: The Minor Gentry in the Rebellion of 1322 in Gloucestershire and Herefordshire', *Speculum*, 52 (1977), 843–69.

Wells-Furby, B., 'The Gower Prelude to the Marcher Rising of 1321: A Question of Evidence', *Welsh History Review*, 27 (2014), 4–27.

Wilkinson, B., 'The Sherburn Indenture and the Attack on the Despensers', *EHR*, 63 (1948), 1–28.

Wood-Legh, K. L., 'The Knights' Attendance in the Parliaments of Edward III', *EHR*, 47 (1932).

Woolgar, C. M., *The Great Household in Late Medieval England* (1999).

Index

Amesbury Priory 4, 8, 9, 11, 16, 35–6, 53, 55, 89, 113, 135, 166, 168, 180
Audley, Hugh, earl of Gloucester 28, 48, 52–5, 57–9, 62–4, 68–70, 73–5, 77–81, 83–4, 88, 90, 95, 97, 101, 107, 121, 134–5, 137–8, 143, 149–50, 156–7, 160–9, 171–3, 179, 181–3, 186, 188, 190–1, 199
Audley, Margaret (d. 1349) 89, 97, 114, 143, 171–2, 184, 186, 189, 192

Badlesmere, Bartholomew and Margaret 46–8, 64, 68, 72, 78–9, 88, 93, 182
Bannockburn, battle of 38–9
Bar, Jeanne de, countess of Surrey 7, 10, 23, 26, 77, 93, 106, 135, 189, 190
Bardolf, John 96, 98, 146, 159, 179–80, 185, 193, 199
Berenger, Ingelram 80, 148, 158
Berkeley, Maurice (d. 1326) 40, 80, 83, 180
Berkeley, Maurice (d. 1368) 176–7, 180
Berkeley, Thomas (d. 1361) 144, 176
Berkeley, Thomas (d. 1417) 176, 201

Bohun, Humphrey, earl of Hereford (d. 1322) 38, 87
Bohun, Humphrey, earl of Hereford (d. 1361) 169
Bohun, John, earl of Hereford 169
Bohun, William, earl of Northampton 164, 169, 173, 179, 198
Bohun, Margaret, countess of Devon 87, 169
Botetourt, John and Maud, 105, 120
Brotherton, Thomas of, earl of Norfolk 12, 13, 77, 100, 136, 166
Bruce, David, king of Scotland 169
Bruce, Robert, king of Scotland 18, 24–6, 38, 61–2, 70, 84
Burgh, Elizabeth, duchess of Clarence 167, 184, 188, 194–8
Burgh, John 18, 19, 24, 30, 36, 49, 51, 59, 94
Burgh, Maud, countess of Gloucester 18, 24, 30, 38–9, 43–4, 47–8, 59, 61–2
Burgh, Richard, earl of Ulster 17, 18, 40, 61, 96, 133–4
Burgh, William, earl of Ulster 30, 59, 106, 133–4, 145–7, 150, 159, 167–8, 188, 196

Caerphilly Castle 6, 62, 100, 120, 138, 140, 145, 150–1, 157, 164
Chaucomb, Cecily and John 25, 113
Chedworth, Robert 127–8, 162
Chedworth, Thomas 128, 162
Clare Castle 106, 127, 134
Clare College, Cambridge 177–8
Clare, Eleanor, Lady Despenser (d. 1337)
  abduction 150, 153
  birth 6, 7
  children 10, 16, 19, 21, 25, 30, 37, 72, 76, 103, 111, 115–16, 118, 124–5, 126, 129–30, 141–2, 148, 152
  death 173–5
  household and attendants 27, 81, 111, 154
  imprisonment 139, 147, 153–4
  lands and income 19–20, 22, 37, 39, 43–4, 46–8, 59–60, 61–2, 79–80, 93, 110–11, 147–8, 150, 153, 155, 161–2, 174
  letters 73, 104–05
  relations with Edward II 21–22, 25, 37, 48, 71–2, 91–3, 101, 103–04, 109–10, 117–18, 120, 123–4, 126–7, 131–3, 136, 148, 158
  relations with Hugh Despenser 25, 72, 76, 102, 104, 116, 129, 136, 148
  relations with Queen Isabella 21, 26, 94, 99–101, 104, 111–12, 122–3, 154–5
  weddings 9, 10, 150–2
Clare, Elizabeth, lady of Clare (d. 1360)
  abduction 45–6
  birth 8
  children and grandchildren 30, 49, 55, 66–7, 96, 133–4, 146–7, 156, 159, 163, 167, 185–6, 192–5, 196
  death 198
  founds Clare College 177–8
  founds Ballinrobe 36
  household and attendants 27, 67, 97–8, 141, 162, 196–7
  imprisonment 87
  lands and income 39–40, 44, 51, 61–2, 82, 87, 94, 105–6, 126–7, 138–9, 144, 168–9
  marriages 18–19, 24, 36, 41, 45, 49, 50, 56, 59
  protest 127–9
  relations with Edward II 45, 49–50, 55, 83, 88, 95, 135
  relations with Edward III 181
  relations with family and friends 95–6, 134, 147, 150, 156, 165–6, 169, 175, 176–7, 179, 184, 188–90, 193–4, 198
  relations with Roger Damory 50–51, 56–7, 63, 74, 85–6
  relations with Theobald Verdon 46, 49
  religious beliefs and practices 74, 86, 188–9
  will 195–7
Clare, Gilbert 'the Red', earl of Gloucester (d. 1295) 2–4, 6–11, 13, 39, 40, 62, 173, 180
Clare, Gilbert, earl of Gloucester (d. 1314) 5–8, 12, 17–19, 22–3, 26, 30, 32, 37–40, 43–4, 48, 59, 103
Clare, Isabella, Lady Berkeley 3, 40, 80, 180

Clare, Joan, countess of Fife 3, 9, 62, 180
Clare, Margaret, countess of Cornwall (d. 1312) 34–5
Clare, Margaret, countess of Cornwall and Gloucester (d. 1342)
  birth 7–8
  children 16, 26, 28, 35–6, 89, 96–7, 113–14, 143, 171–3, 182
  death 182–3
  household and attendants 27, 73
  imprisonment 89–91, 103, 107, 121, 142
  lands and income 16–18, 22, 28, 34–5, 36, 39–40, 52, 58, 61–2, 69, 78, 143, 173
  petition 35
  relations with Edward II 14, 36, 40, 48, 52, 59, 65, 78, 81–2, 88–90, 135–6
  relations with Hugh Audley 52, 58–9, 63, 73–4, 135, 143, 165, 168, 182–3
  relations with Piers Gaveston 14–15, 18, 23–4, 26, 31, 33–4, 42
  weddings 13–14, 57–8
Clare Priory 11, 36, 74
Clare, Richard, earl of Gloucester 3, 11, 36
Clarence, Philippa of, countess of March and Ulster 194–5, 198, 208
Comyn, Elizabeth 120, 125, 163

Damory, Elizabeth 96, 98, 114, 128, 146, 159, 185, 192–3, 196, 199
Damory, Margaret 96, 114, 128, 146, 185

Damory, Richard (d. 1330) 41, 57, 87, 97, 111, 143, 146
Damory, Richard (d. 1375) 97, 146, 193
Damory, Roger (d. 1322) 22, 39–41, 48–51, 53–8, 61–70, 74–5, 78–81, 83–8, 94, 96, 101, 105, 114–15, 126, 128, 150, 156, 159, 168–9, 185, 190, 196–7
Damory, Roger (fl. 1330s) 97
Damory, Nichol 97–8, 177, 196, 199
Despenser, Edward (d. 1342) 10, 25, 30, 37, 76, 94, 116, 148, 177, 181–2, 186, 200–01
Despenser, Edward (d. 1375) 152, 177, 182, 192–3
Despenser, Eleanor (d. 1351?) 76, 115, 141–2, 148
Despenser, Elizabeth, Lady Berkeley 76, 124–6, 130, 148, 176, 180, 192, 200–01
Despenser, Gilbert 37, 76, 93–4, 99, 110, 116, 148, 176, 181, 192, 201
Despenser, Hugh, the Elder, earl of Winchester 10, 11, 19, 22, 24, 27, 38, 41, 68, 70, 80, 83, 88, 91, 93–4, 103, 105–6, 109, 117, 119–20, 136–8, 158
Despenser, Hugh, the Younger, lord of Glamorgan 10, 11, 13, 14, 19, 20, 22, 24–5, 27, 38, 39, 41–4, 47–8, 52–3, 59–62, 64–6, 68, 70–9, 81, 83–5, 88, 92, 94–6, 99, 100, 102–05, 108–12, 115–17, 119–24, 126–9, 131, 133, 136–40, 144–5, 161
Despenser, Hugh or 'Huchon', lord of Glamorgan (d. 1349) 10, 19,

252 Edward II's Nieces: The Clare Sisters

30, 37, 60, 76, 93–4, 115, 138, 145, 152, 157, 163–5, 175, 177, 181–2, 186, 189, 192–3
Despenser, Isabella, countess of Arundel 30, 37, 76–7, 103, 129–30, 148, 177, 182, 187, 200
Despenser, Joan 37, 76, 103, 141–2, 148
Despenser, John 76, 109, 116, 148, 181, 201
Despenser, Margaret 76, 103, 115, 126, 141–2, 148, 175, 177

Edward I, king of England 1–10, 12, 15, 19, 56, 136, 173
Edward II, king of England 2, 5, 9–18, 21–6, 28–31, 33–5, 37–46, 48–50, 52–5, 57–79, 80–1, 83–95, 99–113, 116–24, 126–9, 131–3, 135–41, 143–4, 147–8, 154, 157, 166, 176, 183
Edward III, king of England 30, 36–7, 48, 98, 113, 115–16, 133, 135, 143–4, 147–9, 152–4, 159–67, 169–71, 173–5, 177–8, 180–2, 184–9, 193–5, 199
Edward of Woodstock, prince of Wales 159, 181, 198–9
Eleanor of Woodstock, countess of Guelders 99, 115, 117, 129, 164, 167, 172
Elizabeth, countess of Hereford 12, 16, 32, 48, 169

Ferrers, Anne 177, 184
Ferrers, Elizabeth, countess of Atholl 166, 185, 192, 194
Ferrers, Henry 146–7, 149–50, 156–7, 166, 177, 186, 192

Ferrers, Philippa 166, 186, 192, 194
Ferrers, William 166, 179, 185, 192, 195–6
Fitzalan, Edmund (d. 1381/2) 129–30, 139, 148, 174, 182, 187
Fitzalan, Edmund, earl of Arundel 32–3, 76, 88, 103, 115, 139
Fitzalan, Richard, earl of Arundel 76, 115, 139, 157, 160, 180–1, 187

Gaveston, Amie 26, 114–15, 154
Gaveston, Joan 29, 30, 34–6, 42, 59, 65, 89, 113–14
Gaveston, Piers, earl of Cornwall 11, 13–18, 20–4, 26, 27–9, 31–4, 40–2, 69, 71, 97, 101, 114–15
Grey, John, of Rotherfield 151–3, 164
Greystoke, Ralph 70, 80, 88, 143

Hanley Castle 83, 103, 148, 150–1, 153, 161
Hastings, Isabella 67, 100, 115, 117, 129, 134, 142, 147, 168
Houk, Thomas 103, 111, 115, 141

Inge, John 70–1, 73, 77, 96, 105
Isabella of France, queen of England 16, 21, 24, 26–7, 29, 30, 34, 37, 48, 51, 55, 65, 92–5, 99, 100–04, 108, 111–13, 116, 119, 121–4, 127–8, 131–3, 136–43, 145, 147–50, 153–5, 158–60, 164, 170, 174, 180, 187, 198

Joan of Acre, countess of Gloucester 1–13, 15, 32, 36–7, 56, 62, 67, 75, 88, 156

Index 253

Joan of the Tower, queen of Scotland 99, 115, 117, 169
John of Eltham, earl of Cornwall 52, 65, 99, 112, 127, 137, 139, 180

Lacy, Alice, countess of Lincoln 62, 120, 163, 172
Lacy, Maud, countess of Gloucester 3–5
Lancaster, Maud of, countess of Ulster 27, 145, 167, 188, 194–5
Lancaster, Maud of, duchess of Bavaria 186–7
Lancaster, Henry, earl of 10, 36, 48, 56, 130, 136, 138–9, 141, 144–6, 149–50, 153, 156, 162–3, 167, 186–7, 194
Lancaster, Henry of Grosmont, duke of 145–6, 173, 186–8, 194, 197–9
Lancaster, Thomas, earl of 16, 23, 32–3, 38, 46, 48, 52, 54, 62–4, 68–9, 77, 84–5, 88, 111, 145, 153, 169, 172
Lusignan, Alice, countess of Gloucester 2, 3, 9, 40, 62, 180

MacDuff, Duncan, earl of Fife 2–4, 6, 180
Mary, nun of Amesbury 5, 8, 12, 16, 19, 36, 53, 56, 135–6, 166
Montacute, Elizabeth, Lady Despenser 181–2, 192–3
Montacute, William (d. 1319) 48, 53–4, 62–3, 68, 69, 111, 159, 181
Montacute, William, earl of Salisbury (d. 1344) 54, 69, 111, 159, 181

Monthermer, Edward 9, 12, 39, 157–8, 179
Monthermer, Joan 9, 39, 142, 180
Monthermer, Mary 9, 39, 62, 180
Monthermer, Ralph 9, 23, 39, 67–8, 88, 100, 117
Monthermer, Thomas 9, 39, 117, 156, 177
Mortimer, Roger, earl of March 45, 48, 61, 79, 83, 100, 102–03, 127, 134, 139, 141–2, 147, 149–51, 156, 159, 162, 171, 176, 182, 195
Multon, John 24, 59, 114

Neville, Ralph 143, 160, 163–4

Philip VI, king of France 162, 181, 189
Philippa of Hainault, queen of England 131, 133, 147, 153–4, 195
Prior, Emma and Joan 27, 111, 115, 154

Quincy, Margaret, countess of Lincoln 3, 8

Sadington, John 104
Sempringham Priory 89, 91, 97, 103, 106, 121, 13–5, 137, 141–3
St Pol, Marie of, countess of Pembroke 163, 178, 188, 193, 199
Stafford, Ralph, earl of (d. 1372) 97, 159, 171–3, 180, 182, 184, 187, 189, 190, 192–3, 198
Stafford, Ralph (d. bef. 1347) 186–7

Tonbridge Castle 4, 43–4, 61, 73, 78, 106–07, 120, 165, 173, 179

Valence, Aymer, earl of Pembroke 31, 38, 163, 178
Verdon, Isabella 55, 134, 146–7, 150, 156–7, 163, 166–7, 179, 184–6, 192, 195, 197, 200
Verdon, Theobald 45–6, 49, 51, 54–5, 57, 65, 86, 94, 197

Warenne, John, earl of Surrey 10, 23, 26, 76, 106–7, 190

Woodstock, Edmund of, earl of Kent 12, 13, 16, 122, 136–7, 145, 147, 157–9, 179, 198

Zouche, Alan 98, 151–2, 174–5, 199
Zouche, William (d. 1337) 138, 140, 150–5, 157–8, 160–2, 164–6, 168, 170, 173–5
Zouche, William (d. after 1390) 152, 159, 174, 177, 193, 201